METROWERKS CODEWARRIOR PROGRAMMING FOR THE MAC

Dan Parks Sydow

M&T BOOKS

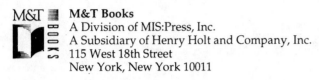 **M&T Books**
A Division of MIS:Press, Inc.
A Subsidiary of Henry Holt and Company, Inc.
115 West 18th Street
New York, New York 10011

ISBN: 1-55851-435-X

Editor-In-Chief: Paul Farrell
Managing Editor: Cary Sullivan
Development Editor: Michael Sprague
Copy Edit Manager: Shari Chappell
Copy Editor: Suzanne Ingrao
Production Editor: Stephanie Doyle

METROWERKS CODEWARRIOR PROGRAMMING FOR THE MAC

Dedication

To Nadine and Taylor Ann

Dan

Table of Contents

CHAPTER 1

Introduction to CodeWarrior 1

Some Terminology 2

    680x0, 68K, PowerPC, and PPC... 2

    CodeWarrior Editions.. 2

    CodeWarrior Versions 4

About the CodeWarrior CD-ROM Package............................... 4

    The Metrowerks C/C++ ƒ Folder 5

    Other Items of Interest on the CodeWarrior CD.................... 7

Chapter Summary 10

CHAPTER 2

CodeWarrior Projects 11

PPC and 68K Projects 12

    The EmptyWindow Resource File 12

The Empty Window MW C/C++ 68K Project 15

The Empty Window MW C/C++ PPC Project 21

Headers, Libraries, and the Toolbox 24

Apple's Universal Header Files 25

The Universal Header Files and the Toolbox 26

MacHeaders and the #include Directive 28

Libraries and the Toolbox 29

The SetVolume Example Program 30

The SetVolume Project 32

The SetVolume Source Code 36

Verifying that Header Files and Libraries are Necessary .. 38

CodeWarrior Projects and Libraries 41

C++ Projects and Libraries 42

ANSI Projects and Libraries 43

SIOUX Projects and Libraries 50

Project Stationary 54

Chapter Summary 55

CHAPTER 3

Understanding the Universal Header Files 57

Errors and the Universal Header Files 58

The PlaySound Project 59

The Faulty PlaySound Source Code 62

Correcting the Type Mismatch Error 63

Correcting Errors Involving the Toolbox 67

The Find Dialog Box and Search Sets 68

The DelaySound Example Program 70

Using the Search Set to Correct an Error 73

Improving the PlaySound Program 75

Using the Search Set 76

Making the Changes 78

Chapter Summary 79

CHAPTER 4

Debugging and MW Debug 81

Installing and Running MW Debug 82

Installing the Debugger 82

Installing the Debugger Nub Files 82

Debugger Basics 84

The ChangingValues68K Program 86

MW Debug Windows 87

Controlling Program Execution 89

Debugging the ChangingValues68K Program 91

Executing the ChangingValues68K Program 91

Variables, Data Structures, and the Debugger 95

Variables and the Locals Pane 95

The Rect Data Type 98

The WindowPtr, WindowRecord, and
      GrafPort Data Types 100

Experimenting with the GrafPort 104

Further Investigation of the GrafPort 108

Chapter Summary 110

Chapter 5

Fat Applications 111

Executable Code and Resources 112

68K Applications and Code Resources 112

PowerPC Applications and Data Fork Code 113

Fat Applications and Executable Code 114

Building a Fat Binary Application 116

Creating 68K and PowerPC Applications 116

Get Ready for the Fat App 119

Get the PPC Project Ready 119

Build the Fat Binary Application 123

Examining the Programs with a Resource Editor 124

Chapter Summary 126

Chapter 6

Getting Started with PowerPlant 129

The Example Application 130

What the PPIntro68K Example Does................................ 130

The Example Source Code Listing................................... 132

The PowerPlant Project.. 133

The PPIntro68K Example Project Folder 133

The Project and PowerPlant Classes 134

PowerPlant Resources 137

The Project Resource File 138

The PowerPlant PPob Resource 141

PowerPlant Classes 143

    PowerPlant Naming Conventions...................................... 144

    The LApplication Class 148

    The LWindow Class 154

    PowerPlant Classes and Static Member Functions 155

    PowerPlant Classes and the Toolbox.................................. 157

Source Code and the PowerPlant Project............................. 158

    The #pragma once Directive and Include Files................ 158

    The LApplication Derived Class.. 160

    The CPPIntroApp Class Constructor 160

    What's Left? 163

    The PPIntroApp.h Header File Source Code Listing....... 164

    The PPIntroApp.cp Source Code Listing........................... 165

    PowerPlant and the MW C/C++ PPC Compiler 167

Chapter Summary 168

CHAPTER 7

Menus and PowerPlant....................... 171

Menus, Resources, and PowerPlant....................................... 172

    The PPIntro68K Program 172

    Adding the MENU and MBAR Resources 173

    Menu Items and the Mcmd Resource 174

    The Mcmd Resource and Resorcerer................................. 178

    The Mcmd Resource and ResEdit....................................... 184

Adding Application-Specific Menu Items 188

    Command Numbers and Application Menus 189

    Adding Resources for a New Menu 189

Menus, Commands, and Commanders 191

Defining Menu Item Constants... 191

Menu Items, Commands, and the Target 192

Commands and the Chain of Command........................... 194

The Target and the LCommander Class 196

ObeyCommand() and the Chain of Command 197

Overriding ObeyCommand().. 201

A Look at the ObeyCommand() Member Function......... 204

Overriding FindCommandStatus() 210

The PPMenu68K Example Application 214

The PPMenu68K Project... 215

The PPMenu68K Resources 217

The PPMenuApp.h Header File Source Code Listing 221

The CPPMenuApp.cp Source Code Listing 222

PPMenu and the MW C/C++ PPC Compiler................... 225

Adding to the PPMenu68K Example 226

The PPMoreMenu68K Project 226

Adding the New Menu-Related Resources....................... 227

Adding the New Menu-Related Source Code 228

PPMoreMenu and the MW C/C++ PPC Compiler 233

Chapter Summary 233

Chapter 8

Panes, Constructor, and PowerPlant 235

Windows, Views, and Panes 236

About PowerPlant Panes 236

Creating Panes.. 237

Using Constructor to Gain an
Understanding of Panes... 237

Creating a PPob Resource with Constructor 241

Using Constructor to Create a PPob................................. 241

Examining the Constructor Output............................. 246

A Pane Example.. 247

Creating the PPob File 249

The PPDemoPane68K Project................................... 253

The PPDemoPane68K Resources 254

The Pane Class.. 255

Registering the Pane 258

Overriding DrawSelf()... 260

Overriding ClickSelf() 261

The CTestPane.h Header Listing............................. 263

The CTestPane.cp Source Code Listing.................... 263

The CPPDemoPaneApp.h Header Listing 265

The CPPDemoPaneApp.cp Source Code Listing 266

Chapter Summary 267

CHAPTER 9

ZoneRanger and Macintosh Memory 269

Macintosh Memory 270

Memory Overview... 270

The Application Heap 272

Relocatable Blocks... 275

Keeping Track of Relocatable Blocks....................... 278

Nonrelocatable Blocks 279

Setting an Application's Heap Size.. 280

What the PictMemBad68K Program Does 281

The PictMemBad68K Resources 282

The PictMemBad68K.c Source Code 283

Setting the Application's Heap Size 286

Estimating an Application's Heap Requirements 288

Changing an Application's Heap Size 294

ZoneRanger Basics 295

Examining a Process Using ZoneRanger 298

Using the ZoneRanger Overview Window 299

The Overview Window and PictMemBad68K.................. 301

Using the ZoneRanger Zone Window 302

Getting Heap Block Information.. 305

Finding the PictMemBad68K Memory Problem 309

Correcting the PictMemBad68K Memory Problem 313

Why Not Just Use the Debugger?..................................... 315

ZoneRanger and Native PowerPC Programs......................... 318

Native PowerPC Applications and Memory 318

Native PowerPC Applications and Virtual Memory 322

Fat Binary Applications and RAM 324

Chapter Summary 327

CHAPTER 10

Profiler and Program Timing 329

Using the CodeWarrior Profiler 330

The CodeWarrior Profiler... 330

Adding Profiling to a Project.................................... 330

The Profiler Functions 332

Adding Profiling to a Project.................................... 335

A Profiler Example 336

The ProfilerIntro68K Source Code...................... 337

The Profiler Output File 340

Examining the Profiler Output File 342

A Further Look at the Profiler Output File......... 344

Speeding Up a Function 345

Getting a Sampling of a Function's Execution Time 346

Improving the OpenDrawWindow() Function?.............. 348

Determining Which Part of a Function Is Slow 350

Analyzing the Drawing Time of PICTs 352

Creating a Simple Test Program.......................... 353

The PictureResource68K Test Program 354

Examining the PictureResource68K Profiler Output 358

Profiler and the Event Loop...................................... 360

The EventLoop68K Program 361

Function Dependencies and the Profiler 362

Chapter Summary 369

INDEX **371**

Acknowledgments

Stephanie Doyle, Production Editor, M&T Books, for a page layout effort that resulted in such a polished looking book.

The many Metrowerks people who were so readily accessible and quick to provide information. Among those at Metrowerks who answered questions or provided input:

Greg Galanos, President; Avi Rappoport, CodeWarrior Documentation; Ron Liechty, Middleman Extrordinaire; Joshua Golub, ZoneRanger; Eric Scouten, Constructor; Jonathan Hess and Greg Dow, PowerPlant; and Steve Nicolai, Profiler.

Carole McClendon, Waterside Productions, for making this book happen.

Mike E. Floyd, for permission to use his Blue Angels picture in Chapter 10.

Introduction

About the CodeWarrior Lite Software

The CD that accompanies this book contains a limited version of both the 68K and PowerPC CodeWarrior C/C++ compilers. By "limited" I mean that while the compilers can be used to work with any of the included projects, you won't be able to create new projects of your own. For that, you'll have to order the full-featured versions that are a part of the Metrowerks CodeWarrior development package. The CD contains a file that holds more specific ordering information.

So what can you use the limited compiler for? As mentioned, you can open any of the twenty projects included on the CD—you'll find them in the folder named Sydow CW Book ƒ. You can use the two CodeWarrior compilers to compile the included code and build applications from the projects. You can also go beyond the material covered in this book by typing in any new source code you want in an existing source code file. While you won't be able to save your work, you will be able to experiment with Macintosh programming and the features of the CodeWarrior compilers.

Finally, the included CD comes with three Metrowerks utilities that can be used to help you in your programming endeavors. ZoneRanger is a memory-checker that allows you to examine how a program makes use of memory. The version of ZoneRanger that's included on this book's CD is a full-featured program that let's you see how the example programs—or any other programs—dynamically allocate memory. Constructor is another utility you'll find on the CD. Constructor is a graphical interface-building tool that can be used in conjunction with PowerPlant—Metrowerks exciting application framework. Finally, the Metrowerks Profiler is included on the CD. This code profiling tool allows you to put a program through its paces, then obtain a detailed report of exactly how much processing time was spent in each of the program's routines. That's handy information for determining how to speed up and fine-tune a program. Like ZoneRanger and Constructor, the version of Profiler included on this CD isn't a limited version.

About This Book

In this book you'll find full descriptions of the elements of the CodeWarrior development environment mentioned on the preceding pages, including the Metrowerks compilers, ZoneRanger, Constructor, Profiler, and PowerPlant in the chapters of this book. You'll also find out how to get the most out of the CodeWarrior package to create standalone Macintosh applications for both older Macs and the new Power Macs.

Chapter 1 introduces you to the CodeWarrior development environment. CodeWarrior, as you'll find out, is more than just a compiler. The Metrowerks CodeWarrior CD consists of several compilers, programming tools and utilities, example code, and documentation.

Chapter 2 explains why the full-featured CodeWarrior CD (and the CD that accompanies this book) comes with two C/C++ compilers. You'll find out how any program created with a CodeWarrior compiler starts out as a project consisting of source code files, resource files, and libraries.

Chapter 3 discusses the often times overlooked, and potentially troubling, topic of Apple's Universal Header files. This collection of over one hundred header files define the function prototypes for each of the thousands of Toolbox routines. Without these function prototype, a Macintosh compiler will not compile code that includes a call to a Toolbox function. Here you'll see why Apple's occasional practice of updating the Universal Header files can lead to headaches for a Mac programmer.

Chapter 4 introduces you to MW Debug, the CodeWarrior debugger included on this book's CD. Using Metrowerks debugger you'll be able to easily step through the execution of a program, view memory, and change variable values in a running program—all without knowing a bit of assembly language. You'll also see how to use the debugger to gain a better understanding of Macintosh data structures.

Chapter 5 explains how the two compilers included on the full-featured version of CodeWarrior (and on this book's CD) can be used to create fat binary applications. A fat binary is a version of a Mac program that is designed to run on both older Macs and the newer Power Macs. Not only will a fat binary run on either type of machine, it will know which type of computer it resides on. And that enables it to be compatible with the older 680x0 family of Macintosh microprocessors, and take advantage of the speed of the new PowerPC CPU.

Chapter 6 is the start of a three-chapter journey that covers PowerPlant—the Metrowerks application framework that takes much of the drudgery out of programming. An application framework is code that handles the tasks common to all programs—such as working with menus. By using the Metrowerks-written code that is the PowerPlant framework, you can concentrate your programming efforts on the fun stuff—such as graphics.

Chapter 7 continues with the description of PowerPlant programming. Here you'll move beyond the introductory topics of Chapter 6 to discover the details of how PowerPlant lets you forget about most of the menu-related Toolbox functions you've used so often.

Chapter 8 concludes the discussion of PowerPlant. In this chapter you'll learn all about panes—the self-contained drawing areas that hold all the text and graphics found in the windows of programs created from projects that use the PowerPlant framework. You'll see how a pane makes graphics-handling easy. You'll also find out how using panes allows you to easily add program features (such as allowing the user to click on a drawing area and drag it about a window) that would take a far greater programming effort using traditional programming practices. In this chapter you'll also see how to graphically define the properties of a pane using the Metrowerks Constructor.

Chapter 9 describes the use of ZoneRanger, the Metrowerks memory-checking tool. Because computer memory is something that's discussed in theory, rather than in practicality, it is a topic that includes many concepts that are difficult to grasp—topics such as pointers, handles, and memory allocation and deallocation. ZoneRanger is a software tool that provides a numerical and graphical look at how each running application is using memory. With this information you'll be able to move beyond theory and gain an understanding of Macintosh memory. You'll see how much memory an application uses, how much free space it leaves unused, and how it can be modified to make more efficient use of memory

Chapter 10 discusses programming timing and Profiler—the Metrowerks utility that keeps track of where a Mac's processor spends its time. By tracking the time spent in each routine of a program, you'll be able to decide where your programming efforts should be directed in order to speed up and optimize your code.

Chapter 1

Introduction to CodeWarrior

The product is named CodeWarrior, yet there is no application named CodeWarrior. That's because CodeWarrior is a *development environment*. It consists of several compilers, programming tools and utilities, example code, and documentation. Before jumping right in and writing some code, it will be worth your while to spend a few minutes discovering just what's included in the CodeWarrior package.

Some Terminology

Terminology usually appears in a glossary at the back of a book, right? Well, Metrowerks doesn't always follow conventions, so I won't either. There are a few words and phrases that will come up time and again throughout this book, so I think it makes sense to define them right up front.

680x0, 68K, PowerPC, and PPC

Before Apple introduced the Power Macintosh computers in 1994, all Macs used a Motorola microprocessor that was part of the *680x0* family. That means each Mac had either a 68000, 68020, 68030, or 68040 central processor unit chip. People often refer to a Macintosh that has one of these CPUs as a *68K-based* Macintosh computers, or *680x0-based* Macintosh.

The Power Macs are driven by the new *PowerPC* chip—a chip developed jointly by Apple, Motorola, and IBM. The first Power Macs used the PowerPC 601 microprocessor. You'll sometimes see PowerPC abbreviated as *PPC*, and a Macintosh computer that has a PowerPC chip as a *PPC-based* or *PowerPC-based* Macintosh.

Because Metrowerks uses the terms 68K and PPC extensively, this book will as well.

CodeWarrior Editions

CodeWarrior comes in two editions, *Bronze* and *Gold*. The less expensive Bronze edition contains two compilers: one that compiles both C and C++ source code and one that compiles Pascal code. The Gold edition contains four compilers: two C/C++ compilers and two Pascal compilers.

The C/C++ compiler that is a part of the CodeWarrior Bronze package will run on either a 68K-based Macintosh or a PowerPC-based Mac. The applications that are created, or *generated*, from this compiler will also run on either type of *machine*, or Macintosh. While it's true that a program generated by the Bronze C/C++ compiler, which is named the

`MW C/C++ 68K` compiler, will run on either a 68K or PowerPC, it will not take advantage of the faster *instruction set* found on PowerPC-based Macs. Instead, it will run in a slower *emulation mode*. This is shown in Figure 1.1. To create an application that makes full use of the fast instructions that are a part of the PowerPC chip, you'll need to use one of the C/C++ compilers found in the CodeWarrior Gold package. The same applies to the Bronze version of the Pascal compiler.

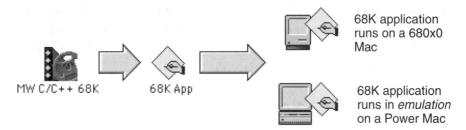

Figure 1.1 *The MW C/C++ 68K compiler generates 680x0 applications.*

The CodeWarrior Gold package includes two C/C++ compilers. Both run on either 68K- or PowerPC-based Macintosh computers. The difference is in the type of program that each generates. One generates code that runs on either machine but doesn't take advantage of the speed of the PowerPC. This is the same `MW C/C++ 68K` compiler found in the Bronze edition. The second C/C++ compiler, named the `MW C/C++ PPC` compiler, generates applications that take full advantage of the PowerPC instructions, but only run on a PowerPC-based Macintosh. An application of this type is said to run in fast *native mode* on a PowerPC-based Mac. Figure 1.2 illustrates this.

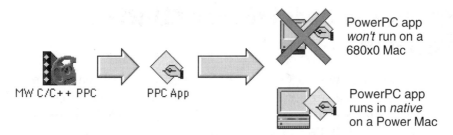

Figure 1.2 *The MW C/C++ PPC compiler generates PowerPC applications.*

N O T E

If it isn't obvious, I'll sum it up here: the CodeWarrior Gold CD contains everything that's on the Bronze CD, and then some.

The advantage of owning the two C/C++ compilers found in the CodeWarrior Gold package is that you can compile your source code twice. The first time you'll use the MW C/C++ 68K compiler to generate a 68K application that owners of 68K-based Macintosh computers can use. The second time, you'll compile with the MW C/C++ PPC compiler to create a PowerPC-only application that will run on PowerPC-based Macs at a speed faster than its 68K version will.

CodeWarrior Versions

Metrowerks is constantly working to improve its products. As a result of those efforts, the company frequently releases enhanced versions of their compilers and other programming tools. When you purchase CodeWarrior, you purchase a CodeWarrior *subscription*. Paying for CodeWarrior once entitles you to three versions of the CD. As new versions are created, they'll be sent to registered owners. As of this writing, CodeWarrior CW5 is available, and CW6 soon will be.

N O T E

Metrowerks releases three new versions of its compilers each year. A new version adds enhancements to previous versions, but it doesn't make code you wrote using a previous version obsolete.

About the CodeWarrior CD-ROM Package

This book comes with a CD that holds a trimmed-down version of CodeWarrior, some supporting files, and several example programs. If you think that's a lot, then double-clicking on the full-featured CodeWarrior CD that's available from Metrowerks may prove downright intimidating. Figure 1.3 shows what you'll see if you have CodeWarrior CW5; other versions are similar.

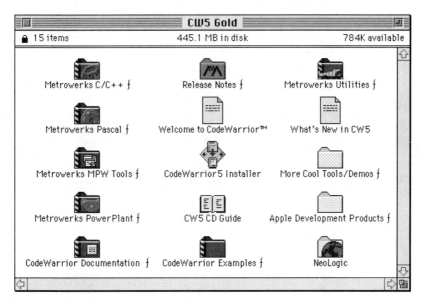

Figure 1.3 *The main CodeWarrior CD-ROM folder.*

 If you own the full-featured CodeWarrior package, your main directory, or folder, may have a different name than mine. Most of the folders within the main folder will have identical, or very similar names, however.

N O T E

As you traverse through the CodeWarrior folders you'll find a variety of applications, utilities, demos, documents, and more folders. Some things you'll immediately recognize, others won't make much sense to you—even after a close look. In this chapter you will learn about some of the main components of the CodeWarrior package, with an emphasis on the software that is covered in this book.

The Metrowerks C/C++ ƒ Folder

For the Macintosh, C and C++ are the languages of choice. If you program in either of these languages, you'll be most interested in the folder named `Metrowerks C/C++ ƒ` (see Figure 1.4). If you own CodeWarrior Gold, this folder contains both the 68K and PPC versions of the Metrowerks C/C++ compiler. It also holds two versions of the Metrowerks debugger, one version for each compiler.

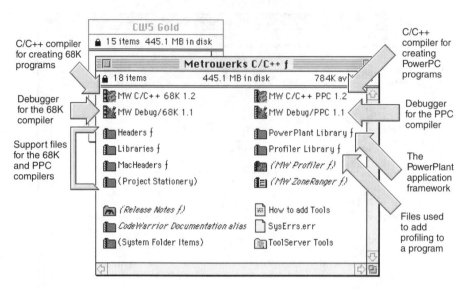

Figure 1.4 *The Metrowerks C/C++ f folder from the CodeWarrior Gold CD.*

In this folder you'll also find several other folders that hold support files for the compilers. You'll seldom need to open these folders.

The Metrowerks C/C++ f folder holds the Metrowerks application framework named PowerPlant. An application framework is code that handles many of the repetitious programming tasks common to most Mac programs. By including this Metrowerks code in your own projects, you'll be able to devote your programming efforts to the fun areas of programming rather than the mundane parts. You'll find several chapters in this book devoted to understanding and getting started with the PowerPlant application framework.

The Metrowerks Profiler allows you to determine the length of time it takes for different parts of your program to execute. Does your program seem to run sluggishly? Are graphics updated slowly? With the Profiler, you'll be able to find out exactly which lines of your code are the ones that need fine-tuning, or *optimization*. The Metrowerks C/C++ f folder houses a folder named Profiler Library f folder. This folder holds the files that allow you to add profiling to any of your Mac programs.

The MW C/C++68K and MW C/C++ PPC compilers are your only real concerns in this folder; they're the only two applications that you'll double-click to execute. The rest of the contents of the Metrowerks C/C++ ƒ folder are less important because:

- The debuggers are run from within the compilers— you don't need to launch them from the Finder.
- Most of the folders in this folder hold support code, such as libraries and header files, that you'll use from within the compiler.

Other Items of Interest on the CodeWarrior CD

Your CodeWarrior Gold CD has several folders besides the Metrowerks C/C++ ƒ folder; one of the them is the Metrowerks PowerPlant ƒ folder, which is shown in Figure 1.5. You saw that the Metrowerks C/C++ ƒ folder holds the files that make up PowerPlant. The Metrowerks PowerPlant ƒ folder holds PowerPlant documents and examples. It also contains an application named Constructor. Constructor is a utility program that helps you create the special resources that are required by PowerPlant.

If you've ever used the resource editor ResEdit, then the idea of a graphics editor like Constructor should make sense to you.

Another folder of interest is the Metrowerks Utilities ƒ folder (see Figure 1.6). This folder holds a Profiler folder that contains the Profiler application. The Profiler support libraries, which were discussed earlier, are held in the Metrowerks C/C++ ƒ folder. The Metrowerks Profiler has a chapter of its own in this book—Chapter 11.

The Metrowerks Utilities ƒ folder also holds a utility application named ZoneRanger. You'll find ZoneRanger in the Metrowerks ZoneRanger ƒ folder. ZoneRanger is a neat program that runs unobtrusively in the background on your Macintosh. If you'd like to see how your program manages memory, just launch it and look at the ZoneRanger windows.

There you'll see specific information about the amount of memory your program uses, and the way in which your program uses it. ZoneRanger is the topic of Chapter 9.

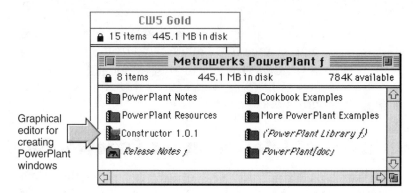

Figure 1.5 *The Metrowerks PowerPlant ƒ folder from the CodeWarrior Gold CD.*

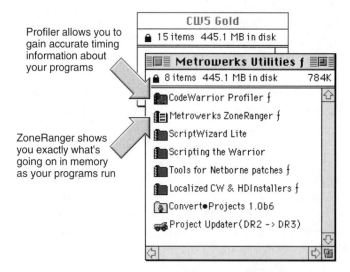

Figure 1.6 *The Metrowerks Utilities ƒ folder from the CodeWarrior Gold CD.*

The More Cool Tools/Demos ƒ folder has a vast assortment of programming tools and utilities, most of them demos of the full-featured versions. This folder is shown in Figure 1.7. One demo in particular is worth mentioning: the demo version of Resorcerer. Resorcerer is a resource editor that allows you to create and edit resources in a graphical manner, just as Apple's ResEdit program does. Resorcerer, however, is a much more powerful resource editing tool. Just in case you haven't bought CodeWarrior yet, I've included a copy of the demo on this book's CD.

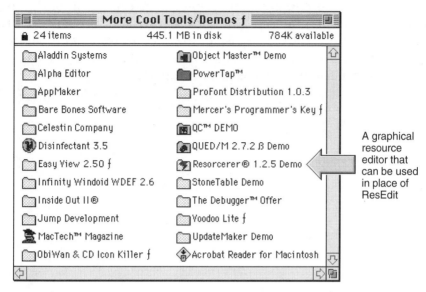

A graphical resource editor that can be used in place of ResEdit

Figure 1.7 *The More Cool Tools/Demos ƒ folder from the CodeWarrior Gold CD.*

Speaking of ResEdit, you'll find a working copy of this popular resource editor in the Apple Development Products ƒ folder (see Figure 1.8).

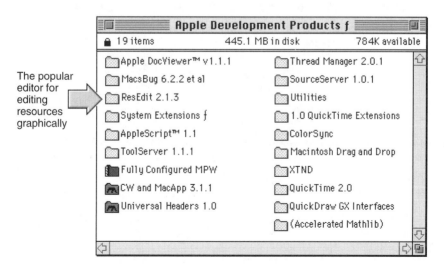

The popular editor for editing resources graphically

Figure 1.8 *The Apple Development Products ƒ folder from the CodeWarrior Gold CD.*

Chapter Summary

CodeWarrior is a development environment that holds all of the compilers, tools, and programming utilities that make it possible to write programs for both older 68K Macintosh computers and the new PowerPC-based Macs. At the heart of the CodeWarrior package lie Metrowerks fast, feature-laden C/C++ compilers.

Chapter  2

CodeWarrior Projects

The CodeWarrior Gold package comes with two C/C++ compilers. In this chapter you'll see why there are two compilers, and you'll use both of these compilers to build two versions of the same simple Macintosh application.

An application starts its life as a CodeWarrior project. Each project may consist of source code files, resource files, and libraries. Additionally, these files rely on several of Apple's Universal Header files. In this chapter you'll see how these different pieces of the puzzle fit together.

Different projects require different libraries of code to be added to them. This can lead to some confusion—as well as to some compile and link errors. This chapter ends with a discussion of some of the different combinations of libraries that need to be added to different project types.

PPC and 68K Projects

If you bought CodeWarrior as the CodeWarrior Gold package, you have two C/C++ compilers. One, the MW C/C++ 68K compiler, generates executable programs that run on both 680x0-based Macintosh computers and Power Macs—though they won't run in the faster PowerPC native mode on the Power Macs. The other compiler, the MW C/C++ PPC, generates fast native PowerPC applications that will only run on Power Macintosh computers.

When it comes time to develop a Mac application, you'll choose one compiler or the other. You'll also have the option of using *both* compilers to develop a *fat binary* application—a single program that runs on a 680x0-based Mac using 680x0 instructions and runs on a Power Mac using the faster native PowerPC instructions. Fat binary application are discussed at length in Chapter 5. In this chapter I'll focus on creating programs that are just one type or the other, 680x0 or PowerPC.

 If fat binary applications sound like your cup of tea, you might be tempted to skip this section. Please reconsider— everything that you'll read here will serve as background information for discussions in Chapter 5.

NOTE

In this section you'll learn the steps for building a small application named EmptyWindow. When launched, this program simply opens an empty window. There are no menus, and the window can't be moved. Clicking the mouse button ends the program. It's a bare minimum Mac program, but it's enough to see how a source code file, resource file, and libraries all work together in either a 68K or PPC project.

I make two versions of the same program, one using the MW C/C++ 68K compiler and the other using the MW C/C++ PPC compiler. To keep the projects and resulting applications separate, I'll give them similar but different names. I'll keep all of the files together in one folder—a folder I've created in my folder of Chapter 2 examples and named Empty Window ƒ.

The EmptyWindow Resource File

Almost all Macintosh programs that have a Macintosh interface are based on a project that includes a resource file. The resource file for the EmptyWindow program is named EmptyWindow.rsrc and holds just a single resource, a WIND with an ID of 128.

If you use `ResEdit` as your resource editor, read on. If you prefer `Resorcerer`, skip ahead a couple of pages to the discussion of creating the `EmptyWindow.rsrc` resource file using `Resorcerer`.

Begin by launching `ResEdit`. Select **New** from the File menu to create a new resource file. You'll see the New File dialog box pictured in Figure 2.1. Use its pop-up list menu to move to the `Empty Window ƒ` folder. Type in the resource file name, then click on the **New** button.

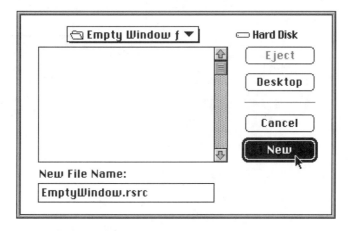

Figure 2.1 *Creating a new resource file in ResEdit.*

To add a `WIND` resource to the empty file, select **Create New Resource** from the Resource menu. Scroll to the `WIND` item in the list in the Select New Type dialog box that appears. Click once on `WIND`, then click the **OK** button, as shown in Figure 2.2.

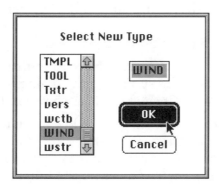

Figure 2.2 *Creating a WIND resource in ResEdit.*

For the EmptyWindow program, it's not important what type or size window you use. Enter the values shown in Figure 2.3, or use window dimensions of your own choosing. When you're done, select **Save** from the File menu and quit ResEdit.

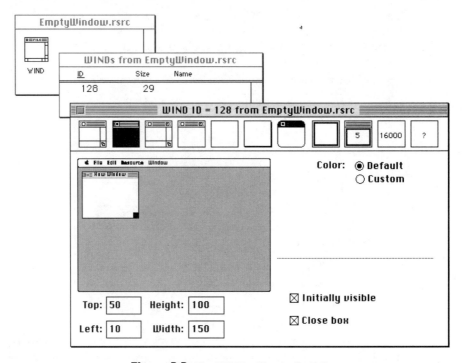

Figure 2.3 *The WIND editor in ResEdit.*

If you use Resorcerer rather than ResEdit, go ahead and launch it now. Select **New File** from the File menu. Use the list menu in the dialog box to move to the Empty Window ƒ folder, type in the name of the resource file, and click on the **Save** button (see Figure 2.4).

To add the WIND resource, select **New Resource** from the Resource menu. Scroll down to the WIND item in the dialog box and click on the item once. Then click the **Create** button, as shown in Figure 2.5.

Select **Set Window Info** from the Window menu to change the size or type of the new window. Figure 2.6 shows the dimensions I've entered for the window—you're free to use your own values. When you're finished, select **Save File** from the File menu and quit Resorcerer.

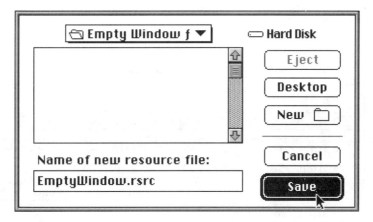

Figure 2.4 *Creating a new resource file in Resorcerer.*

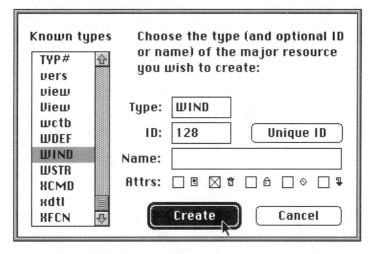

Figure 2.5 *Creating a WIND resource in Resorcerer.*

The Empty Window MW C/C++ 68K Project

If you own the CodeWarrior Gold package, you have two C/C++ compilers: a 68K version and a PowerPC (PPC) version. Others have just one, the 68K version. Even if you have a Power Mac and both compilers, it's a good idea to know how to work with projects for both compilers. In this section you'll see how to create a typical MW C/C++ 68K project. In the next section you'll work with the PPC compiler.

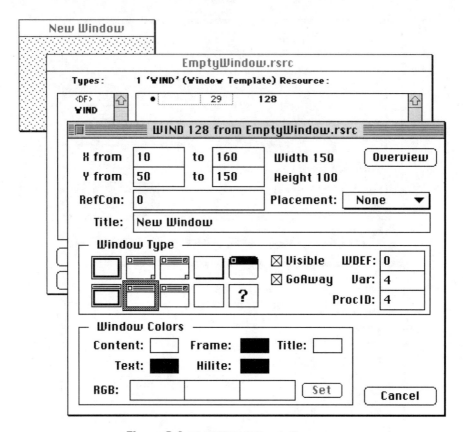

Figure 2.6 *The WIND Editor in Resourcer*

Begin by launching the MW C/C++ 68K compiler and selecting **New Project** from the File menu. Use the list menu to move to the Empty Window ƒ folder, then type in a name for the project, as I've done in Figure 2.7. Metrowerks projects should abide by the following naming convention:

1. End the project name with either 68K or PPC to indicate which compiler the project is used with.

2. Add an extension of .µ (create the µ character by typing the **Option** and **m** keys simultaneously).

As you can see from the project name in Figure 2.7, I'm using the MW C/C++ 68K compiler to create this version of the EmptyWindow program.

After typing in the project name, click the **Save** button. When you do, you'll see a new, empty project window (see Figure 2.8).

Figure 2.7 *Creating a new CodeWarrior project.*

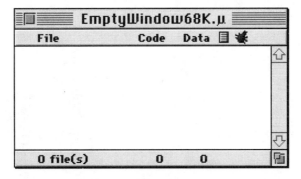

Figure 2.8 *The new, empty CodeWarrior project window.*

Now, select **New** from the File menu to open a new, empty file. Type in the source code shown in Figure 2.9. Then select **Save** from the File menu and name the source code file. Typically, you'll give the source code file the same name as the project—without the 68K or PPC. For a C language program, give the source file a .c extension, as I've done in Figure 2.10.

```
void  main( void )
{
    WindowPtr   theWindow;

    InitGraf( &qd.thePort );
    InitFonts();
    InitWindows();
    InitMenus();
    TEInit();
    InitDialogs( 0L );
    FlushEvents( everyEvent, 0 );
    InitCursor();

    theWindow = GetNewWindow( 128, nil, (WindowPtr)-1L );

    while ( !Button() )
        ;
}
```

Figure 2.9 *The source code file for the EmptyWindow project.*

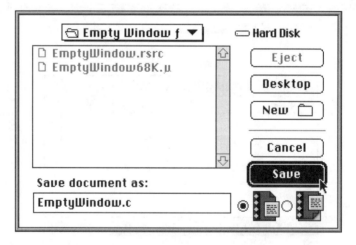

Figure 2.10 *Saving the source code file to disk.*

Add the file to the empty project by selecting **Add Window** from the Project menu. To add a file other than an open source code file, select **Add Files** from the File menu. Click on the EmptyWindow.rsrc resource file name, then click the **Add** button. Before clicking the **Done** button, use the dialog box list menu to work your way into the MacOS 68K ƒ folder. Once there, add the MacOS.lib library, as is being done in Figure 2.11. Refer to Figure 2.12 to see the folder path that leads to this library.

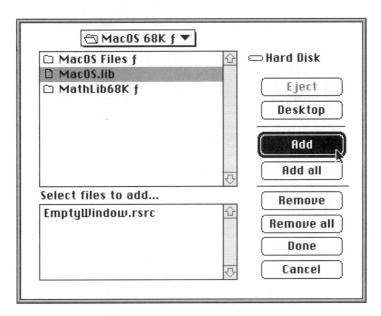

Figure 2.11 *Adding files to the CodeWarrior project.*

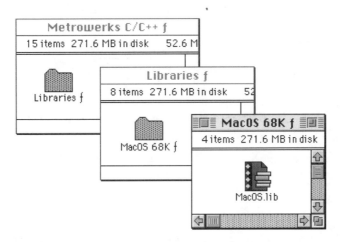

Figure 2.12 *The folder path to the MacOS.lib library.*

Your `EmptyWindow68K.µ` project window should now look like Figure 2.13.

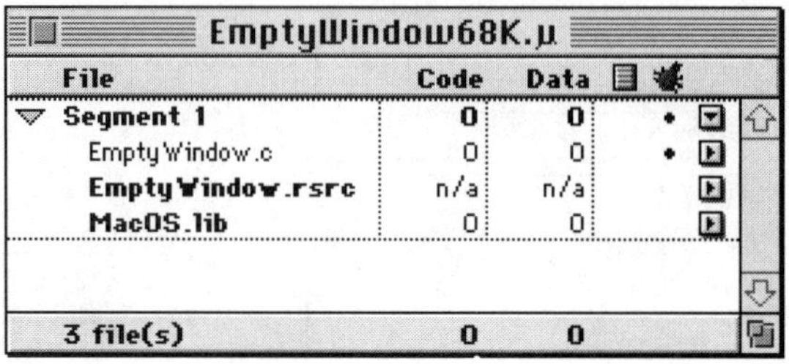

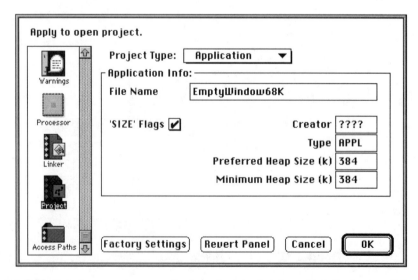

Figure to follow shows the project window:

File	Code	Data		
▽ **Segment 1**	**0**	**0**	•	☑
Empty Window.c	0	0	•	▶
Empty Window.rsrc	n/a	n/a		▶
MacOS.lib	0	0		▶
3 file(s)	**0**	**0**		

Figure 2.13 *The EmptyWindow68K project with all the necessary files added to it.*

You'll want to include the `MacOS.lib` library in all of your 68K projects. You'll read a lot more about this important library later in this chapter.

N O T E

Before building the application, select **Preferences** from the Edit menu. Click on the **Project** icon, then type in a name for the program that is generated from this project. Because you'll be making two versions of this program (if you own both C/C++ compilers), append **68K** to the end of the program's name, as I've done in Figure 2.14. Then click the **OK** button.

Figure 2.14 *Entering a program name in the project panel of the project's Preferences dialog box.*

To test out the application, select **Run** from the Project menu. This menu item will compile and link the files listed in the project window to create a 68K version of the EmptyWindow program. It will also take the program for a test drive. When that happens, you'll see an empty window on the screen. Click the mouse button to end the EmptyWindow68K program.

The Empty Window MW C/C++ PPC Project

If you own the PowerPC version of the Metrowerks C/C++ compiler, launch it now. Select **New Project** from the File menu, as you did for the 68K project. Use the list menu to move to the Empty Window ƒ folder, then type **EmptyWindowPPC.µ** as the name of the project (see Figure 2.15).

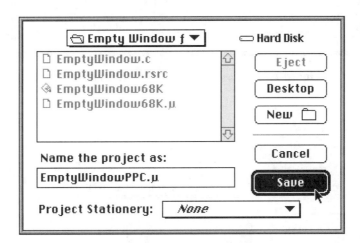

Figure 2.15 *Creating a PowerPC version of the EmptyWindow project.*

To add the necessary files to the empty project window, select **Add Files** from the Project menu. Because you've already created a 68K version of the EmptyWindow program, some of the files you need for the PPC version will already be in the Empty Window ƒ folder. Add the source code file and resource file, as I've done in Figure 2.16. Before clicking the **Done** button, work your way into the MacOS PPC ƒ folder and add the InterfaceLib library. Then move to the Runtime PPC ƒ folder and add the MWCRuntime.Lib. The paths to these two libraries are shown in Figure 2.17.

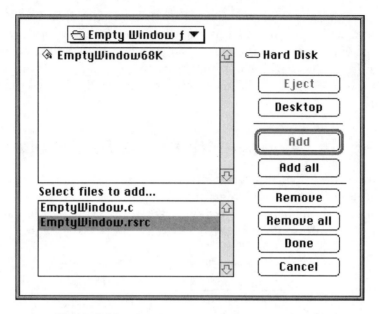

Figure 2.16 *Adding files to the EmptyWindow project.*

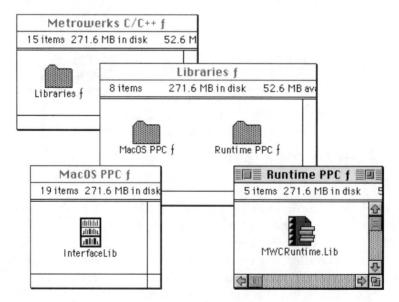

Figure 2.17 *The folder path to the InterfaceLib and MWCRuntime.Lib libraries.*

When complete, your project window should look like Figure 2.18. It's important to note that both the 68K and PPC versions of the EmptyWindow project use the same EmptyWindow.c source code file and the same EmptyWindow.rsrc file. Figure 2.19 emphasizes this fact.

Figure 2.18 *The EmptyWindowPPC project with the necessary files added to it.*

 Add both the InterfaceLib and MWCRuntime.Lib libraries to all of your PPC projects. Like the MacOS.lib library used in 68K projects, you'll read more about the PPC libraries later in this chapter.

NOTE

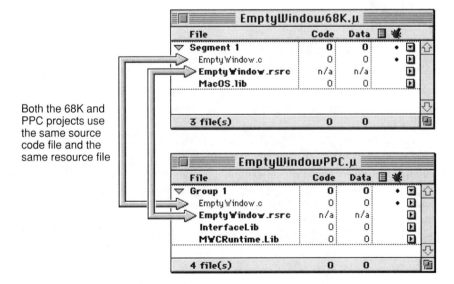

Both the 68K and PPC projects use the same source code file and the same resource file

Figure 2.19 *Both 68K and PPC versions of a project can use the same source code and resource files.*

Before building the EmptyWindow application, select **Preferences** from the Edit menu. Click the **Project** icon to bring up the project panel. Here, enter the program's name. Append **PPC** to the name to make it clear that this is a PowerPC-only application (see Figure 2.20). After clicking the **OK** button, build the application. If you're working from a Power Mac, select **Run** from the Project menu to build the application and to give it a test run. If you're using a 680x0-based Macintosh, you'll be able to build the application, but you won't be able to run it. In that case select **Make** from the Project menu.

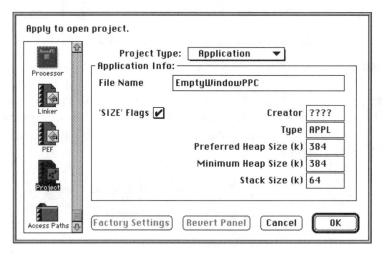

Figure 2.20 *Entering a program name in the project panel of the project's Preferences dialog box.*

Congratulations—you've successfully used CodeWarrior to create both a 68K and a PowerPC-only program! Now, to get a better understanding of the libraries that were added to the two projects, as well as a look at how header files are used in a project, continue on to the next section.

Headers, Libraries, and the Toolbox

A CodeWarrior project consists of one or more source code files, one or more library files, and usually a resource file. And while you won't see the names of any header files in a project window, a project also uses several Universal Header files. The purpose of the Universal Header files, and of one of the library files, is to allow your project to communicate with the Macintosh Toolbox. In this section you'll see the relationship between Universal Header files, libraries, and the Toolbox. In the section following this one ("The SetVolume Example Program"), you'll see a short example program named `SetVolume` that drives these points home.

Apple's Universal Header Files

The Toolbox is a collection of Apple-written functions that have been compiled and placed in the ROM chips of each Macintosh. In order to include a call to one of the Toolbox routines, your source code must provide the compiler with the calling convention of the routine. That is, the compiler needs a function prototype for a called Toolbox function so that it can verify that the parameters and function return type you supply are correct. The Apple Universal Header files contain function prototypes for each Toolbox function. A few of the more than 100 Universal Header files are shown in Figure 2.21.

N O T E

Apple occasionally adds new functions to the thousands of existing Toolbox routines. When that happens, the header files need to be updated. That's one reason there are different versions of the Universal Header files. As of this writing the current version is 2.0a3.

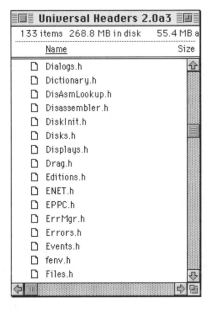

Figure 2.21 *Some of the many Apple Universal Header files.*

The Universal Header Files and the Toolbox

As an example of when a Universal Header file is needed, consider the Toolbox function GetNewWindow(). Its prototype is supplied in the Universal Header file Windows.h. If one of my CodeWarrior projects includes a call to GetNewWindow(), then it will also need to include the Windows.h header file. That enables my project to use the GetNewWindow() function that's found in ROM (see Figure 2.22).

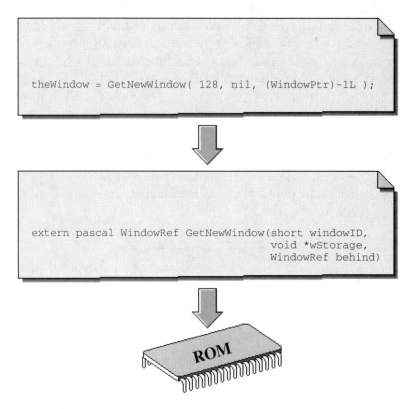

```
theWindow = GetNewWindow( 128, nil, (WindowPtr)-1L );
```

```
extern pascal WindowRef GetNewWindow(short windowID,
                                     void *wStorage,
                                     WindowRef behind)
```

ROM

Figure 2.22 *The function prototype of a Toolbox function, necessary to use the Toolbox function located in ROM, is found in a Universal Header file.*

None of the more than 100 Universal Header files are a part of your project unless you specifically include them. To do so, use the #include compiler directive. Figure 2.23 shows the Windows.h Universal Header file being included in a source code file.

```
#include <Windows.h>

theWindow = GetNewWindow( 128, nil, (WindowPtr)-1L );
```

Figure 2.23 *Use an #include directive in a source code file to make use of a Toolbox function.*

As your source code grows and you make more and more calls to Toolbox routines, keeping track of which Universal Header files are needed in a project can become difficult. To simplify things, Metrowerks has taken several of the most commonly used Universal Header files and created a single precompiled header file. By using this single header file in a project, you eliminate the need to include several individual Universal Header files. For 680x0 projects, the precompiled header file is named MacHeaders68K. For a PowerPC project, you'll instead use MacHeadersPPC. Once a MacHeaders file is included in a project, you'll seldom have to use #include directives with the Universal Header files. In Figure 2.24 you can see that I've commented out the inclusion of Windows.h.

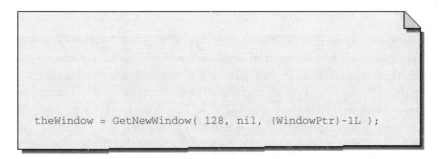

```
theWindow = GetNewWindow( 128, nil, (WindowPtr)-1L );
```

Figure 2.24 *With MacHeaders included in a project, few of the Universal Header files will need to be included in source code.*

To include one of the two precompiled headers in a project, enter its name in the **Prefix File** edit box in the Language panel of the Preferences dialog box. Figure 2.25 shows this being done for an MW C/C++ 68K project. The file named in this edit box will be compiled before any other files in the current project.

```
Apply to Metrowerks defaults.

                    Source Model: [ Custom      ▼ ]

    ┌─ Language Info: ────────────────────────────────────┐
    │   ☐ Activate C++ Compiler    ☐ ANSI Strict          │
    │   ☐ ARM conformance          ☐ ANSI Keywords Only   │
    │   ☐ Direct Destruction       ☐ Expand Trigraphs     │
    │   ☐ Don't Inline                                    │
    │                              ☐ MPW Newlines         │
    │   ☐ Pool Strings             ☐ MPW Pointer Type Rules│
    │   ☐ Don't Reuse Strings      ☐ Enums Always Int     │
    │                                                     │
    │   ☐ Require Function Prototypes                     │
    └─────────────────────────────────────────────────────┘

        Prefix File [MacHeaders68K                    ]

    [ Factory Settings ]  [ Revert Panel ]  [ Cancel ]  [  OK  ]
```

Figure 2.25 *A MacHeaders file is added to a project by naming it in the Prefix File edit box of the Language panel in the Preferences dialog box.*

NOTE

You'll find that CodeWarrior adds the appropriate precompiled header (MacHeaders68K or MacHeadersPPC) when you create a new project.

Including the appropriate MacHeaders precompiled header file in your project makes things simpler than using a #include directive for each needed Universal Header file. There's a second advantage to using a MacHeaders file, though. Because the MacHeaders68K and MacHeadersPPC files are precompiled, they add almost no time to the building of an application. The compiler doesn't need to compile the file's contents (as might be the case if you named a different file as the prefix file). In contrast to this, each Universal Header file that is added to a project through the use of a #include directive must be compiled once.

MacHeaders and the #include Directive

With a MacHeaders header file as your project's prefix file, you might think that there'd be no need to use the #include directive with any Universal Header files. Recall, however, that the MacHeaders files contain the compiled code of the most commonly used header files—not the code of *all* the header files. For example, QuickDraw.h, Windows.h, Dialogs.h, Events.h, and Resources.h are a few of the header files that are a part of MacHeaders, but the Sound.h header file is not. On occasion, you'll make a call to a less commonly used Toolbox function that doesn't have its prototype listed in MacHeaders—such as the SndPlay() Toolbox routine which is defined in Sound.h. In a project such as this, you must use a MacHeaders file and an #include <Sound.h> directive.

N O T E

This chapter's SetVolume program, discussed in just a bit, is an example of a project that uses both a MacHeaders file (MacHeaders68K) and the #include directive to incorporate a Universal Header file (Sound.h) into a project.

Libraries and the Toolbox

By now you should understand the relationship between the Universal Header files and the Toolbox: Macintosh programs make calls to Toolbox functions that reside in ROM, and the Universal Header files provide the Metrowerks compiler with the definitions of these functions. That takes care of working with many Toolbox functions, but not all of them.

A decade ago, when the first Macs came out, there were several hundred Toolbox functions at a programmer's disposal. As time went on, Apple improved the Mac interface by adding more and more Toolbox functions—now there are several *thousand*. Each time Apple added a new set of Toolbox routines, they created new ROM chips for the new Macintosh models. But what about the millions of existing Macintosh computers in homes, stores, and businesses? How could these models, with the older ROM chips, gain the functionality that was offered by the new Toolbox routines? The answer lies in the System file found on every Macintosh computer.

When new Toolbox routines are created by Apple, Apple places them in both the ROM chips of new Macs *and* in a new version of the System file. The new ROM chips are useless to owners of existing Macs, but the new version of the System file is useful. Any Mac owner can get a copy of a new version of the System file and use it in place of his or her current version. When a Mac owner does that, the new Toolbox routines make their way into the owner's machine.

Thankfully, the fact that some Toolbox routines exist in ROM and some in the System file isn't much of a concern to Macintosh software developers. Metrowerks has seen to that by creating the MacOS.lib and the InterfaceLib libraries.

A *library* is nothing more than a set of functions that are precompiled and stored together in a single file. You won't find any source code in a library—just the compiled versions of the functions. Your projects can use the functions in a library, even though you can't open the library to view the source code from which the compiled code originated. If you're creating a 680x0 project, you'll add the MacOS.lib library to your project. It holds code that helps the MW C/C++ 68K compiler use any Toolbox routines found in the System file. If you're creating a PowerPC project, you'll instead add InterfaceLib—the PPC version of this library—to your MW C/C++ PPC project.

Figure 2.26 summarizes why a project might need a MacHeaders precompiled header file as the prefix file, a Universal Header file included in a #include directive, and a library added to the project. On the left side of the figure, a source code file named Test.c makes a call to the Toolbox function GetNewWindow(). The prototype of this older Toolbox routine, which is found in the ROM of any Macintosh, is defined in the Windows.h Universal Header file. This header file is one of the many that is a part of the MacHeaders68K precompiled header file.

On the right side of the figure is the same source code file, this time making a call to the newer Toolbox function SetSoundVol(). This routine is defined in the Universal Header file Sound.h. Because Sound.h is not a part of MacHeaders68K, an #include <Sound.h> directive will need to be included in the Test.c source code file. Not only that, but since the SetSoundVol() function won't be found in the ROM of every Macintosh, the library MacOS.lib needs to be in the project so that the compiler can find this Toolbox routine in the System file.

The SetVolume Example Program

In this section we'll take a look at a very simple Mac program that exists merely for the purpose of demonstrating the last section's discussion

about the various file types found in a CodeWarrior project. The
SetVolume program uses the Toolbox function SetSoundVol() to set the
user's Macintosh speaker volume to its highest setting. Running
SetVolume produces no on-screen effects—you won't see any menus or
windows. Instead, the program starts up, beeps the speaker twice, then
quits. If you open your Sound control panel after running SetVolume,
you'll see that the speaker volume slider is set to the highest level,
regardless of where it was before SetVolume ran. Figure 2.27 shows the
Sound control panel, found in the Control Panels folder.

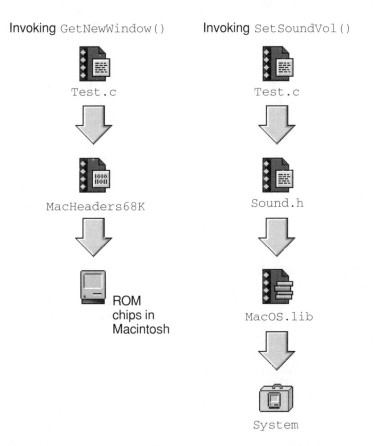

Figure 2.26 *Some Toolbox functions are not mentioned in the MacHeaders files,
making it necessary to include a Universal Header file.*

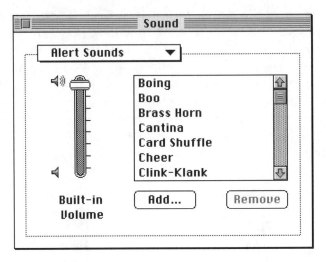

Figure 2.27 *The Sound Control Panel.*

 NOTE You can change the volume setting on your own computer, and leave it changed, any time you want. But it's considered a bit rude to change a *systemwide feature*, such as speaker volume or desktop pattern, on someone else's Mac. I'll remedy the impolite behavior of the SetVolume program in Chapter 3 when I write another short sound-related program.

The SetVolume Project

If you're using a 680x0-based Macintosh, use the MW C/C++ 68K compiler to create the SetVolume68K.µ project. If you're working on a Power Mac, you can use either the MW C/C++ 68K or MW C/C++ PPC compiler to create the SetVolume project. You might, however, decide to go with the 68K compiler so that your efforts match the figures in this section.

Create a new, empty folder and name it Set Volume ƒ. The SetVolume project won't require any resources, so there's no need to run your resource editor. Instead, jump right in and launch your compiler, then select **New Project** from the File menu. In the dialog box that opens (see Figure 2.28), enter the name of the project. I'm using the MW C/C++ 68K compiler to compile my version of SetVolume, so I've named my project **SetVolume68K.µ**. After typing in the project name, click the **Save** button.

Set Volume ƒ
Hard Disk
Eject
Desktop
New
Name the project as:
SetVolume68K.µ
Cancel
Save
Project Stationery:
None

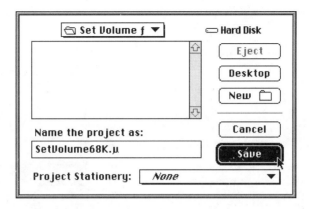

Figure 2.28 *Creating the SetVolume68K project.*

Now, select **New** from the File menu to open a new, empty file. Type in the source code shown in Figure 2.29. We'll take a close look at the code a little later. For now, just select **Save** from the File menu and name the source code file. As you saw earlier, you'll typically give the source code file the same name as the project, without the 68K or PPC. Now that you've seen that the same source code file can be used in both a 68K and PPC project, it should make sense that the source code file name doesn't include a reference to either compiler. Because this is a C language program, I've added a `.c` extension to the file name, as shown in Figure 2.30.

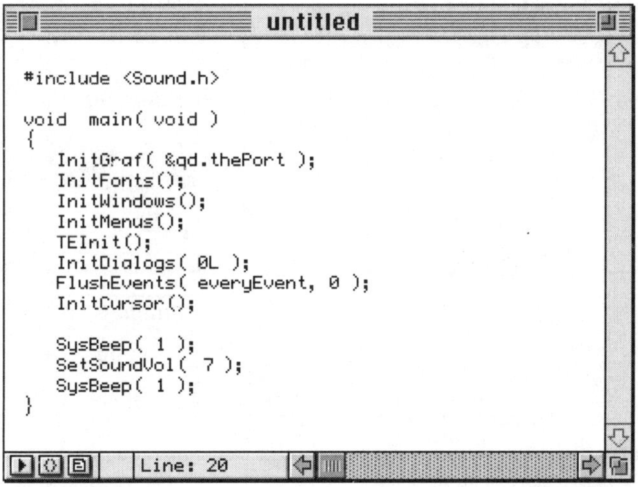

untitled
#include <Sound.h>
void main(void)
{
InitGraf(&qd.thePort);
InitFonts();
InitWindows();
InitMenus();
TEInit();
InitDialogs(0L);
FlushEvents(everyEvent, 0);
InitCursor();
SysBeep(1);
SetSoundVol(7);
SysBeep(1);
}
Line: 20

Figure 2.29 *The source code file for the SetVolume project.*

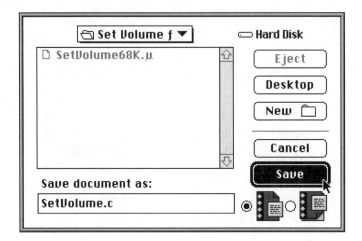

Figure 2.30 *Saving the Set Volume source code file to disk.*

Add the file to the empty project by selecting **Add Window** from the Project menu. Then add the MacOS.lib library to the project by selecting **Add Files** from the File menu and working your way into the MacOS 68K ƒ folder, as I've done in Figure 2.31. Refer to Figure 2.32 if you need a reminder of the folder hierarchy.

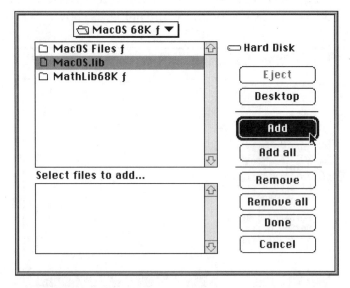

Figure 2.31 *Adding a file to the Set Volume project.*

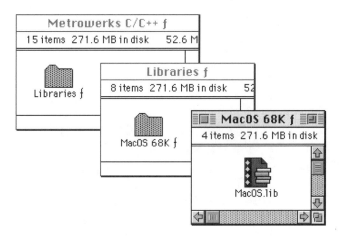

Figure 2.32 *The folder path to the MacOS.lib library.*

I've created a 68K version of the SetVolume project—its project window is shown on the left side of Figure 2.33. If you decide to use the PPC compiler instead, your project window should match the one on the right side of this same figure. If you're making a PowerPC project, and you can't remember just where the InterfaceLib and MWCRuntime.Lib libraries are located, refer to Figure 2.34.

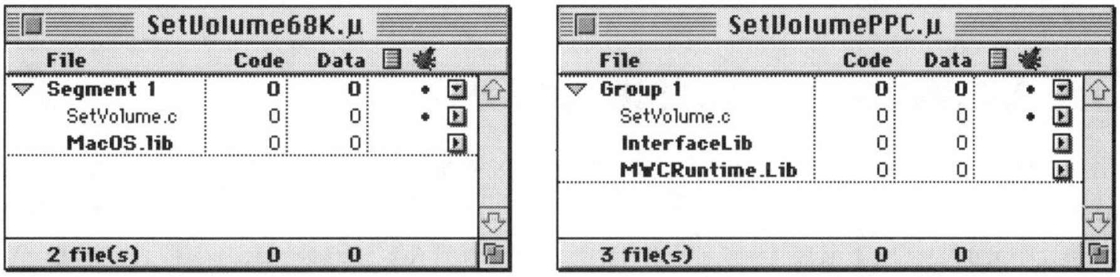

Figure 2.33 *The 68K and PPC versions of the SetVolume project.*

Notice in Figure 2.33 that the project for the 68K compiler uses the MacOS.lib library, while the PPC project uses the InterfaceLib library, as discussed in the previous section. Additionally, the PPC project uses a library named MWCRuntime.Lib. This library contains the code for certain Code Fragment Manager routines. The way a program is stored in memory differs on a 680x0-based Macintosh and on a Power Mac. It's the job of this new manager to make sure that a program gets properly loaded into memory when running on a Power Mac.

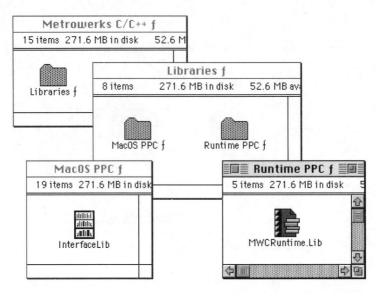

Figure 2.34 *The folder path to the InterfaceLib and MWCRuntime.Lib libraries.*

Always add MacOS.lib to a CodeWarrior 68K project, and *always* add InterfaceLib and MWCRuntime.Lib to a CodeWarrior PPC project.

N O T E

The SetVolume Source Code

The SetVolume.c source code file has a single *application-defined function*, the main() function. To distinguish between functions written by a programmer for this one application and those that are a part of the Macintosh Toolbox, you'll see the phrase "application-defined function" used throughout this book. Here's a look at main():

```
void  main( void )
{
   InitGraf( &qd.thePort );
   InitFonts();
   InitWindows();
   InitMenus();
   TEInit();
   InitDialogs( 0L );
   FlushEvents( everyEvent, 0 );
```

```
    InitCursor();

    SysBeep( 1 );
    SetSoundVol( 7 );
    SysBeep( 1 );
}
```

The `SetVolume main()` function consists of nothing more than 11 calls to Toolbox routines. The first eight are standard initialization routines that should appear in the given order in every program that makes use of the Macintosh Toolbox. The three remaining function calls are made to the Toolbox routines `SysBeep()` and `SetSoundVol()`.

The `SysBeep()` function sounds the Mac's speaker one time. In the old days, when the Mac had just entered the computer market, this function did just what its name implies—it sounded a beep. You could vary the length, or duration, of the beep by changing the value of the one parameter `SysBeep()` requires. Now, `SysBeep()` works a little differently. A call to this function plays whatever sound the user has selected in the Sound Control Panel. And while the one parameter to `SysBeep()` is still required (for backwards compatibility with older Macintosh computers), its value doesn't matter.

The prototype for the `SysBeep()` function can be found in the `OSUtils.h` Universal Header file. This header file is one of the many that is included in the `MacHeaders68K` precompiled header file, so there's no need to use an #include directive in the source code to bring `OSUtils.h` into the file.

The `SetSoundVol()` function is a Toolbox routine that sets the volume level of the user's Macintosh. Normally, the user will set this level using the Sound control panel found on all Macs. Including a call to `SetSoundVol()` in a program will override whatever sound level the user currently has. The level will be changed to a value that is based on the one parameter passed to `SetSoundVol()`. This parameter should be in the 0–7 range, with 0 turning off the volume, and 7 setting the volume to its highest level.

The prototype for `SetSoundVol()` can be found in the Universal Header file `Sound.h`. The `Sound.h` file is a header file that is not a part of `MacHeaders68K`—and that's worthy of noting. This means that the `Sound.h` file needs to be included in the source code file. The `SetVolume` program does that with the following line:

```
#include <Sound.h>
```

Figure 2.35 summarizes the purpose of the source code that makes up
the `SetVolume` program.

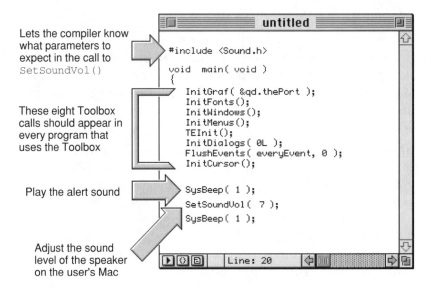

Lets the compiler know
what parameters to
expect in the call to
`SetSoundVol()`

These eight Toolbox
calls should appear in
every program that
uses the Toolbox

Play the alert sound

Adjust the sound
level of the speaker
on the user's Mac

```
                              untitled
#include <Sound.h>

void  main( void )
{
    InitGraf( &qd.thePort );
    InitFonts();
    InitWindows();
    InitMenus();
    TEInit();
    InitDialogs( 0L );
    FlushEvents( everyEvent, 0 );
    InitCursor();

    SysBeep( 1 );
    SetSoundVol( 7 );
    SysBeep( 1 );

                              Line: 20
```

Figure 2.35 *An explanation of the SetVolume source code.*

Verifying that Header Files and Libraries are Necessary

In this section I'll do a few simple experiments with the `MacHeaders` precompiled header file, the Universal Header files, and libraries to see the
effect of forgetting to add one or more of these elements to a project. In
doing so, you should gain a better understanding of the purpose of each.

Begin by opening the **SetVolume68K.µ** project by double-clicking
on its icon in the Finder, or by selecting it from the dialog box that
appears when you choose **Open** from the File menu of the MW C/C++ 68K
compiler. Open the Preferences dialog box and click on the **Language**
icon. Then click on the **Require Function Prototypes** check box, as
shown in Figure 2.36. Now any error messages you get will match mine
when you attempt to compile and link the `SetVolume` project.

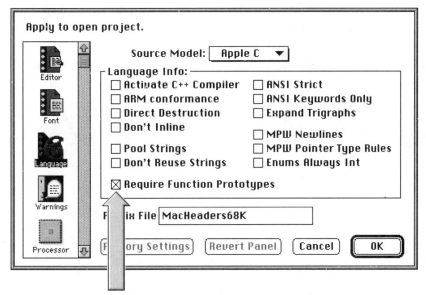

Check this checkbox to guarantee that the
compiler will report missing prototypes as errors

Figure 2.36 *Requiring prototypes to appear in a
project forces the compiler to check code closely.*

Close the Preferences dialog box and open the SetVolume.c source code
file by double-clicking on its name in the SetVolume68K.µ project window.
Comment out the #include <Sound.h> line, then select **Run** from the
Project menu to recompile and run the program. As you may have
guessed, commenting out the inclusion of the Sound.h file will prevent the
project from successfully compiling. Before looking at Figure 2.37, try to
guess at what kind of an error message might be displayed in the Message
Window.

The compiler informs you that without the Sound.h file, it can't
determine what the Toolbox function SetSoundVol() should look like.
Notice, however, that the compiler didn't report any errors regarding
the ten other Toolbox function calls. Why? They're commonly used routines, and the Universal Header files that define their prototypes are all
a part of the MacHeaders68K precompiled header file. To further prove
that this is the case, open the Preferences dialog box and click on the
Languages icon. Then cut or backspace over the string that's in the

Prefix File edit box—**MacHeaders68K**. After clicking the **OK** button, again select **Run** from the Project menu. After you do that, you'll see a message window much like the one shown in Figure 2.38. Notice that without MacHeaders68K in the project, the compiler doesn't recognize what any of the common Toolbox routines look like.

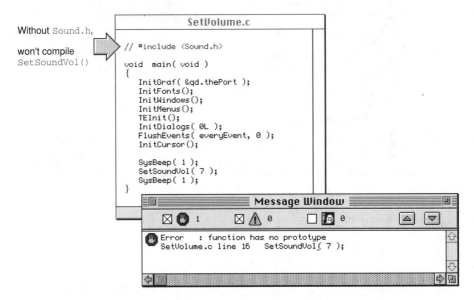

Figure 2.37 *Without the Sound.h header file, the compiler doesn't know what parameters should be passed to the SetSoundVol() routine.*

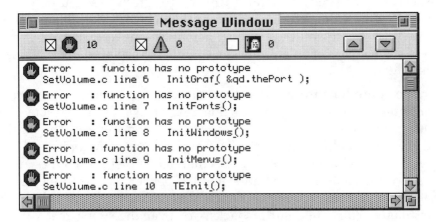

Figure 2.38 *Without MacHeaders, the compiler doesn't recognize any of the Toolbox functions.*

You've seen the effects of keeping both the `Sound.h` header file and the `MacHeaders68K` precompiled header file out of a project. There's one final test you can perform to gain a better understanding of the relationship between the files of a project. First, bring `Sound.h` back into the project by removing the double slash from in front of the `#include` directive at the top of the `SetVolume.c` source code listing. Then add `MacHeaders68K` by typing its name into the **Prefix File** edit box in the Languages panel of the Preferences dialog box. Next, click once on the `MacOS.lib` library in the project window, then select **Remove Files** from the Project menu. Now select **Run** from the Project menu.

As was the case when the `#include` directive was commented out earlier, once again only `SetSoundVol()` is listed in the message window, as shown in Figure 2.39. This time the compiler successfully compiled the code (because it knew what `SetSoundVol()` looks like from the `Sound.h` header file), but CodeWarrior reports that a link error occurred. The commonly used Toolbox routines are found in ROM, and a program such as `SetVolume` can access them without any help from a library. But the `SetSoundVol()` Toolbox routine is a different story. This is a function that didn't exist before System 7. Now, it exists, but not in ROM. Instead, its code appears in the new versions of the `System` file. CodeWarrior needs the code in the `MacOS.lib` library to make this connection.

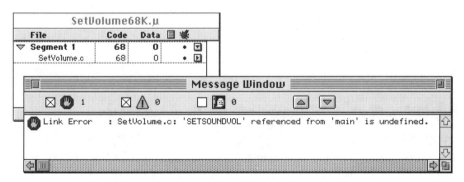

Figure 2.39 *Without the MacOS.lib library, the compiler doesn't recognize SetSoundVol() as a Toolbox function.*

CodeWarrior Projects and Libraries

In this chapter you've seen the importance of the `MacHeader` precompiled header file, the Universal Header files, and the `MacOS.lib` and

InterfaceLib libraries. I'll finish with a short summary of some of the other libraries your projects might need to use.

Different types of projects require the addition of different libraries. Knowing which of the dozens of libraries to use in a project will go a long way to avoiding compile and link errors. In this section I'll cover several project types, and the libraries they require. On the included CD you'll find a 68K and PPC project—along with a source code file—for each example.

C++ Projects and Libraries

If you're programming in C++ rather than C, and you're using the MW C/C++ PPC compiler, then you don't need to do anything special to create a C++ project. If you're using the MW C/C++ 68K compiler, you'll need to use one additional library.

THE MW C/C++ PPC COMPILER AND C++ LIBRARIES

CodeWarrior PowerPC projects that access the Toolbox using C++ need to use the InterfaceLib library. As you read earlier, this library, along with MWCRuntime.Lib, should already be a part of any of your PowerPC projects. For an example of a C++ object-oriented project, look at the OOPexample on the book's CD. Figure 2.40 shows a part of the OOPexample.cp source code file, along with the window that is the result of running the program. Figure 2.41 shows the project window for the PPC version.

THE MW C/C++ 68K COMPILER AND C++ LIBRARIES

If your 68K project uses C++ and the Toolbox, include the CPlusPlus.lib library in your project, along with the MacOS.lib library you're used to adding. Figure 2.42 shows the path to the CPlusPlus.lib. You'll find a 68K version of a C++ object-oriented project on the book's CD. Figure 2.43 shows the project window. You can look at Figure 2.40 to see the source code file and the window that appears when you run the program.

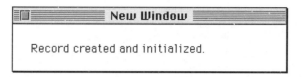

```
class  StudentInfo
{
    private:
        long   studentID;

    public:
        StudentInfo( void );        // constructor
};


StudentInfo :: StudentInfo( void )
{
    this->studentID = 0;
    MoveTo( 20, 30 );
    DrawString( "\pRecord created and initialized." );
}


StudentInfo   *theStudent;
```

Figure 2.40 *The source code file and program output for the OOPexample project.*

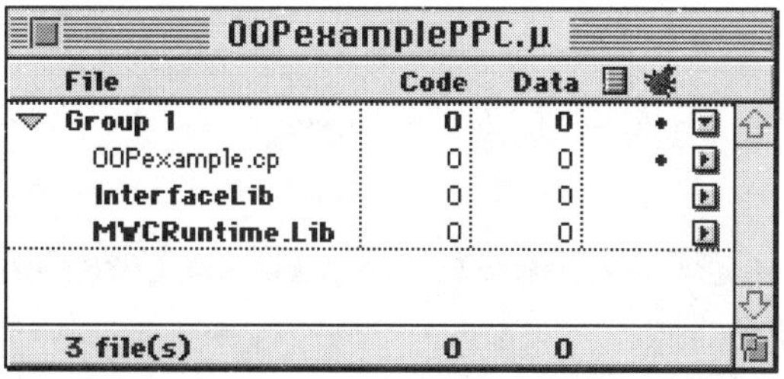

OOPexamplePPC.µ			
File	Code	Data	
▽ Group 1	0	0	• ▽
OOPexample.cp	0	0	• ▶
InterfaceLib	0	0	▶
M▼CRuntime.Lib	0	0	▶
3 file(s)	0	0	

Figure 2.41 *The project window for the PowerPC version of OOPexample.*

ANSI Projects and Libraries

If you're writing a Mac program that uses ANSI C or ANSI C++ functions, you'll need to include one of the ANSI libraries in your project.

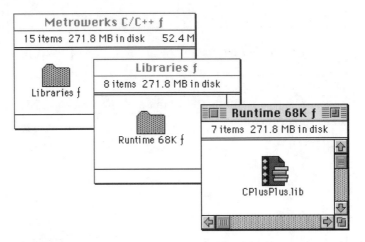

Figure 2.42 *The folder path to the CPlusPlus.lib library.*

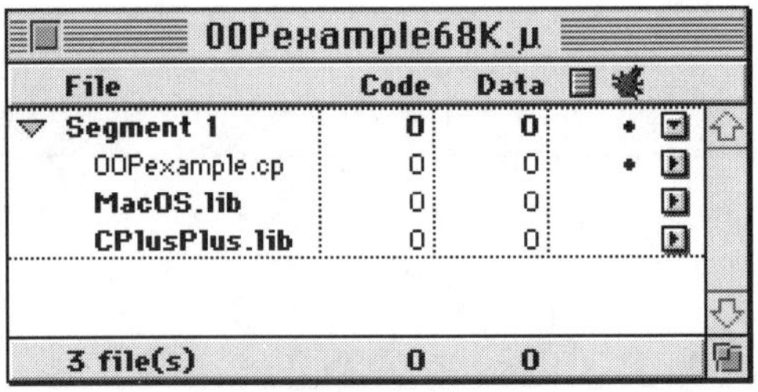

File	Code	Data		
▽ **Segment 1**	0	0	•	▣
OOPexample.cp	0	0	•	▣
MacOS.lib	0	0		▣
CPlusPlus.lib	0	0		▣
3 file(s)	**0**	**0**		

Figure 2.43 *The project window for the 68K version of the OOPexample.*

THE MW C/C++ PPC COMPILER AND ANSI LIBRARIES

If your PPC project uses ANSI C functions, use the ANSI C.PPC.Lib. If your project uses ANSI C++ functions, use *both* the ANSI C.PPC.Lib and the ANSI C++.PPC.Lib. On the left of Figure 2.44, you'll see the path to these two libraries. Whether you're doing a C or C++ project, you'll also want to add the appropriate ANSI header files in your source code. Figure 2.45 shows part of the source file for a Mac program that uses the ANSI C function toupper() to convert lowercase characters to uppercase. Notice that the ctype.h header file, which holds the definition of the toupper() function, is used in a #include directive. The figure also shows the window that results from running this program.

Figure 2.46 shows the PPC project window. You'll find the project and source for this ANSIexample program on the included CD.

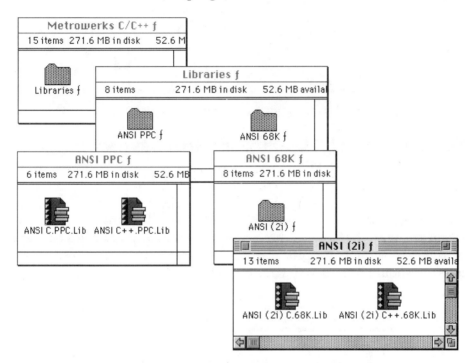

Figure 2.44 *The folder path to some of the ANSI libraries.*

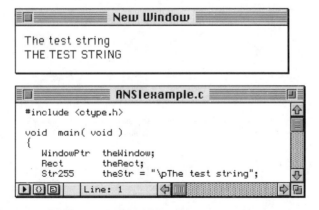

Figure 2.45 *The source code file and program output window of the ANSIexample.*

File	Code	Data		
▽ **Group 1**	**0**	**0**	•	▽
ANSIexample.c	0	0	•	▶
InterfaceLib	**0**	**0**		▶
MWCRuntime.Lib	**0**	**0**		▶
ANSI C.PPC.Lib	**0**	**0**		▶
4 file(s)	**0**	**0**		

ANSIexamplePPC.µ

Figure 2.46 *The project window for the PPC version of the ANSIexample.*

The MW C/C++ 68K Compiler and ANSI Libraries

When choosing the right library to add to a 68K project that uses ANSI C or C++, you must take into consideration different processor settings. This is a "good news, bad news" situation. The bad news is, there are eight 68K ANSI folders holding a total of a few dozen different libraries. Figure 2.47 shows these eight folders. The good news is, there is a very systematic approach to determining which of these many libraries should be added to your project.

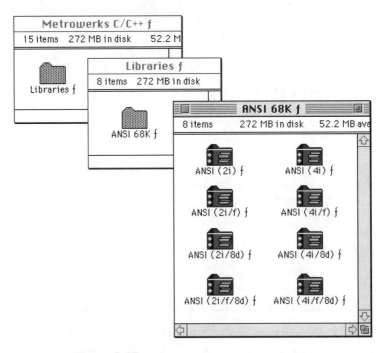

Figure 2.47 *The folder path to the ANSI folders.*

To determine which ANSI library to add to a project, you'll use the processor panel in the Preferences dialog box of your 68K project. The first thing to look for in this panel is whether the Factory Settings button is dim. If it is, use the ANSI (2i) ƒ folder. *This will most often be the case.*

Looking back at Figure 2.47 you can see that part of each ANSI folder's name is enclosed in parentheses. You can select the correct folder by matching settings in the Preferences dialog box with the numbers and letters in the parentheses—Figure 2.48 shows you how. You'll look at three check boxes in the Preferences dialog box. If the **4-Byte Ints** check box is checked, the ANSI folder name should include "4i" in it. If the **8-Byte Doubles** check box is checked, the folder name should include "8i." And, if the **68881 Codegen** check box is marked, the folder name should include the letter "f."

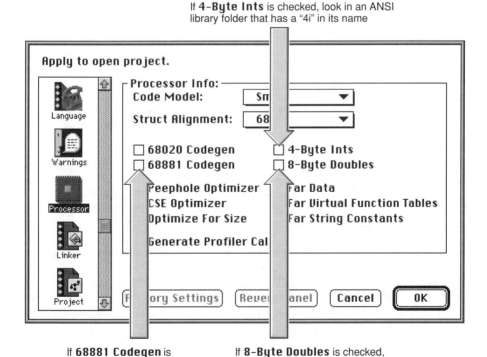

Figure 2.48 *Settings in the processor panel of the Preferences dialog box determine which ANSI library to use in a project.*

Consider a project that has a preferences processor panel like Figure 2.49. Because the **4-Byte Ints** and **8-Byte Doubles** check boxes are checked, the ANSI folder to use should include both a "4i" and an "8d." In this figure I've marked the correct folder.

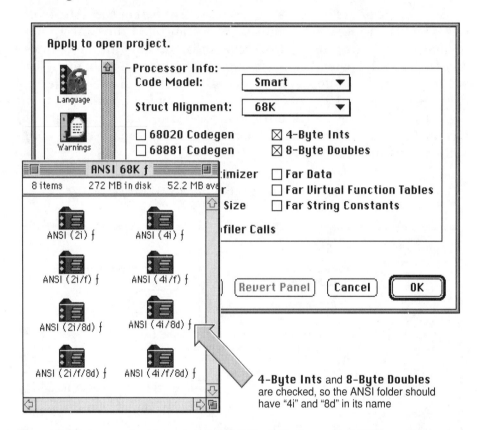

Figure 2.49 *An example of determining which folder holds the proper ANSI library for a project.*

Once you've determined which ANSI folder to use, you'll need to determine which one of the libraries in that folder belongs in your project. Typically you'll use one of two libraries—the C or C++ library. Figure 2.50 shows the two most commonly used libraries in the ANSI (4i/8d) ƒ folder—the folder that would be used in the example given in Figure 2.49.

N O T E

Remember, if the Factory Settings button in the preferences processor panel is dim, you'll use a library from the ANSI (2i) ƒ. Most likely, this library will be the ANSI (2i) C.68K.Lib library (for projects that use ANSI C) or the ANSI (2i) C++.68K.Lib library (for projects that use ANSI C++).

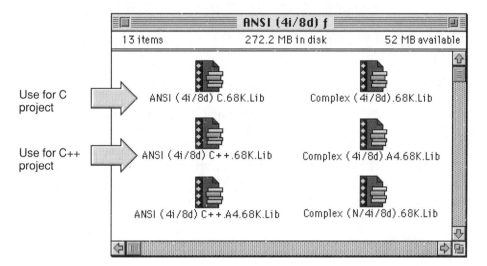

Use for C project

Use for C++ project

Figure 2.50 *The ANSI libraries to use for C and C++ projects that have 4-byte integers and 8-byte doubles.*

If your project will use ANSI C++, include the appropriate ANSI C++ library (as determined above) along with the ANSI C version of the same library and the CPlusPlus.lib library. For example, an ANSI C++ project that requires the ANSI (2i) C++.68K.Lib library would also need to have the ANSI (2i) C.68K.Lib library and the CPlusPlus.lib library.

Figure 2.51 shows the 68K project window for the ANSIexample68K project that can be found on this book's CD. Look back to Figure 2.45 to see a part of this project's source code file, as well as the window that appears when the program executes. Because the preferences processor panel is dim, I've used the ANSI (2i) C.68K.Lib library.

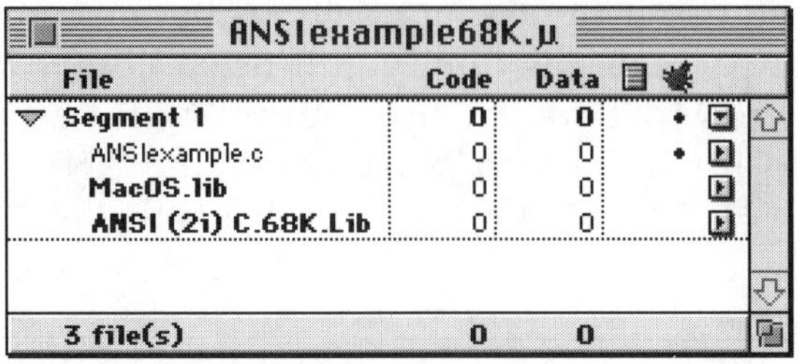

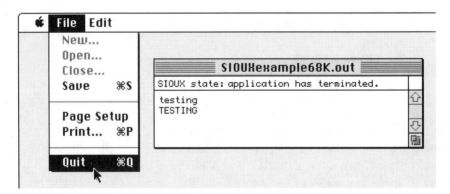

Figure 2.51 *The project window for the 68K version of the ANSIexample.*

SIOUX Projects and Libraries

If you're writing a simple program that doesn't need a Mac interface, you might use the standard CodeWarrior console window. If you use the console, your program will include menus and a window like Figure 2.52, without your having to write any supporting code. To make use of the console you need to include a SIOUX (Standard Input Output User eXchange) library in your project.

Figure 2.52 *The output of the SIOUXexample.*

THE MW C/C++ PPC COMPILER AND THE SIOUX CONSOLE

If your PowerPC project is to use the SIOUX console, include the `SIOUX.PPC.Lib` library and the `MathLib` library. The paths to these two libraries are shown in Figure 2.53. Because this console is often used for simple ANSI C or C++ programs, make sure you also add the `ANSI C.PPC.Lib` library (for an ANSI C project) or the `ANSI C.PPC.Lib` library *and* the `ANSI C++.PPC.Lib` library (for an ANSI C++ project).

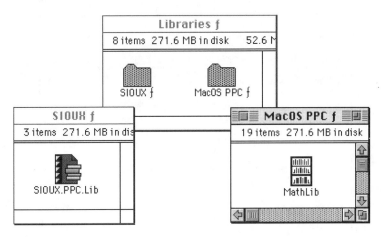

Figure 2.53 *The folder path to the SIOUX.PPC.Lib and MathLib libraries.*

The example SIOUX program included with this book is named `SIOUXexample`. Figure 2.54 shows the entire source code listing for it. Because the ANSI function `toupper()` is used, the ANSI header file `ctype.h` is included. And because the program calls the ANSI function `printf()`, the ANSI header file `stdio.h` is also included. To see the program's output, refer back to Figure 2.52. Figure 2.55 shows the PPC project for this example.

THE MW C/C++ 68K COMPILER AND THE SIOUX CONSOLE

For 68K projects that use the SIOUX console, add the `SIOUX.68K.Lib` library. If you're using ANSI code with the console, as is often the case, also add the appropriate ANSI libraries (such as `ANSI C (2i) C.68K.Lib` for an ANSI C project or `ANSI C++ (2i) C++.68K.Lib` and `CPlusPlus.lib` for an ANSI C++ project), as discussed earlier in this section. Also add the appropriate math library. You'll find a 68K math library with a name that includes parenthetical text to match whichever ANSI library you're using. For example, if you're using the `ANSI C (2i) C.68K.Lib` library, you'll use the `MathLib68K (2i).Lib` math library. Figure 2.56 shows the path to the 68K math libraries.

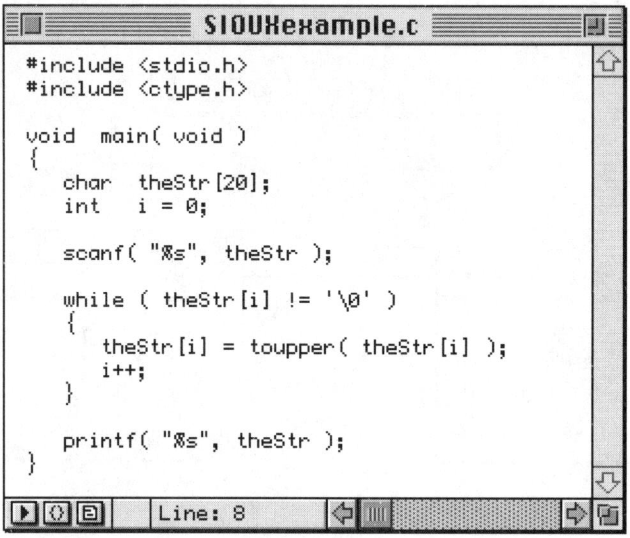

```
#include <stdio.h>
#include <ctype.h>

void  main( void )
{
   char  theStr[20];
   int   i = 0;

   scanf( "%s", theStr );

   while ( theStr[i] != '\0' )
   {
      theStr[i] = toupper( theStr[i] );
      i++;
   }

   printf( "%s", theStr );
}
```

Figure 2.54 *The source code file of the SIOUXexample.*

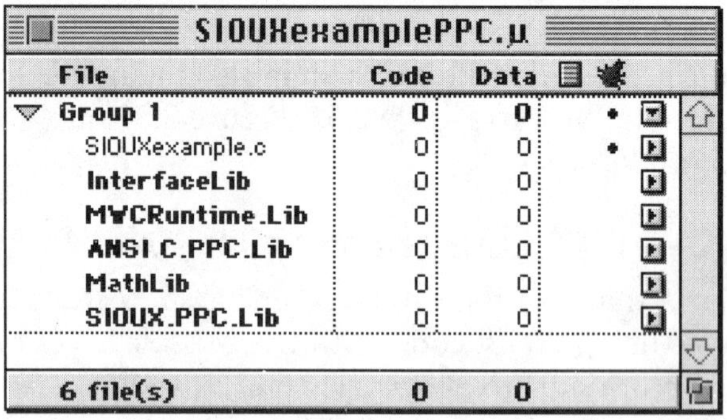

File	Code	Data		
▽ Group 1	0	0	•	▽
SIOUXexample.c	0	0	•	▷
InterfaceLib	0	0		▷
MWCRuntime.Lib	0	0		▷
ANSI C.PPC.Lib	0	0		▷
MathLib	0	0		▷
SIOUX.PPC.Lib	0	0		▷
6 file(s)	0	0		

Figure 2.55 *The project window for the PPC version of the SIOUXexample.*

The 68K project window for this book's SIOUX example is shown in Figure 2.57. To see the source code listing and program output, refer back to Figure 2.54 and Figure 2.52, respectively.

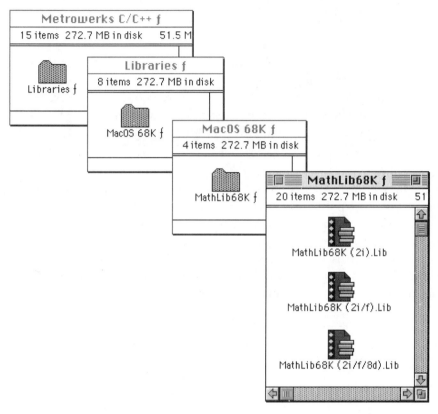

Figure 2.56 *The folder path to the MathLib libraries.*

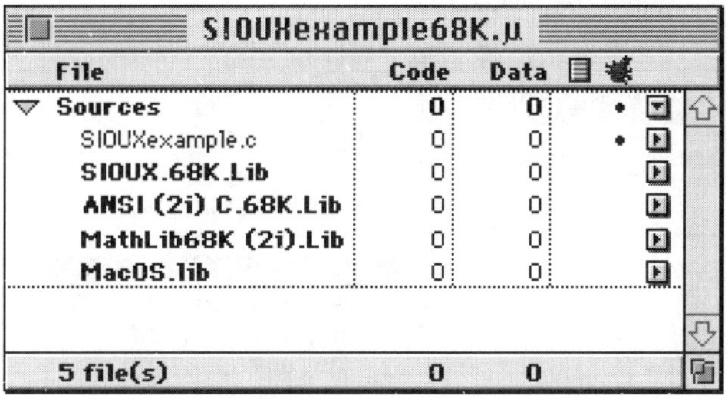

Figure 2.57 *The project window for the 68K version of the SIOUXexample.*

Project Stationary

When you select **New Project** from the File menu of either the MW C/C++ 68K or MW C/C++ PPC compiler, you'll face the New Project dialog box. At the bottom of that dialog box is a pop-up menu that allows you to select an optional stationary on which the new project should be based. The stationary is nothing more than a template which opens a project with the appropriate libraries already added to it.

In Figure 2.58 you can see that I'm creating a new project based on the ANSI 68K (2i) C stationary. From previous discussions you'd guess that when the project window opens, it should include the MacOS.lib library (as most 68K projects do), and the ANSI (2i) C.68K.Lib library. Metrowerks goes one step further and makes the assumption that you might be using the SIOUX console window in your program, so this stationary should also add the SIOUX.68K.Lib library and the MathLib68K(2i).Lib library. Figure 2.59 shows that this is exactly what does in fact appear in the new project window.

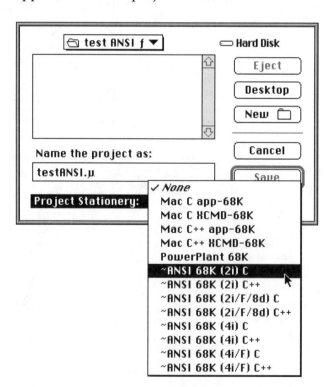

Figure 2.58 *The pop-up Project Stationary menu in the New Project dialog box.*

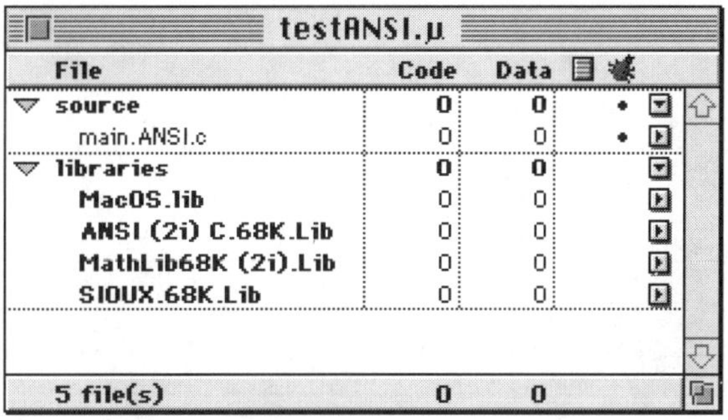

File	Code	Data	📄	🐞	
▽ source	0	0	•	▼	⬆
main.ANSI.c	0	0	•	▶	
▽ libraries	0	0		▼	
MacOS.lib	0	0		▶	
ANSI (2i) C.68K.Lib	0	0		▶	
MathLib68K (2i).Lib	0	0		▶	
SIOUX.68K.Lib	0	0		▶	⬇
5 file(s)	**0**	**0**			

Figure 2.59 *The new project that results from selecting the ANSI 68K (2i) C stationary.*

So why didn't I bring up the topic of project stationary before all the discussion about how to determine which libraries to add to a project? Because I knew that once you found out about project stationary, you wouldn't bother to learn about why different projects require different libraries. And when it comes to tracking down compile and link errors, that's an important topic to understand.

Chapter Summary

The CodeWarrior Gold package comes with two C/C++ compilers—one for generating 68K applications, the other for creating PowerPC-only programs. Regardless of which compiler you use, a program starts out as a CodeWarrior project. Each project consists of source code files, resource files, and libraries.

The files in a project rely on Apple's Universal Header files. This collection of more than 100 header files lists the prototype for *every* Toolbox function currently available.

Different projects will use different libraries of code. For example, a project that uses ANSI C will need an ANSI C library added to it. This is a cause of confusion for many programmers and can result in compile and link errors if the wrong libraries are used.

Chapter 3

Understanding the Universal Header Files

The Universal Header files are a collection of more than 100 header files that define the function prototypes for each of the thousands of Toolbox routines. Toolbox function prototypes are of great importance—without a function prototype, the MW C/C++ 68K and MW C/C++ PPC compilers will not compile code that includes a call to a Toolbox function.

For very small projects, a knowledge of what the Universal Header files are, and how they work, might not be necessary. But as your project grows larger, the chances of successfully compiling that project get smaller. That's because the more code your write, the more Toolbox routines you'll call, and the greater the likelihood that one of your function calls will not match the prototype listed in the header file. To add to the problem, Apple periodically modifies some of the Universal Header files. If you attempt to compile code that was written using an older set of the Universal Header files, you'll find many incompatibilities that result in compiler errors.

In this chapter you'll learn all about the Universal Header files. You'll see that a knowledge of how these files work will eliminate countless compile-time headaches.

Errors and the Universal Header Files

Consider the following scenario. You buy a programming book, which of course includes example source code. Perhaps the author and publisher were even kind enough to provide project files and source code files on an included disk. You attempt to compile the example code, following the book's instructions word-for-word. But instead of seeing a Mac program come to life on your screen, you end up looking at a Message Window that holds one or more errors like Figure 3.1.

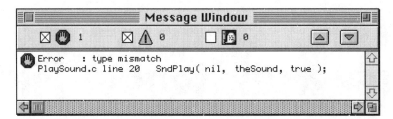

Figure 3.1 *The CodeWarrior Message Window displaying a compiler error message.*

If you've attempted to compile even just a couple of examples that someone else has written, whether from a book or downloaded from an online service library, you've no doubt encountered the dreaded type mismatch error. If the example code came from a programming book, you of course immediately cursed the author's so-called competence and vowed to never purchase another book with his or her name on the cover. But wait! This incompatible code might not in fact be the fault of the author. Instead, Apple and the Universal Header files may be to blame. Fortunately, Chapter 2 supplied you with a thorough understanding of just what these header files are used for, and why they are so important. Armed with that knowledge, you'll be able to get many projects up and running—projects that you had given up on and left dormant on your hard drive.

The PlaySound Project

The `type mismatch` errors can of course occur in your own projects as well as those you've obtained from other sources. The reason I mentioned projects obtained from other sources is that there is a likelihood that a project you've received with a book or downloaded from an online service may be several months, or even a few years, old. In the time between the project's creation and your obtaining it, one important thing may have changed—Apple's Universal Header files. If these files have changed, the chances of the project successfully compiling are greatly diminished.

For the sake of this discussion on `type mismatch` errors, let's assume you're trying to compile a multimedia project that was included in a Macintosh programming book you've purchased. The book's disk also included a compiled, executable version of the program, which is named `PlaySound68K`. When double-clicked, the program plays the sound of a telephone ringing, then quits. No, it may not exactly be a multimedia showcase, but at least it does more than simply write "Hello, World!" to a window! Figure 3.2 shows what the CodeWarrior project window looks like for the `PlaySound68K.µ` project.

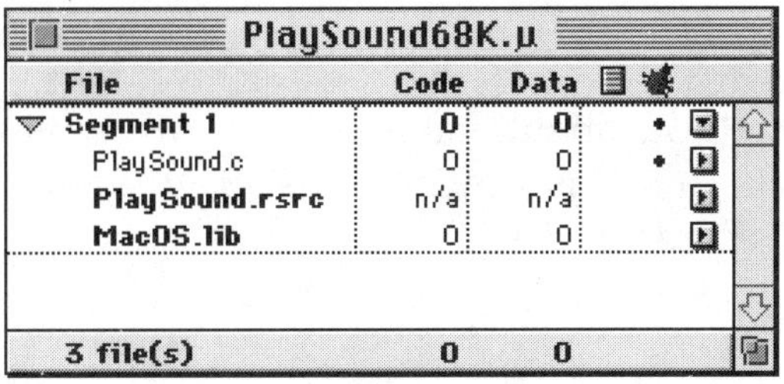

Figure 3.2 *The project window for the PlaySound68K program.*

Like most Macintosh 68K projects, this one includes the `MacOS.lib`, as discussed in Chapter 2. It also includes a resource file. To view the contents of the resource file, double-click on the file name in the project window. That's a neat Metrowerks trick that launches the resource editor that created the file (such as ResEdit or Resorcerer), and then opens that file within the resource editor. Figure 3.3 shows the PlaySound.rsrc file, as viewed from ResEdit.

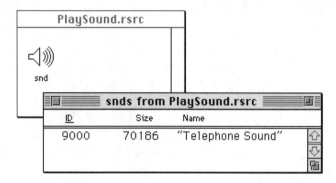

Figure 3.3 *The resource file for the PlaySound68K project.*

From Figure 3.3 you can see that the PlaySound.rsrc file holds a single resource—a snd resource with an ID of 9000. This resource holds the digitized recording of a telephone ringing and will be used by the code in the PlaySound.c source code file.

For obscure reasons that I won't delve into, snd resources that are *not* distributed by Apple should have IDs greater than 8191.

N O T E

Another note about snd resources: All resource types have a four-character name, such as WIND, DLOG, and ALRT. The fourth character in the snd resource name is a blank space.

N O T E

For the curious, a snd resource usually starts as a sound in a sound file. For a project to make use of it, it gets copied to the project's resource file. Figure 3.4 shows that the Play Sound ƒ folder found on this book's CD includes a sound file named Telephone Sound.

Figure 3.4 *A sound can be stored in a file, as is the telephone ringing sound here.*

 Where do sound files come from? Well, buying this book just got you one—the Telephone Sound file. That doesn't help if you're looking for more than a ringing telephone, though. Other sources of sounds are:

- Online services such as America Online and CompuServe have libraries of sound files that are yours for the downloading.
- You can buy a CD-ROM of a thousand sounds through a mail-order vendor for about 30 dollars.
- You can buy a MacRecorder sound digitizer for less than 200 dollars and digitize your own sounds.

To copy the sound in a sound file, launch your resource editor. Use its **Open** menu item to open the sound file. Then open your project's resource file. Copy the sound from the sound file and paste it into the project's resource file. That's all there is to it. Figure 3.5 summarizes this process.

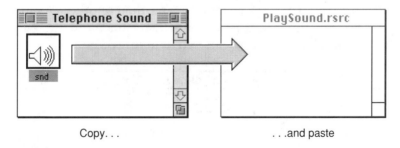

Figure 3.5 *A sound in a file is a resource that can be copied and pasted to a project's resource file.*

The Faulty PlaySound Source Code

Figure 3.6 shows the source code for the PlaySound68K program. Like the short programs in Chapter 2, about half of the code of PlaySound.c is devoted to Toolbox initializations. The rest of the code is explained in the figure.

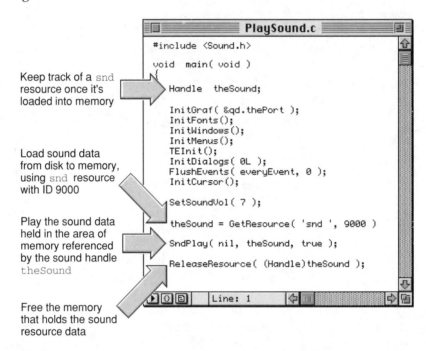

Keep track of a snd resource once it's loaded into memory

Load sound data from disk to memory, using snd resource with ID 9000

Play the sound data held in the area of memory referenced by the sound handle theSound

Free the memory that holds the sound resource data

Figure 3.6 *The PlaySound source code has code to load and play a sound resource.*

Selecting **Run** from the Project menu starts the compile. A short way through, though, the compile will abruptly end and the Message Window will open with the error shown in Figure 3.7.

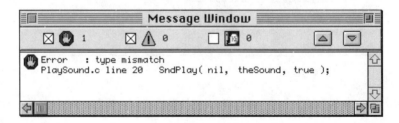

Figure 3.7 *The CodeWarrior Message Window displaying a type mismatch error.*

Correcting the Type Mismatch Error

If a type mismatch involves a Toolbox function, look at the Universal Header file that holds the function's prototype. In some instances you'll know, or be able to quickly guess, which header file holds the prototype. By its name, you'd guess that the SndPlay() routine is defined in the Sound.h Universal Header file. The fact that Sound.h is used in an #include directive lends further support to this guess.

There are two ways to open one of the project's header files. The traditional way to open a file using a compiler is to select **Open** from the File menu, then use the pop-up list menu to move to the folder that holds the file. In Figure 3.8 I've shown the path to the Universal Header files. Of course, your hard disk and CodeWarrior folder may have names that differ from mine. Next, scroll down to the Sound.h header file name in the list and double-click on it.

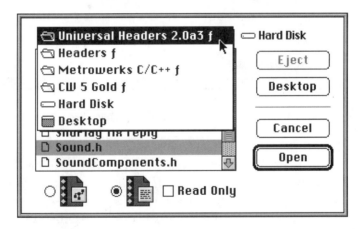

Figure 3.8 *Opening the Sound.h Universal Header file.*

The second, and much more convenient way to open a header file is available to you only if you've successfully compiled a source code file. To open a header file with this method, click on the **Triangle** icon located at the lower-left corner of the source code window. When you do that, a pop-up menu will appear. In that menu is an alphabetized list of header files included in the source code file. Selecting a file from this list opens that file, regardless of where it's located on disk. Figure 3.9 shows how I could open the Sound.h header file if PlaySound.c had been compiled successfully.

NOTE If your source code file doesn't compile, and your project consists of more than one source code file—as many do—then you may still be able to open the header file with this method. You can open the header file from any one of the other source code files if:

1. The file lists the header file you want to open in a #include directive.

2. The file has been successfully compiled.

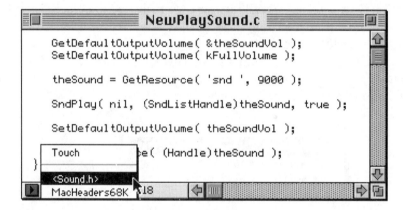

Figure 3.9 *Using the Triangle icon to see a list of header files included in a source code file.*

NOTE The **Touch** item in the menu doesn't have anything to do with the header files. Instead, if you select **Touch** it will tell the compiler to recompile the source code file during the next compile, whether or not there's been changes to the file. Normally, only modified source code files get compiled.

With the Sound.h header file open, begin the search for the SndPlay() function. Select **Find** from the Search menu. Type **SndPlay** in the Find edit box, then click the **Find** button. In Figure 3.10 you can see I've done exactly that.

Once you've found the prototype to the questionable function, note the *types* of parameters that should be used with it. For SndPlay(), the three parameter types are SndChannelPtr, SndListHandle, and Boolean. Now compare the parameter types found in your source code function call with the types listed in the header file. Here's how SndPlay() is listed in the Sound.h file:

```
SndPlay(SndChannelPtr chan, SndListHandle sndHdl, Boolean async);
```

Here's how the function is called from the `PlaySound.c` source code file:

```
SndPlay( nil, theSound, true );
```

Find

Find:	SndPlay	▼	Find
Replace:		▼	Replace
			Replace & Find

☐ Batch   ☒ Ignore Case   ☐ Regexp   Replace All
☐ Wrap   ☐ Entire Word

```
Sound.h
    ONEWORDINLINE(0xA807);
    extern pascal OSErr SndDisposeChannel(SndChannelPtr chan, Boolean quietNow)
    ONEWORDINLINE(0xA801);
    extern pascal OSErr SndPlay(SndChannelPtr chan, SndListHandle sndHdl, Boolean async)
    ONEWORDINLINE(0xA805);
    extern pascal OSErr SndAddModifier(SndChannelPtr chan, Ptr modifier, short id, long i
    ONEWORDINLINE(0xA802);
    extern pascal OSErr SndControl(short id, SndCommand *cmd)
```

Line: 532

Figure 3.10 *Searching Sound.h Universal Header file for the SndPlay() function.*

In Figure 3.11 I've made a side-by-side comparison of the above. I've taken the liberty of inserting a little white space between parameters to make the comparison clear.

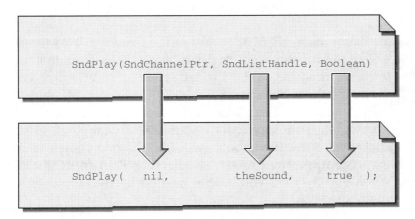

```
SndPlay(SndChannelPtr, SndListHandle, Boolean)



SndPlay(    nil,        theSound,      true  );
```

Figure 3.11 *Comparing the Universal Header file prototype*
of SndPlay() to a source code call to the function.

Let's examine each of the three parameters. The header file says the first should be of type `SndChannelPtr`. You may not be familiar with the `SndChannelPtr` type, but it should make sense to you that a value of `nil` won't lead to a type mismatch error—any type of pointer can be assigned a value of `nil`.

The header file states that the second parameter to `SndPlay()` should be a `SndListHandle`. Looking back at Figure 3.6 you can see that `PlaySound.c` declares `theSound` to be of type `Handle`. When the compiler expects to see a particular type of handle, such as a `SndListHandle`, and it instead finds a generic handle, it will consider it a type mismatch. The solution is simple enough: cast the generic `Handle` variable `theSound` to a `SndListHandle`. Here's how:

```
SndPlay( nil, (SndListHandle)theSound, true );
```

Recall that to cast a variable is to change its type—for the moment. By preceding a variable *name* with a variable *type*, you're telling the compiler to view the variable as being of this type. In the above example, `theSound` will be considered again a variable of type `Handle` after the `SndPlay()` function call.

N O T E

To make sure that there isn't another type mismatch in the call to `SndPlay()`, continue the parameter comparison. The header file states that the last parameter to `SndPlay()` should be of type `Boolean`. The `PlaySound` program passes `SndPlay()` a value of true as the third parameter, so this parameter won't cause a compile error.

Don't make changes to any of the Universal Header files to get the function prototypes to match a Toolbox function call in your source code! Instead, change your source code to match the prototype.

WARNING

Now, go back to the source code file and make the change. After you do that, your `PlaySound.c` file should look like the one shown in Figure 3.12. Next, recompile the project by selecting **Run** from the Project menu. When you do that, you'll be rewarded by the sound of a telephone ringing!

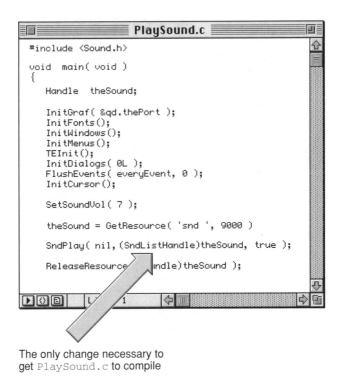

```
                    PlaySound.c
  #include <Sound.h>

  void  main( void )
  {
      Handle   theSound;

      InitGraf( &qd.thePort );
      InitFonts();
      InitWindows();
      InitMenus();
      TEInit();
      InitDialogs( 0L );
      FlushEvents( everyEvent, 0 );
      InitCursor();

      SetSoundVol( 7 );

      theSound = GetResource( 'snd ', 9000 )

      SndPlay( nil, (SndListHandle)theSound, true );

      ReleaseResource    ndle)theSound );
```

The only change necessary to
get `PlaySound.c` to compile

Figure 3.12 *The PlaySound.c source code file, after the parameter to SndPlay() has been corrected.*

Correcting Errors Involving the Toolbox

You've just seen how to solve a `type mismatch` error for a Toolbox function that has its prototype in a known header file. What if this same error occurs in a Toolbox function that you aren't as familiar with? If the error is in a call to, say, `TickCount()`, `GetDateTime()`, or `Delay()`, which header file do you look at? The `type mismatch` error is a common error. Another error you'll see when making calls to Toolbox functions is the `function call does not match prototype` error. In this section I'll demonstrate a general technique for quickly tracking down the causes of these errors.

The Find Dialog Box and Search Sets

One of the features of the CodeWarrior Find dialog box is its ability to search multiple files. This in itself isn't extraordinary—other compilers offer this search option. What *is* helpful is the fact that you can save any number of files as a *search set*. This set can be saved and used in any and all projects you create.

If you create a file search set composed of all of the Universal Header files, correcting compile-time errors that involve Toolbox functions becomes much easier. When the compilation of a project results in an error involving a call to a Toolbox routine, a single click of the mouse causes a search that quickly results in the opening of the Universal Header file that holds the Toolbox function's prototype.

To create the file set, begin by selecting **Find** from the Search menu. When you do, you'll see a dialog box like the one pictured in Figure 3.13. This figure only tells half the story—for the rest, click on the small **Triangle** icon, as shown in Figure 3.14. That expands the Find dialog box from its collapsed state. This lower half of the dialog box is used for multiple file searches. If the Multiple File icon is displaying a single file, click on it now. The icon will change to one that shows two files, and the items in the lower half of the dialog box will become enabled. Once enabled, click on the **Others** button, as shown in Figure 3.14.

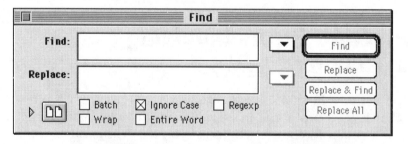

Figure 3.13 *The CodeWarrior Find dialog box, collapsed.*

Clicking on the **Others** button brings up the same dialog box you see when you select **Add Files** from the Project menu. Here, however, you won't be adding files to the project. Instead, you'll be adding files to a file set—a collection of files used in a multiple file search. Use the pop-up list menu in this dialog box to move to the folder that holds the Universal Header files, as I've done in Figure 3.15. Once there, click the **Add all** button, then click on the **Done** button.

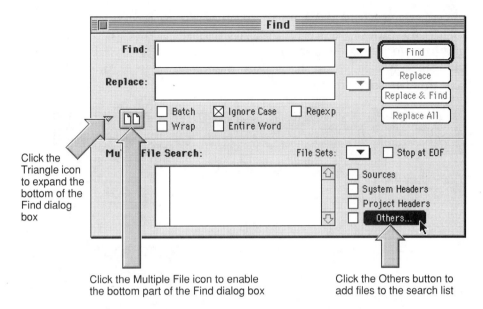

Click the Triangle icon to expand the bottom of the Find dialog box

Click the Multiple File icon to enable the bottom part of the Find dialog box

Click the Others button to add files to the search list

Figure 3.14 *The CodeWarrior Find dialog box, expanded—with files about to be added to the search list.*

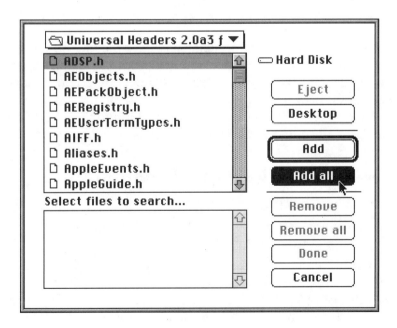

Figure 3.15 *Adding all of the Universal Header files to the list of files to search.*

When you return to the Find dialog box, you'll notice that all of the Universal Header files now appear in the Multi-File Search list. It's now time to save this collection of files to a file set. Click on the File Sets **Triangle** icon to bring up the pop-up menu shown in Figure 3.16. Select **Save this file set** from the menu.

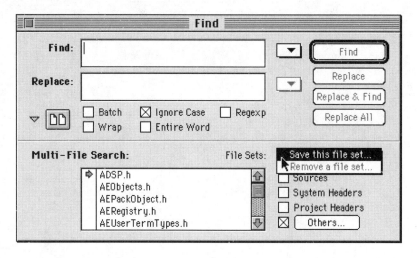

Figure 3.16 *Saving the Universal Header files as a set of files that can be collectively searched.*

In the dialog box that appears, type in a name for the file set. This set will be saved to disk and will be usable in any of your CodeWarrior projects, now and in the future. Because CodeWarrior allows you to save any number of file sets, be sure to give the file set a name that distinguishes it from future sets you might create. Before clicking the **Save** button, select the **Global, for all projects** radio button, as shown in Figure 3.17.

The DelaySound Example Program

Now that you have a file set saved, it's time to use it. On the book's CD you'll find a folder for an example program named `DelaySound68K`. Figure 3.18 is the source code file for this project.

The only difference between the `DelaySound.c` code and the code found in this chapter's `PlaySound.c` file is the addition of a single Toolbox call. `DelaySound.c` includes a call to `Delay()`. This function accepts a parameter that determines the length of the delay that should appear in a program. The delay is in sixtieths-of-a-second increments, so a parameter of 30 will yield a half-second delay, a parameter of 60 will give a one-second delay, and so forth. I've decided upon a 10-second delay. When the program runs, that delay will give me enough time to leave the room before the program plays the digitized telephone ring, removing suspicion from myself when everyone else in the room looks around to find the telephone.

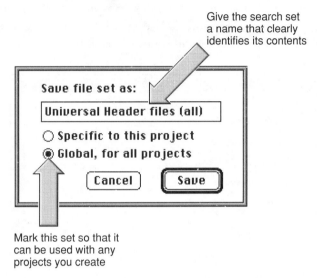

Figure 3.17 *Giving the search set a name, and marking the set for use by any CodeWarrior project.*

After selecting **Run** from the Project menu, the Message Window shown in Figure 3.19 appeared. Notice the error type—it's not a `type mismatch` error this time. Instead, it's a `function call does not match prototype` error.

Like `SndPlay()`, `Delay()` is a Toolbox function. Yet the error message isn't the same as the one I experienced when compiling the `PlaySound` project. That's because in this new example, the number of parameters in the source code function call doesn't match the number of parameters in the header file prototype. This error isn't the result of a change to the Universal Headers. Instead, I got my hands on a project that never compiled properly in the first place.

Now, here's the dilemma: I don't know *which* Universal Header file holds the prototype for the `Delay()` function. The source code `#include` directive lists only the `Sound.h` header file, and I'm guessing that the

`Delay()` function isn't a sound-related Toolbox function. Since there's no other header file given in a `#include` directive, and `Delay()` must have a prototype listed somewhere, what conclusion can I make? That the header file that holds the prototype for `Delay()` is one of those that are precompiled into the `MacHeaders68K` header file that is included in this project. You can refer back to Chapter 2 if you have questions about `MacHeaders68K`. Since `MacHeaders68K` is compiled code, I can't open it to find any prototypes. Instead, the solution to my problem is, of course, to use the search set I created a little earlier.

```
                    DelaySound.c
#include <Sound.h>

void  main( void )
{
    Handle  theSound;

    InitGraf( &qd.thePort );
    InitFonts();
    InitWindows();
    InitMenus();
    TEInit();
    InitDialogs( 0L );
    FlushEvents( everyEvent, 0 );
    InitCursor();

    theSound = GetResource( 'snd ', 9000 );

    SetSoundVol( 7 );

    Delay( 600 );

    SndPlay( nil, (SndListHandle)theSound, true );

    ReleaseResource( (Handle)theSound );
}

 Line: 1
```

Figure 3.18 *The source code file for the DelaySound program.*

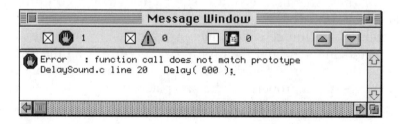

Figure 3.19 *The CodeWarrior message window displaying a compile error.*

Using the Search Set to Correct an Error

To find the prototype for the `Delay()` function, begin by selecting **Find** from the Search menu. Enter the phrase to search for in the Find dialog box. Because "delay" is a common computer term, it's bound to appear in at least two of the more than 100 Universal Header files, most likely as part of an Apple-defined constant. Because I'm looking for "Delay" as a function, I know an opening parentheses will follow the word; I can narrow the search by including an opening parentheses. Next, make sure the bottom half of the Find dialog box is expanded and enabled. If it's not, click the **Triangle** icon at the far left of the dialog box, and make sure that the Multiple File icon is displaying two files. Then click on the **File Sets Triangle** icon and select the file set from the pop-up list menu, as shown in Figure 3.20.

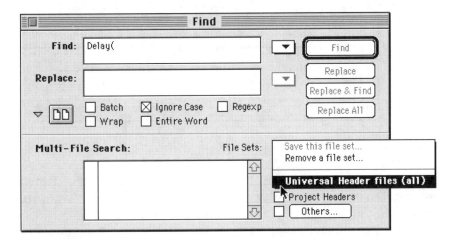

Figure 3.20 *Opening a saved file search set in the Find dialog box.*

Now click on the **Find** button to start the search. As the search takes place, the arrow at the bottom of the Find dialog box will move down the list of file names, always pointing at the file that is currently being searched. When "Delay(" is found, the search ends and the proper header file is opened, as shown in Figure 3.21.

Searching more than 100 files to find a single function prototype? Don't worry about search time, the CodeWarrior search engine is fast. It will take only a few seconds to locate any Toolbox function prototype.

N O T E

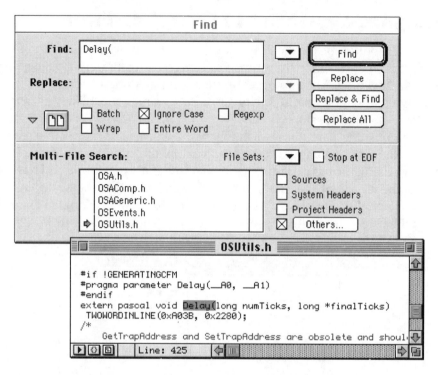

Figure 3.21 *Searching for the Delay() function in the Universal Header files search set.*

In Figure 3.21 you can see that the prototype for the Delay() function appears in the OSUtils.h Universal Header file—a fact that you probably would not have determined on your own. Looking at the prototype, you can see that Delay() requires two parameters, not the one parameter that appears in my incorrect code. The first parameter is the length of the delay, while the second is a pointer to a long variable. When the Delay() function completes, the Toolbox will fill this second parameter with the number of ticks (the number of 60th seconds) since the computer was turned on.

N O T E   No, you probably couldn't deduce the purpose of the second parameter to Delay() from the Universal Header file prototype. But you would be able to see the correct number and type of parameters, even if you wouldn't be able to know the purpose of each. For the Delay() function, you could simply declare a long variable and pass it in by reference (using the & operator, as shown next).

Now that I know the correct way to call the Delay() function, I'll make the changes to the DelaySound.c code. In Figure 3.22 you can see that I've added a long variable named finalTicks and passed its address to Delay().

```
┌─────────────────────────────────────────────────┐
│ ▤▣  ════════════ DelaySound.c ════════════  ▣▤  │
├─────────────────────────────────────────────────┤
│ #include <Sound.h>                           ⇧  │
│                                                 │
│ void  main( void )                              │
│ {                                               │
│    Handle   theSound;                           │
│    long     finalTicks;                         │
│                                                 │
│    InitGraf( &qd.thePort );                     │
│    InitFonts();                                 │
│    InitWindows();                               │
│    InitMenus();                                 │
│    TEInit();                                     │
│    InitDialogs( 0L );                           │
│    FlushEvents( everyEvent, 0 );                │
│    InitCursor();                                 │
│                                                 │
│    theSound = GetResource( 'snd ', 9000 );      │
│                                                 │
│    SetSoundVol( 7 );                             │
│                                                 │
│    Delay( 600, &finalTicks );                   │
│                                                 │
│    SndPlay( nil, (SndListHandle)theSound, true );│
│                                                 │
│    ReleaseResource( (Handle)theSound );         │
│ }                                           ⇩  │
├─────────────────────────────────────────────────┤
│ ▶◀▣  │ Line: 1  │ ◀▥▓▓▓▓▓▓▓▓▓▓▓ ▶▣             │
└─────────────────────────────────────────────────┘
```

Figure 3.22 *The DelaySound.c file after the parameters to the Delay() function have been corrected.*

To see if the change worked, again select **Run** from the Project menu. When it successfully compiles, expect a 10-second delay before the telephone sound plays.

Improving the PlaySound Program

In Chapter 2 I stated that a Mac program shouldn't make lasting changes to the system-wide settings of the program user's Macintosh. Then I went ahead and violated my own advice in both last chapter's SetVolume program and this chapter's PlaySound application. Now that you have a solid understanding of the Universal Header files and Toolbox functions, I'll use the remainder of this chapter to make a couple of changes to the PlaySound program to make it a little more user-friendly. The result will be a program I call NewPlaySound.

Using the Search Set

Before playing the digitized telephone sound, the PlaySound68K program sets the volume of the user's Mac speaker to its highest setting. Because the user might have his or her volume turned off (via the Sound control panel), I want to make sure the volume is on before playing the sound. What a well-behaved Mac program really should do is take note of the user's speaker volume *before* changing it, then set the volume back to its original setting *after* playing the sound. You will see this done in this section.

In PlaySound68K I rely on the Toolbox function SetSoundVol() to change the volume level. Knowing the completeness of the Toolbox, it would make sense that there is a companion routine to SetSoundVol() that allows me to get the current volume. To find it, I'll search for "SetSoundVol" in my Universal Header file set. When I did that, the search ended in Sound.h, as shown in Figure 3.23. In this figure you can see that just below SetSoundVol() is a routine named GetSoundVol(), which seems like it might be exactly what I'm looking for.

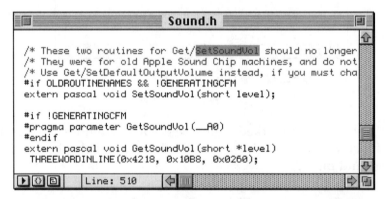

Figure 3.23 *Searching for the SetSoundVol() function in the Universal Header files.*

Before jumping right in and adding a call to GetSoundVol() to my program, I should look at the comment that appears above SetSoundVol() in the Sound.h file. When I enlarged the window and read it, I was grateful that I took the time to do so. It seems that the SetSoundVol() function

I've been using has fallen out of favor and is being phased out. In its place is a function named `SetDefaultOutputVolume()`. The same applies to the `GetSoundVol()` routine I was about to add to my program. Using the Find dialog box, it's a simple matter to search for these new routines to see what their prototypes look like (see Figure 3.24).

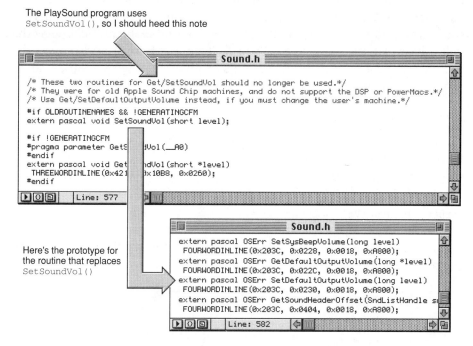

The PlaySound program uses `SetSoundVol()`, so I should heed this note

Here's the prototype for the routine that replaces `SetSoundVol()`

Figure 3.24 *The Sound.h Universal Header file notes that some of the existing Toolbox routines are being phased out.*

From Figure 3.24 you can see that `SetDefaultOutputVolume()` requires a `long` variable as its one parameter, while `GetDefaultOutputVolume()` requires a pointer to a `long`. Now that I know there's more than a couple of changes to the `Sound.h` file, I'll take a few minutes to scroll through it to see if I come across anything else of interest; it just so happens that I did. Near the top of the file is the definition of a constant named `kFullVolume`. This sounds useful for my purpose, so I'll make note of it. Figure 3.25 shows the section of `Sound.h` that holds this constant.

Making the Changes

For my improved sound-playing program I've made copies of the PlaySound project and its associated files and renamed them NewPlaySound. I then edited the source code to use the new Toolbox functions. First, I declared a long variable named theSoundVol. Then I used the GetDefaultOutputVolume() routine to obtain the current sound level and save it to the theSoundVol variable. Next, I changed the volume level with a call to SetDefaultOutputVolume() and played the sound. Finally, I reset the volume to its original level with another call to SetDefaultOutputVolume():

```
long  theSoundVol;

GetDefaultOutputVolume( &theSoundVol );
SetDefaultOutputVolume( kFullVolume );

// load and play the sound

SetDefaultOutputVolume( theSoundVol );
```

Figure 3.26 shows the complete source code listing for the NewPlaySound program.

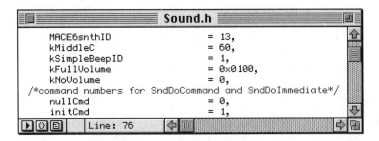

Figure 3.25 *The Universal Header files define constants as well as function prototypes.*

Thanks to a knowledge of the Universal Header files and a CodeWarrior file search set, I've made the sound-playing program a little more user-friendly. You'll find that this simple exercise in exploring the Universal Header files can be applied on a grander scale to eliminate compile errors and improve your programs.

```
╔══════════════════ NewPlaySound.c ══════════════════╗
║ #include <Sound.h>                                  ║
║                                                     ║
║ void  main( void )                                  ║
║ {                                                   ║
║    Handle   theSound;                               ║
║    long     theSoundVol;                            ║
║                                                     ║
║    InitGraf( &qd.thePort );                         ║
║    InitFonts();                                     ║
║    InitWindows();                                   ║
║    InitMenus();                                     ║
║    TEInit();                                        ║
║    InitDialogs( 0L );                               ║
║    FlushEvents( everyEvent, 0 );                    ║
║    InitCursor();                                    ║
║                                                     ║
║    GetDefaultOutputVolume( &theSoundVol );          ║
║    SetDefaultOutputVolume( kFullVolume );           ║
║                                                     ║
║    theSound = GetResource( 'snd ', 9000 );          ║
║                                                     ║
║    SndPlay( nil, (SndListHandle)theSound, true );   ║
║                                                     ║
║    SetDefaultOutputVolume( theSoundVol );           ║
║                                                     ║
║    ReleaseResource( (Handle)theSound );             ║
║ }                                                   ║
╚═══════════════ Line: 18 ═══════════════════════════╝
```

Figure 3.26 *The source code file for the NewPlaySound68K program.*

Chapter Summary

Apple's Universal Header files are a collection of more than 100 header files. Any compiler designed to generate Macintosh executables needs to have access to these header files. Without them, the compiler will not know if the parameters in your calls to Toolbox functions match the parameter list the Toolbox is expecting.

The CodeWarrior compilers allow you to save file search sets. A search set is a group of files that can be collectively searched with a single click of the mouse button. By creating a search set that consists of all of the Universal Header files, you make it easy to find the function prototype for any one Toolbox function. Once you find a function's prototype, you can compare it to the call you're making in your own source code. That makes correcting function parameter errors fast and simple.

Chapter  4

Debugging and MW Debug

MW Debug is the name of the CodeWarrior high-level debugger. A high-level debugger like MW Debug allows you to examine variable values as your program runs, without your having to know any assembly language. A high-level debugger also includes a feature-laden Mac interface that allows you to use menu commands to slowly step through the execution of your program, view the contents of memory, and change the values of variables as your program runs. In this chapter you'll learn the basic terminology of MW Debug and walk though a short debugging session.

Macintosh data structures, and their placement in memory, are topics that can be explained in a book, but only become clear when viewed in practice. Because MW Debug displays the address and contents of variables in an easy to understand format, the debugger is an excellent tool for understanding Macintosh memory. In this chapter you'll use MW Debug to examine memory to gain a better understanding of some of the common Macintosh data types.

Installing and Running MW Debug

The Metrowerks debugger is easy to use—once it's set up. Before you can fire up the debugger, there are a couple of steps you'll want to perform to make sure the debugger does indeed execute when you call upon it to do so.

Installing the Debugger

Just as there are two versions of the Metrowerks C/C++ compiler, there are dual versions of the Metrowerks debugger. For debugging 68K applications compiled with the MW C/C++ 68K compiler, you'll use the MW Debug/68K application. For MW C/C++ PPC projects, you'll use the MW Debug/PPC application. If they aren't already in your Metrowerks C/C++ ƒ folder, copy each to that folder now.

N O T E   A CodeWarrior compiler looks for its corresponding debugger in the same folder in which the compiler resides, so make sure that the MW C/C++ 68K compiler and the MW Debug/68K debugger are together in the same folder. The same applies to the MW C/C++ PPC compiler and the MW Debug/PPC debugger.

Installing the Debugger Nub Files

The Metrowerks debuggers work with the help of one or more support files, or *debugger nubs*. You'll find these debugger nub files on this book's CD, as well as the Bronze and Gold CodeWarrior CDs. Depending on which Macintosh you own (68K or PPC), which system you're running (pre–System 7.5 or System 7.5 or later), and which types of projects you'll be debugging (68K or PPC), you'll need some or all of the various nub files installed on your Mac.

If you'll be using the MW C/C++ 68K compiler, and want to debug your projects, refer to Figure 4.1. That figure shows that regardless of the Mac you use, you'll want the Debugger INIT extension in your computer's Extensions folder. If you want Drag and Drop capabilities added to the debugger, then you should also have the Macintosh Drag and Drop extension in your Extensions folder.

The Macintosh Drag and Drop extension works with many Mac applications—not just the Metrowerks debugger—so you may already have a copy of this extension in your Extensions folder. If that's the case, there's no need to copy this extension from the CD to your Mac's System Folder.

N O T E

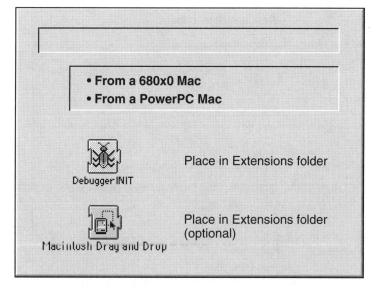

- **From a 680x0 Mac**
- **From a PowerPC Mac**

Debugger INIT — Place in Extensions folder

Macintosh Drag and Drop — Place in Extensions folder (optional)

Figure 4.1 *Debugger support files for debugging 68K projects.*

If you want to debug MW C/C++ PPC projects, you'll have to be programming on a PowerPC-based Macintosh.

Remember, if you're using a 680x0-based Mac, you can still run the MW C/C++ PPC compiler and generate PowerPC-only applications. You just won't be able to debug or run them on your 68K Mac.

N O T E

Copy the PPCTraceEnable nub to the Extensions folder in your Mac's System Folder. Additionally, you'll want to copy the Power Mac DebugServices file to your Startup Items folder, also found in your computer's System Folder. If your system is a version earlier than System 7.5, you'll also need to copy the ObjectSupportLib file to your Extensions folder. If you want Drag and Drop capabilities, and you don't already have the Macintosh Drag and Drop extension in your Extensions folder, copy it to that folder as well. Figure 4.2 summarizes the files you'll want in your System Folder.

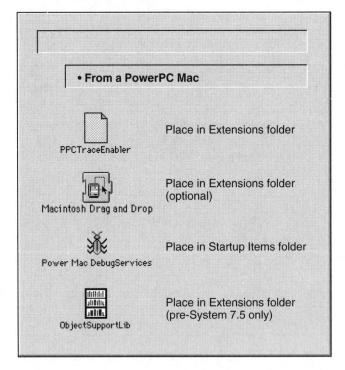

Figure 4.2 *Debugger support files for debugging PPC projects.*

After copying all of the necessary files to your Mac, restart your computer to ensure that the files are all properly loaded into memory.

Debugger Basics

During the course of writing a Mac program that has moved beyond the trivial stage in complexity, you're bound to discover a *bug*. When you make a *syntax* error (writing code that violates the programming language you're using), the compiler quickly catches it and reports back to you. This type of error doesn't require a debugger to locate—the compiler does that. When you make a *semantic* error (an error in logic), your code will compile successfully, but won't run properly. This is the type of error that requires a debugger.

A debugger is a program that runs concurrently with your own program. MW Debug is just such an application. It allows you to run your program line-by-line, observing changes in variable values at each step. By keeping a close watch over everything your program does and reporting this information back to you in a manner that's easy to understand, a debugger helps you pinpoint the section of code that isn't working as you intended.

You can debug any project by simply selecting **Enable Debugging** from the compiler's Project menu, as shown in Figure 4.3. That turns debugging on for that one project. Now, each time you select **Run** from the Project menu, the debugger steals the show. Instead of your program immediately executing, two debugger windows open. From within these windows you control the running of your program, and you observe what happens in memory as your program executes.

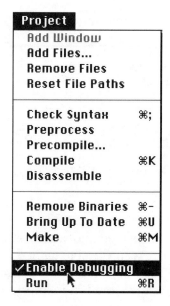

Figure 4.3 *Check* **Enable Debugging** *in the compiler's Project menu to allow MW Debug to gain control of your project.*

The ChangingValues68K Program

This chapter has a single example program, the ChangingValues68K application. When run, this program opens a window and draws a string to it, as shown in Figure 4.4. Figure 4.5 shows the project window for this program. You'll notice in Figure 4.5 that there is no resource file included in this project. Rather than obtaining window specifications from a WIND resource, the program's window is created based on information passed to the Toolbox in a call to NewWindow( ). Figure 4.6 shows the source code listing for the ChangingValues68K program, including the call to NewWindow( ).

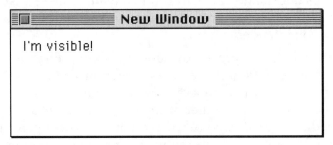

Figure 4.4 *The window that's displayed when running ChangingValues68K.*

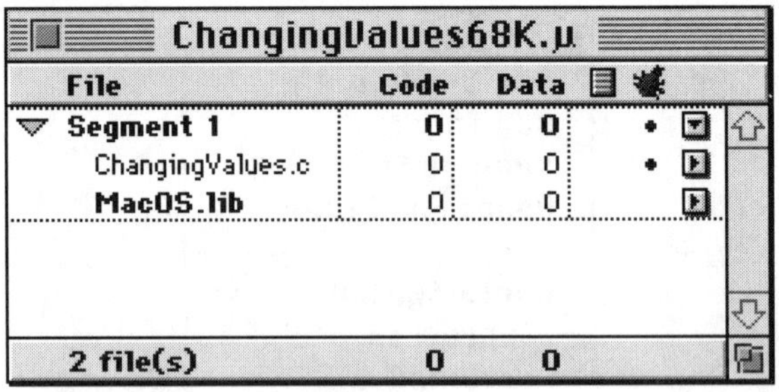

Figure 4.5 *The ChangingValues68K project window.*

ChangingValues68K uses a call to NewWindow( ) to open and display a new window. It then uses an if-else statement to determine whether to hide the window or to keep it displayed and write a string to it. This decision is based on the value of a Boolean variable named showWindow. Throughout this chapter I'll use MW Debug to find a bug in ChangingValues68K, to discover how data structures are stored in memory, and to make changes to variable values as the program executes.

```
                       ChangingValues.c
void  main( void )
{
    WindowPtr   theWindow;
    Rect        theRect;
    Boolean     showWindow = false;

    InitGraf( &qd.thePort );
    InitFonts();
    InitWindows();
    InitMenus();
    TEInit();
    InitDialogs( 0L );
    FlushEvents( everyEvent, 0 );
    InitCursor();

    SetRect( &theRect, 50, 50, 350, 150 );
    theWindow = NewWindow( 0L, &theRect, "\pNew Window", true,
                           noGrowDocProc, (WindowPtr)-1L, true, 0 );

    if ( showWindow = false )
    {
        HideWindow( theWindow );
    }
    else
    {
        ShowWindow( theWindow );
        SetPort( theWindow );
        MoveTo( 10, 20 );
        DrawString( "\pI'm visible!" );
    }

    while ( !Button() )
        ;
}

Line: 1
```

Figure 4.6 *The ChangingValues68K source code file.*

MW Debug Windows

With **Enable Debugging** checked in the Project menu, the Project menu's **Run** command will start the debugger, not your project's application. You'll then use the debugger to start your program. If you select **Run** with **Enable Debugging** checked for the `ChangingValues68K` project, you'll see two windows and a floating toolbar, as shown in Figure 4.7.

The Program window holds the source code from the file that holds the currently executing routine. Some projects consist of more than one source code file. For projects such as these, the code for any of these other files can be viewed in the second debugger window—the SYM window. The toolbar consists of a half dozen buttons that control how the code in the Program window gets executed.

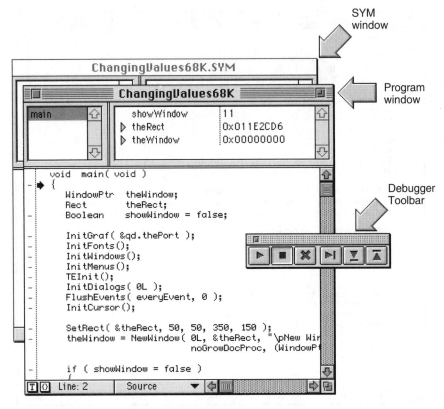

Figure 4.7 *The MW Debug interface.*

 When you build an application using a CodeWarrior compiler, you'll notice that CodeWarrior creates not one, but two files: the application itself and a *SYM file*. The SYM file holds information (such as variable names and variable locations within the code) that will be used by MW Debug when you debug a project.

NOTE

The Program window is divided into three panes: the Source pane, the Call Chain pane, and the Locals pane (see Figure 4.8). The Source pane holds the source code listing for the file that contains the currently executing function. The Call Chain pane lists all of the functions found in the source code file that is currently being displayed in the Source pane. The ChangingValues68K project has just one source code file, so it of course is displayed in the Source pane. This simple program consists of just one function—main()—which is listed in the Call Chain pane.

The Locals pane lists variables (and their values) that are local to the currently executing routine. In Figure 4.8, main() is running, so the three variables declared in main() are listed in the Locals pane. You can tell which line of code is about to execute by looking at the *current statement arrow* in the Source pane. You can specify a particular line at which the program should next stop execution by clicking on the dash by that line. This adds a *breakpoint* to the code.

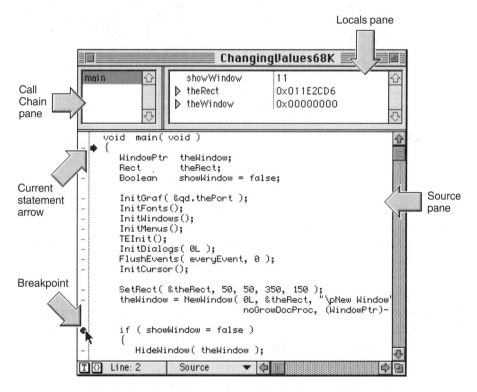

Figure 4.8 *The Program window consists of three panes.*

Controlling Program Execution

To control execution of a program you use either the Control menu or the toolbar, whichever is easier for you. The functionality of the first six menu items in the Control menu is repeated in the six buttons on the toolbar. For you lovers of numbers, Figure 4.9 uses circled numbers to pair each toolbar button with its corresponding Control menu item.

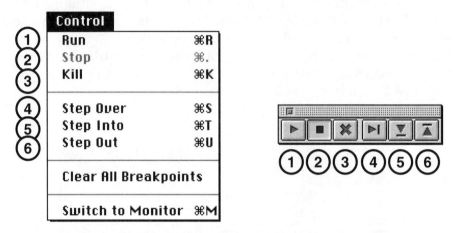

Figure 4.9 *Each program execution menu item has a corresponding button in the toolbar.*

You'll start your program running by selecting **Run** from the Control menu. You can temporarily stop the program at any time by selecting **Stop** from the Control menu, or by clicking on the toolbar **Stop** button. You can completely end program execution by instead selecting **Kill** from the Control menu or by clicking on the **Kill** button in the toolbar. If you don't go with one of these options, and you haven't set any breakpoints in the Source pane, your program will run on screen just as it normally would. If you've set a breakpoint, and the program reaches the line of code that is marked with that breakpoint, your program will stop executing and the current statement arrow in the Program window Source pane will move to the breakpoint line. It's now up to you to decide what to do.

Once your program has stopped, you can view the values of some or all of the variables in the Program window's Locals pane, you can restart your program (by again selecting **Run** from the Control menu or by clicking on the toolbar **Run** button), or you can execute just a single line of code from your program (by selecting **Step Over**, **Step Into**, or **Step Out** from the Control menu or by clicking the appropriate toolbar button).

The three step buttons (or menu items) all perform exactly the same when an application-defined function *isn't* involved. For instance, if the current statement arrow was at the following line of code, then clicking on any one of these three buttons would execute the line of code and move the current statement arrow down to the next line of code:

```
squareValue = num * num;
```

If, on the other hand, the line of code at which the current statement arrow is pointing contains a function call, such as the below line, the buttons behave differently:

```
squareValue = SquareWholeNumber( num );
```

The Step Over button would execute the above line and move the current statement arrow down to the next line. The Step Into button behaves differently. The debugger would find the listing for the SquareWholeNumber() function and would then move the current statement arrow to the start of this function. You could then use the Step Over or Step Into buttons repeatedly to execute this function one line at a time. Once inside this function, you could exit by clicking the **Step Out** button. That would have the effect of executing the remaining lines in the SquareWholeNumber() routine and then returning the current statement arrow to the line of code that follows the call to SquareWhole Number().

Debugging the ChangingValues68K Program

ChangingValues68K is a short, simple program—perfect for a quick look at how the MW Debug debugger works. Begin by launching the MW C/C++ 68K compiler and opening the ChangingValues68K.µ project. Check **Enable Debugging** from the Project menu, then select **Run** from that same menu. When you do, you'll see the MW Debug Program window, SYM window, and toolbar.

Executing the ChangingValues68K Program

Running a program from within the debugger is simple; just select **Run** from the Control menu or click the **Run** button on the toolbar. When you do that, program execution begins at the point of the current statement arrow, as shown in Figure 4.10.

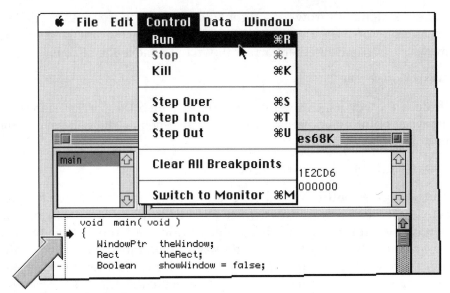

Program execution begins at
the current statement arrow

Figure 4.10 *Program execution always starts at the current statement arrow.*

If you run ChangingValues68K without setting a breakpoint, the program executes from start to finish as it would without the debugger present. What you'd rather do is set a breakpoint so that the debugger stops at a predictable spot in the program. What I've done is set a breakpoint at the if (showWindow = false) line before selecting **Run** from the Control menu. After selecting **Run**, the program executes up to the line that has the breakpoint. As shown in Figure 4.11, the call to NewWindow() results in a new window opening.

In Figure 4.11, the if statement is about to execute. If I select one of the Step menu items from the Control menu, the program will perform the if test. The current statement arrow will then move down to the next line that is to be executed. Should the if test pass, then the current statement arrow will end up at the HideWindow() line. Should the if test fail, the arrow will appear at the ShowWindow() line.

I know that the Boolean variable has a value of false; it was set to false when it was declared. After running the program up to the breakpoint, I can confirm that showWindow is still false by looking at the Locals pane. There, showWindow has a value of 0, or false. So I know that the if test will pass (showWindow *is* false), and the HideWindow() function will get called. Right? Figure 4.12 shows where the current statement arrow moved to after selecting **Step Into** from the Control menu. Depending on how closely you've looked at the ChangingValues68K source code, the result may or may not surprise you.

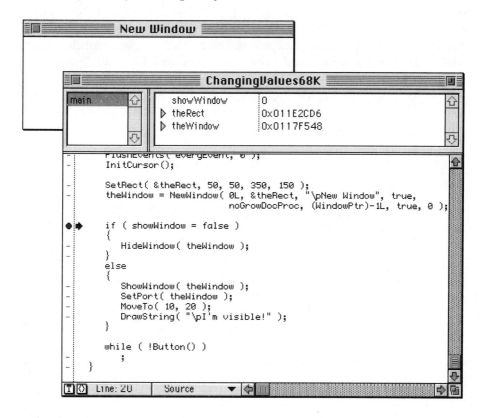

Figure 4.11 *After the call to NewWindow(), a window appears on the screen.*

The debugger makes it clear that the code took the else path rather than the if path. Because the debugger clearly showed that showWindow had a value of false at the time the program was at the if statement, I know that there must be a problem within the line of code that makes up the if test. Knowing just where to focus my problem-solving energies, it doesn't take me long to realize that the if test is *assigning* showWindow a value of false—it isn't *comparing* showWindow to false, as it should! To remedy the problem the if test needs to be changed from:

```
if ( showWindow = false )
```

to:

```
if ( showWindow == false )
```

Now select **Quit** from the File menu to exit the debugger. If the debugger posts an alert asking if it should kill the process, click the **Kill** button. You'll then find yourself back in the MW C/C++ 68K compiler. If the ChangingValues.c source code file isn't open, open it now. Type in the code change to correct the erroneous if statement; then rerun the program. Again step through the source code. This time you'll see that the HideWindow() call gets executed, and the window becomes hidden. Click the mouse to end the program.

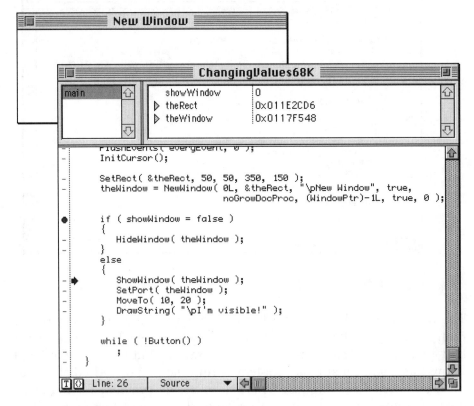

Figure 4.12 *The else section of code executes—not the if section.*

Variables, Data Structures, and the Debugger

Information about data structures and Macintosh memory can be found in several texts, including the *Inside Macintosh* series, this text, and other books by M&T Books. While the information found in these books is helpful, it can be greatly enhanced by using the MW Debug debugger to watch the changing values of variables as a program executes. This is especially true for a complicated concept such as the WindowPtr/WindowRecord/GrafPort relationship—one of the topics covered in this section.

 The Metrowerks ZoneRanger application, the topic of Chapter 9, is another great way to become familiar with Macintosh memory.

N O T E

While the main purpose of a debugger like MW Debug is to help you correct faulty code, you shouldn't overlook another potential use for it. Because MW Debug makes looking at the contents of memory simple and intuitive, the debugger is an excellent tool for exploring and understanding Macintosh memory. In this section I'll again rely on the ChangingValues68K program to demonstrate the power of MW Debug.

Variables and the Locals Pane

To get some further use out of the ChangingValues68K project, I'll use it in the following discussions. First, I'll make one change to the source code (in addition to correcting the faulty if statement). I'll change the declaration of the showWindow variable from

```
Boolean  showWindow = false;
```

to

```
Boolean  showWindow = true;
```

After making sure **Enable Debugging** is checked, I'll select **Run** from the Project menu to start up the debugger.

The upper-right corner of the debugger source window holds the Locals pane—an area that displays the variables declared in the routine currently being executed. Figure 4.13 shows the Program window immediately after selecting **Run** from the compiler's Project window. In this figure you can see that the currently executing routine, main(), is highlighted in the Call Chain pane, and the three variables of main() are displayed in the Locals pane.

Figure 4.13 shows the values for the main() variables at the start of the program; note that the current statement arrow is at the start of main(). Here the variables in main() have values, but not necessarily the values they'll have once the program executes.

 Because it's up to the Memory Manager where to place data structures in memory, the addresses you see will differ of course from those shown in the figures in this chapter.

N O T E

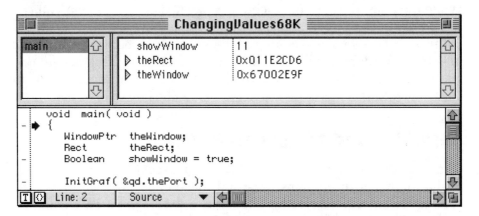

Figure 4.13 *Program execution begins at the start of main().*

 Some programs test to see if a window is open by checking to see whether the window's WindowPtr has a value of nil:

N O T E
```
if ( theWindow == nil )   // theWindow isn't open
    // open the window
```

In Figure 4.13 the debugger shows that a `WindowPtr` variable isn't automatically assigned a value of `nil` when it's declared; you'll have to do this yourself:

```
WindowPtr  theWindow = nil;
```

Next, I'll set a breakpoint at the if statement, then select **Run** from the Control menu. Figure 4.14 shows the state of the program as the breakpoint is reached. The value of the `Boolean` variable `showWindow` is 1, or true—that occurred during the declaration of variable. The rectangle variable `theRect` never gets assigned a new value, so its value remains the same. After the program reaches the breakpoint, the `NewWindow()` routine will have executed, and the `WindowPtr` variable `theWindow` will hold the memory address of the start of a `WindowRecord`.

NOTE

Compare the values of the three variables in Figure 4.14 with the values shown in Figure 4.13 to see the changes that took place.

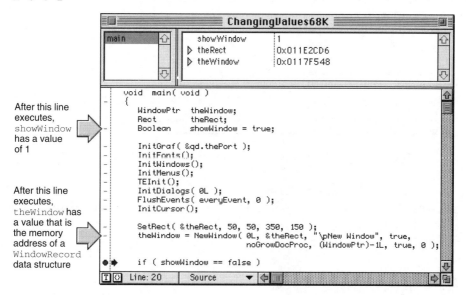

Figure 4.14 *Variable values after the program reaches the breakpoint.*

Up to this point, the figures have shown addresses as the values for the theRect and theWindow variables. It's more likely that you'll want to see the contents of these variables, not the memory address where each is located. The Locals pane allows you to easily do that. But first, give yourself some room by stretching the Locals pane out a little. To do that, click the mouse button on the double horizontal line that lies just beneath the Locals pane and, with the mouse button still held down, drag downward (see Figure 4.15).

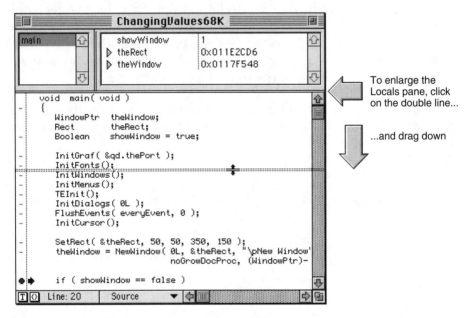

Figure 4.15 *The Locals pane can be enlarged with a click of the mouse button.*

Now, I'll take the remainder of this section to explore the data types of the theRect and theWindow variables. The topics I'll cover here will be useful in learning about any of the many data types unique to Macintosh programming.

The Rect Data Type

If a variable has a Triangle icon beside its name, then that variable has more data than is displayed by the variable's name. For example, a Rect is a structure with four fields: the top, left, bottom, and right pixel coordinates of a rectangle. Clicking on the Triangle icon that's beside the variable's name reveals the fields of the structure that's being pointed to. In Figure 4.16 the contents of theRect rectangle data structure have been displayed.

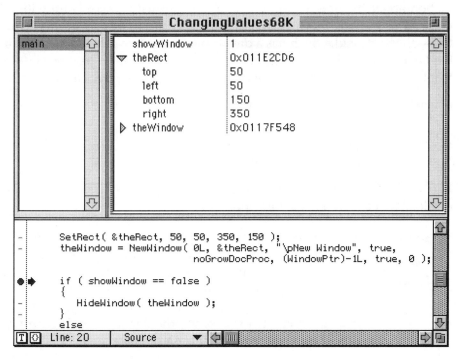

Figure 4.16 *A Rect variable is a data structure that holds the four coordinates of a rectangle.*

N O T E Notice from the placement of the current statement arrow in Figure 4.16 that at the time that the data structure is being viewed, program execution has passed the call to the SetRect() Toolbox function. That's why the values of the rectangle coordinates match those provided as parameters to the SetRect() function. If you view theRect before the call to SetRect() is reached, you'll see entirely different numbers. Since no assignment is made to theRect initially, these values would be considered *garbage*—random "leftovers" from whatever program last used these memory locations.

The WindowPtr, WindowRecord, and GrafPort Data Types

When a window is created using a call to NewWindow() or GetNewWindow(), the Toolbox creates a WindowRecord data structure in which to hold information about the new window. The WindowRecord is a structure with 17 fields. The Toolbox then returns a pointer to the first field in this structure—the port field, which has a data type of GrafPort. That means that in the ChangingValues68K program, the result of the call to NewWindow() is that the variable theWindow points to a GrafPort. Here's that function call:

```
WindowPtr  theWindow;
...
...
theWindow = NewWindow( OL, &theRect, "\pNew Window", true,
                    noGrowDocProc, (WindowPtr)-1L, true, 0 );
```

Figure 4.17 illustrates that it's the GrafPort, this first field of the WindowRecord, that a WindowPtr points to.

A data structure starts at a smaller address and ends at a larger address. Because Macintosh memory is conceptually viewed as having small addresses at the bottom of memory and larger addresses at the top, data structures appear "upside down" in figures. For example, the first field of a WindowRecord is a GrafPort, yet the GrafPort in Figure 4.17 appears to be at the bottom of the WindowRecord.

So, does a WindowPtr hold the starting address of a GrafPort or of a WindowRecord? The answer is "both." Because the GrafPort is the first field in a WindowRecord, they share the same address. As you're about to see, it's the many fields of the GrafPort data structure that hold the window information commonly accessed by programmers, so it's the GrafPort that is accessed via the WindowPtr.

As it turns out, a GrafPort itself is a data structure consisting of several fields—more than two dozen, in fact. In Figure 4.18 I've expanded the GrafPort to show a few of these fields, the first three and the last two.

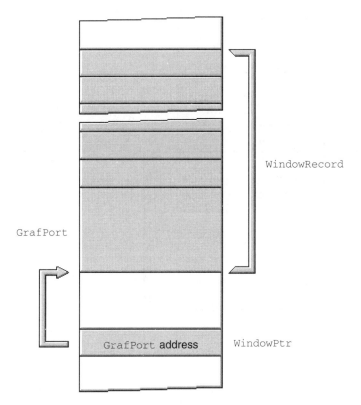

Figure 4.17 *A WindowPtr holds the address of a GrafPort.*

If the preceding discussion seems at all confusing, don't be alarmed. Window data structures is a topic that troubles many programmers. To see how MW Debug can help, again run the ChangingValues68K program with **Enable Debugging** checked in the Project menu. Make sure there's a breakpoint set at a line past the NewWindow() call, then select **Run** from the debugger's Control menu. When the program stops at the breakpoint, click on the **Triangle** icon next to theWindow in the Locals pane.

Figure 4.19 shows part of the data structure that the pointer variable theWindow points to. You know from Figure 4.18 that the first three fields of the GrafPort are the device, portBits, and portRect fields. Figure 4.19 confirms this.

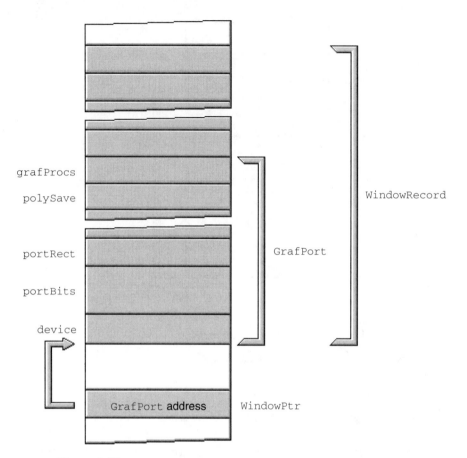

Figure 4.18 *A GrafPort is a data structure that consists of several fields.*

Scrolling through the Locals pane reveals all of the remaining fields in the GrafPort structure. A field that has a single value is displayed as that value. A field that is a data structure is displayed as a pointer; the address of the data structure is shown. You'll seldom have a reason to want to know the address of a variable or the address of a field of the data structure a variable points to. After all, you want to know *what* a variable is, not *where* the Memory Manager placed it in memory. You'll want to know the actual numerical (or string) contents of a variable or field. You can see that value by clicking on the **Triangle** icon next to a pointer's name. In Figure 4.20 you can see that the pnLoc field is a data structure consisting of a v field and an h field, both of which have a value of 0.

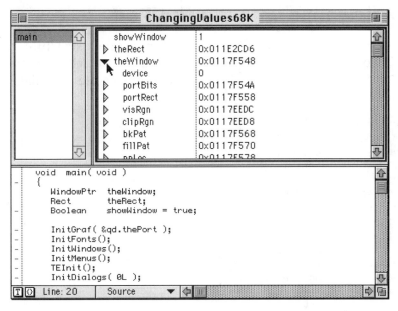

Figure 4.19 *The many fields of the GrafPort data structure can be viewed in MW Debug.*

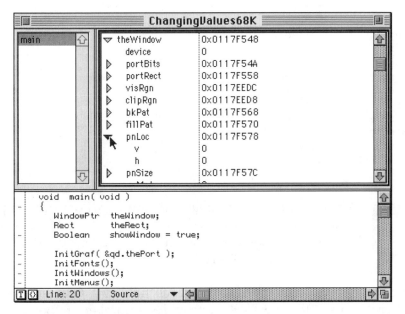

Figure 4.20 *A variable that is displayed as an address can
also be viewed as the underlying data structure.*

Experimenting with the GrafPort

If you'd like to see the definition of any Toolbox data structure, refer to the Universal Header files. The structure that a WindowPtr points to—a GrafPort—is defined in the QuickDraw.h header file. I've listed it as follows.

```
struct GrafPort
{
    short       device;
    BitMap      portBits;
    Rect        portRect;
    RgnHandle   visRgn;
    RgnHandle   clipRgn;
    Pattern     bkPat;
    Pattern     fillPat;
    Point       pnLoc;
    Point       pnSize;
    short       pnMode;
    Pattern     pnPat;
    short       pnVis;
    short       txFont;
    Style       txFace;
    SInt8       filler;
    short       txMode;
    short       txSize;
    Fixed       spExtra;
    long        fgColor;
    long        bkColor;
    short       colrBit;
    short       patStretch;
    Handle      picSave;
    Handle      rgnSave;
    Handle      polySave;
    QDProcsPtr  grafProcs;
};
```

What if you didn't *know* that the GrafPort data type is defined in the QuickDraw.h header file? You'd open your Universal Header search set in the compiler Find dialog box and search for "GrafPort"!

NOTE

Rather than have to memorize what each field of a GrafPort is, and what each is used for, the Toolbox provides a number of Toolbox functions that allow you to indirectly change these fields. For example, the pnLoc field holds the current location of the graphics pen. When you call DrawString(), the starting point of the drawing is determined by the values in this field. To change the pnLoc field, you don't tamper with the field directly. Instead, you call Move() or MoveTo() to let the Toolbox change the values in pnLoc to those that you specify. To satisfy yourself that this is indeed what happens, again run the ChangingValues68K program with the debugger turned on.

Set a breakpoint at the program's call to MoveTo(), then select **Run** from the debugger's Control menu. The program will stop at the MoveTo() call, *before* the call takes place. When it stops, click on the **Triangle** icon by theWindow in the Locals pane. Then scroll down to the pnLoc field and click on its **Triangle** icon. Note that both the vertical pen coordinate (v) and the horizontal pen coordinate (h) have a value of 0, as shown in Figure 4.21.

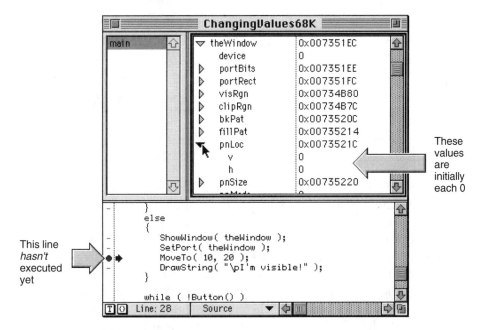

Figure 4.21 *MW Debug shows that the location of the graphics pen in a window is initially at the point (0,0).*

Now select **Step Into** (or type **Command-S**) to step. When you do, the MoveTo() statement will execute and the current statement arrow will move down to the DrawString() line. More importantly, you'll notice that the values in the v and h fields of the pnLoc field of the GrafPort that theWindow points to will have changed (see Figure 4.22).

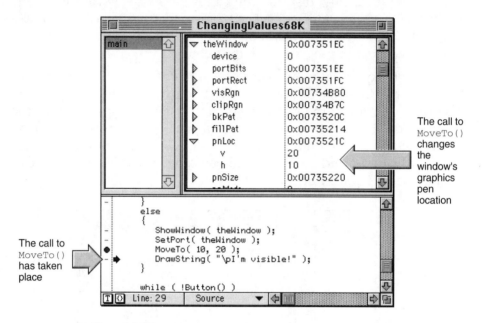

Figure 4.22 *MW Debug shows that after a call to MoveTo(),*
the graphics pen position has been changed.

An interesting feature of MW Debug is that the debugger allows you to change the value of a variable during the execution of a program. When you double-click on a variable's current value in the Locals pane, the value becomes surrounded by an edit box. To change the value of the variable, all you need to do is type in the desired number. To gain a better understanding of how fields of a GrafPort work, try changing one or both of the pnLoc fields in this way. Rerun ChangingValues68K and step through the program until the current statement arrow stops at the DrawString() line. Because the MoveTo() call will have been made, the values of the pnLoc fields v and h will be 10 and 20, respectively. Double-click on the value of the h field (10) to surround the value with an edit box, as I've done in Figure 4.23. Then type in a new value. In the figure I've entered a value of 150. Before selecting **Step Into** from the Control menu, you should be able to accurately predict what will happen. Match your guess with the result shown in Figure 4.24.

Double-click on a value to display an edit box...

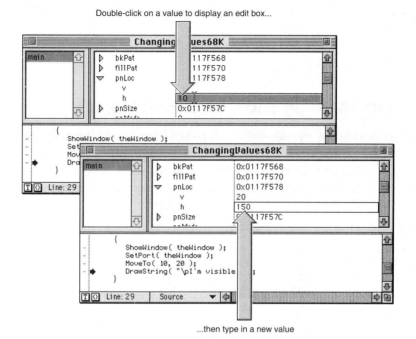

...then type in a new value

Figure 4.23 *A variable's value can be changed by double-clicking on the value and then typing in a new number.*

The horizontal location of the pen was set to 150, so the `DrawString()` text now starts 150 pixels from the window's left edge

After the `DrawString()` line executes, the Toolbox updates the `h` field to the new pen location—the end of the "I'm visible!" text

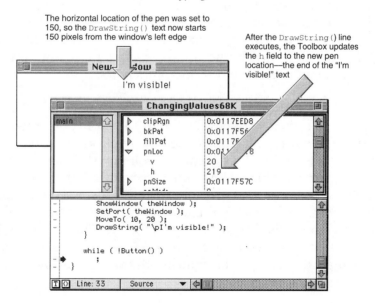

Figure 4.24 *Changing the graphics pen location affects subsequent text drawing.*

Finally—the reason the program is named "Changing Values"!

Further Investigation of the GrafPort

The pnLoc field of the GrafPort data structure isn't the only field you can alter, of course. The fgColor field is responsible for selecting which one of eight colors foreground objects (such as text and graphics) will be drawn in. If you look in the QuickDraw.h Universal Header file you'll find that each of the eight colors has a corresponding constant defined for it:

```
blackColor     =    33
whiteColor     =    30
redColor       =   205
greenColor     =   341
blueColor      =   409
cyanColor      =   273
magentaColor   =   137
yellowColor    =    69
```

Color Macs are capable of using more than eight colors, of course, but only in color graphics ports (using the CGrafPort data type). The fgColor and bkColor fields of the GrafPort provide a quick and simple means of adding a minimal amount of color to basic graphics ports.

To see how the GrafPort affects window color, run ChangingValues68K again. Break at or before the DrawString() line of code. Then display the fields of the GrafPort data structure by clicking on the **Triangle** icon by theWindow in the Locals pane. Scroll down to the fgColor field and note its current value—33. Looking back at the color constants, you can see that a value of 33 represents black. That's as you'd expect. By default, drawing takes place in black, so you know that the window foreground color is black. Double-click on the **fgColor** value to display an edit box, then type in one of the color constant values. In Figure 4.25 I've entered a value of 137. This matches the magentaColor constant, so you'd expect writing and drawing to now take place in a purplish red color. Of course, the black and white figure can't illustrate this—all the more reason for you to try it out on your color Mac!

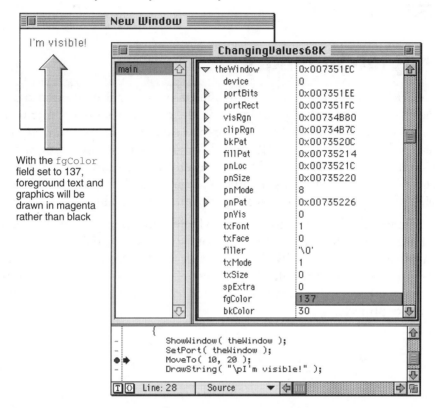

Figure 4.25 *The fgColor field of the GrafPort holds the foreground color for a window.*

A few of the other GrafPort fields a program manipulates are listed as follows, along with the Toolbox routines your program can use to make the changes. Try adding calls to some or all of these routines and see how they affect the window. Then try changing these fields directly using MW Debug.

```
bkColor    BackColor()    // changes the window background color
txFont     TextFont()     // changes the text font
txFace     TextFace()     // changes the text style
txSize     TextSize()     // changes the text point size
```

NOTE

In the `ChangingValues68K` program, changing the background color won't have an effect on window. That's because there's no event loop in the program, and the window never gets updated.

Chapter Summary

The CodeWarrior debugger, `MW Debug`, takes control of your program when you check **Enable Debugging** in the compiler's Project menu and then select **Run**. You use the debugger to execute your program up to a breakpoint and then to single-step through a part of your program. In this way you can carefully observe the effects each line of code has on variable values. Using this technique, you'll be able to accurately pinpoint where you've made mistakes in your source code.

Macintosh data structures, and Macintosh memory, can be topics that are difficult to master. If you devote some time to using `MW Debug` to examine memory, you'll gain a better understanding of how the Macintosh works with data. This investment in time will pay off in the future; the knowledge you gain will help you quickly track down bugs in future projects.

Chapter 5

Fat Applications

A program generated with the MW C/C++ 68K compiler runs best on a 680x0-based Macintosh. A program generated with the MW C/C++ PPC compiler runs only on a PowerPC-based Macintosh. If your application will be used by owners of 68K Macs, you'll need to supply them with a 68K version. If your application will be used by owners of PowerPC-based Macs, you should provide them with a faster, native PowerPC version. Rather than distribute two separate applications, wouldn't it be better if you could somehow combine the two versions into one program? Better still, wouldn't it be ideal if this one program knew which type of computer was launching it—a 68K or a PowerPC Mac? A fat binary application is just such a program.

This chapter describes how executable code is stored in 68K, PowerPC-only, and fat binary applications. After that, you'll take a step-by-step walk through the creation of a fat binary application.

Executable Code and Resources

Before the PowerPC-based Macs existed, all Macintosh applications stored the program's executable code within resources. With the arrival of PowerPC-only applications and fat applications, this is no longer true.

68K Applications and Code Resources

Macintosh files (and an application is a file) can consist of two *forks*—a resource fork and a data fork. For a 68K application file, both the program's executable object code and the resources that the program uses are stored in the resource fork. The data fork is generally empty. Figure 5.1 illustrates this.

N O T E   To programmers, the resource fork is the more familiar of the two forks. The resource fork holds the application resources that programmers edit with a resource editor such as ResEdit or Resorcerer. Programmers generally don't work directly with the data fork because in an application, this fork is empty. In document files, however, the situation is usually reversed—the data fork holds the documents text and graphics, while the resource fork has few or no resources.

Most of the resources shown in Figure 5.1 will be recognizable to you except, perhaps, the CODE resource. When a compiler builds a 68K application, it stores the compiled executable code in CODE resources. Because a single CODE resource is prohibited from exceeding 32K in size, most programs house more than one CODE resource.

When the user of a 68K program double-clicks the program's icon, it is the Segment Manager that finds the application's CODE 0 resource and loads the executable code that is stored in that resource.

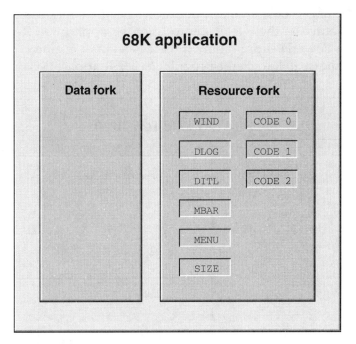

Figure 5.1 *The data fork of a 68K application is generally empty.*

PowerPC Applications and Data Fork Code

A PowerPC application, like a 68K program, consists of a data fork and a resource fork. There is a key difference in how executable code is stored in the two application files, however. In a PowerPC application, the executable code is stored in a *code fragment* in the data fork. The PowerPC code can be stored together like this because there is no 32K size limit on a fragment, as there is on a CODE resource.

The resource fork of a PowerPC application holds all of the resources that you'll typically find in the resource fork of a 68K application, with the exception of the CODE resource. Additionally, you'll find a single resource not present in a 68K resource fork—a resource of type cfrg (for "code fragment") (see Figure 5.2).

When an application icon is double-clicked, it is the Process Manager that is responsible for launching that application. Before it does that, the

Process Manager looks in the application's resource fork to see if there is a `cfrg` resource. If there is, it knows that the application it is about to launch is a PowerPC application. If there is no `cfrg` resource, the Process Manager knows to launch the program as a 68K application.

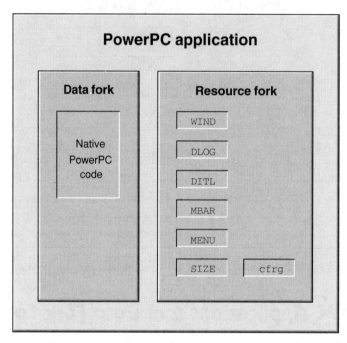

Figure 5.2 *The data fork of a PowerPC application holds the application's executable code.*

Fat Applications and Executable Code

A fat binary application contains two versions of executable code. One version is the native PowerPC code and is stored in the application's data fork. The other version is 68K code and is held in `CODE` resources in the application's resource fork. When this one application is copied to a PowerPC-based Macintosh and launched, the native PowerPC code gets loaded into memory. If this same application is copied to a 680x0-based Mac and launched, the 68K code will instead be loaded into memory.

How does the Process Manager know which set of code to use? The answer lies in the `cfrg` resource. When an application on a PowerPC-base Mac is double-clicked, the Process Manager first looks for a `cfrg` resource in the program's resource fork. If there is a `cfrg` resource, the

Process Manager knows there's native PowerPC code to load. In this scenario the PowerPC code in the application's data fork gets loaded, while the 68K code in the CODE resources gets ignored.

 I'm generalizing a bit. Actually, a CODE resource could get loaded on a PowerPC-based Mac. If a CODE resource has its preload attribute set, it will always get loaded into memory, but on a PowerPC-based Mac, it won't ever execute. The code from the data fork will be used instead. So for all practical purposes, you can consider the CODE resources ignored on a PowerPC-based Macintosh.

Now consider this same fat binary application on the hard drive of a 68K Mac. The 68K Mac knows nothing of cfrg resources—they're defined only on PowerPC-based Macs. So when a fat binary is double-clicked on a 68K Mac, the cfrg resource is ignored, and the version of code that's housed in the CODE resources gets used. Figure 5.3 shows how a fat binary holds two versions of executable code, the resources that are common to both versions, and a cfrg resource.

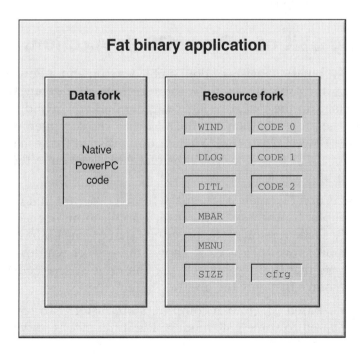

Figure 5.3 *A fat binary application holds two complete versions of an application's executable code.*

NOTE What if an application that's on the hard drive of a PowerPC-based Mac doesn't have a `cfrg` resource? Then it is a 68K application—not a native PowerPC-only application or a fat binary application. A PowerPC-based Mac can run such programs, but they'll run in something called *emulation mode*. 68K code running in emulation mode is slower than native PowerPC code running directly on the PowerPC processor.

Building a Fat Binary Application

If you want to build an application that will run on older, 680x0-based Macs, you'll compile your code using the MW C/C++ 68K compiler to generate a 68K application. If you'd rather your application be a fast, native PowerPC program that runs only on PowerPC-based Macs, you'll use the MW C/C++ PPC compiler. If you want your application to run on 68K Macs and to run in native mode on PowerPC-based Macs, you'll use both compilers to create a fat binary application. This section describes the steps to carry this out.

Creating 68K and PowerPC Applications

Because a fat binary consists of both a 68K version and a PowerPC version of the same program, you'll want to compile and debug two separate projects. Run the MW C/C++ 68K compiler and create and test a 68K version of the program, then run the MW C/C++ PPC compiler and do the same with a PowerPC version. When you're satisfied that each separate application runs as expected, you'll be ready to move on to the creation of a fat binary.

In this section I'll create a fat binary from a program that was developed in Chapter 3—the NewPlaySound68K application. In that chapter I created only a 68K version of the program. That means I'll have to make a PPC version as well. Figure 5.4 shows the project window for both versions. Note that the two projects use the same source code file and the same resource file; only the libraries differ.

PowerPC-based Macintosh computers are faster than 680x0-based Macs. Compared to some 68K models, the difference is very considerable. If you're developing on a Power Mac, you may end up adding certain features to your program that work just fine on a PowerPC-base Mac, but bog down a slower 68K model. You can resolve this dilemma by including *conditional directives* in your source code file. A conditional directive tells the compiler to compile the code that follows the directive only under certain circumstances.

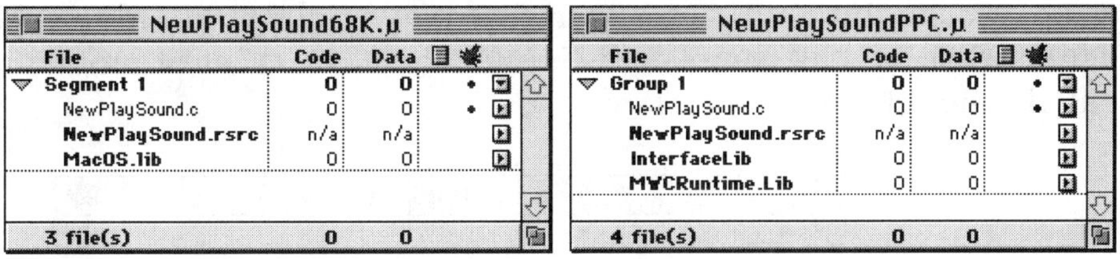

Figure 5.4 *68K and PPC versions of the NewPlaySound project.*

The #ifdef powerc conditional directive tells the compiler to compile the code that follows the #ifdef powerc line only if the compiler is the MW C/C++ PPC compiler. If the compiler is the MW C/C++ 68K version, then the code following the #ifdef should be skipped. If there is an optional #else section, then the code that follows that line should be compiled by the MW C/C++ 68K compiler instead. By using the #ifdef powerc directive, you can include sections of code that get compiled differently depending on which compiler is used. Here's the format of the #ifdef conditional directive:

```
#ifdef powerc
    // code designed to run only if the user has a PowerPC-based Mac
#else
    // code designed to run only if the user has a 68K-based Mac
#endif
```

Just to prove to myself that the #ifdef powerc directive works, I've added one to the NewPlaySound.c source code file. Here's what it looks like:

```
#ifdef powerc
    SndPlay( nil, (SnListHandle)theSound, true );
#else
```

```
      SndPlay( nil, (SnListHandle)theSound, true );
      SndPlay( nil, (SnListHandle)theSound, true );
#endif
```

Remember, the same `NewPlaySound.c` file is a part of both the 68K project and the PPC project. When I compile and build my 68K version of the `NewPlaySound` program, I'll generate code that plays the telephone ring sound twice. When I compile and build the PowerPC version of `NewPlaySound`, I'll have a program that plays the sound only once. Figure 5.5 shows the complete listing for the `NewPlaySound` program, with the `#ifdef` directive in place.

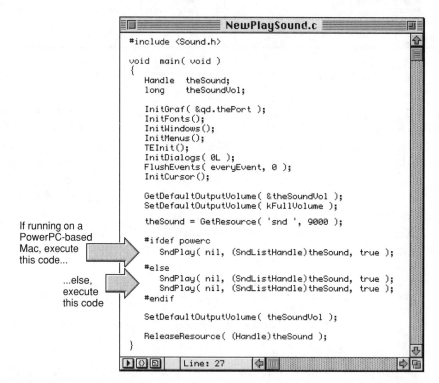

If running on a PowerPC-based Mac, execute this code...

...else, execute this code

Figure 5.5 *The NewPlaySound.c source code file, with the addition of a conditional directive.*

N O T E

In this book I just touch on the differences between PowerPC code and 68K code. For complete information on the particulars of programming the PowerPC-based Macintosh, refer to the M&T book *Programming the PowerPC*, or Apple's *PowerPC System Software* volume of the *Inside Macintosh* series.

Get Ready for the Fat App

To keep your fat application separate from your other versions of NewPlaySound, create a new, empty folder in the same directory that holds the existing NewPlaySound files. Figure 5.6 shows what my New Play Sound ƒ folder now looks like.

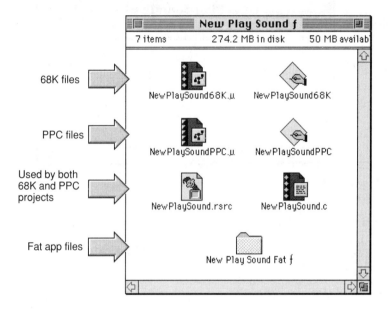

Figure 5.6 *The folder that holds the different versions of the NewPlaySound files.*

Next, make a copy of the existing 68K version of the NewPlaySound application and place it in the fat binary folder. Do the same with the PPC version of the project. Figure 5.7 shows what my "fat" folder now holds.

Get the PPC Project Ready

Go into the New Play Sound Fat ƒ folder and double-click on the **NewPlaySoundPPC.µ** project to launch the MW C/C++ PPC compiler and to open the project. Select **Preferences** from the Edit menu, then click on the **Project** icon to display the project panel. Enter an appropriate name for the fat binary, such as **NewPlaySoundFat**.

Because you've copied the project to a new folder, the CodeWarrior compiler might not be able to find some of the files listed in the project window. If you tried to compile the project now, you'd probably see an alert like the one pictured in Figure 5.8.

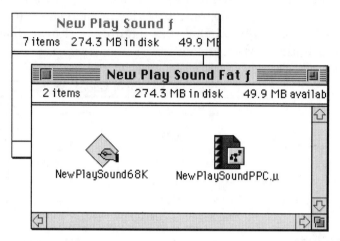

Figure 5.7 *The folder that will hold the fat binary version of NewPlaySound.*

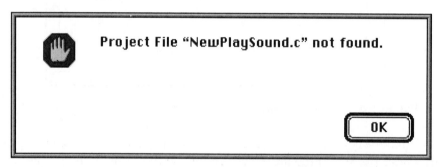

Figure 5.8 *The alert box displayed when a CodeWarrior compiler can't find a file.*

To circumvent this problem, update the compiler access paths. Select **Preferences** from the Edit menu. Then click on the **Access Paths** icon to bring up the Access Paths panel in the Preferences dialog box. Click the **Add** button so that you can add a new path to the list of paths the compiler searches when compiling (see Figure 5.9).

When you click on the **Add** button, you'll see a dialog box like the one shown in Figure 5.10. Use the pop-up list menu at the top of the dialog box to move back out of the New Play Sound Fat ƒ folder and into the New Play Sound ƒ. This is the folder that holds the NewPlaySound.c source code file and the NewPlaySound.rsrc file. Click the **Select "New Play Sound ƒ"** button to add this folder to the compiler's search list. When you do, you'll be returned to the Preferences dialog box. Click the **OK** button to dismiss that dialog box.

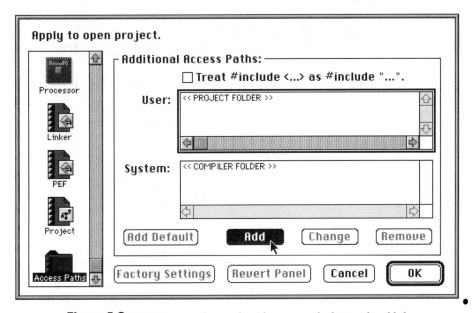

Figure 5.9 *The Access Paths panel, with a new path about to be added.*

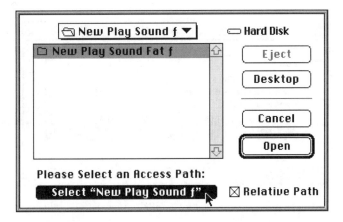

Figure 5.10 *Selecting a path to add to the access paths list.*

Finally, add the NewPlaySound68K application to the PPC project. Yes, that's right. You'll be adding the application itself to the project window. Select **Add Files** from the Project menu, then add the 68K application, as I'm doing in Figure 5.11.

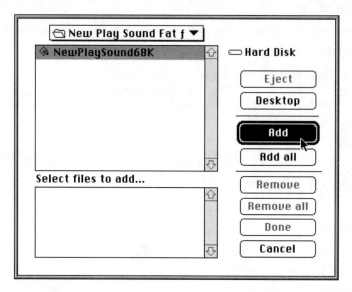

Figure 5.11 *Adding the 68K version of the NewPlaySound program to the fat binary project.*

After adding the application, your NewPlaySoundPPC.µ project window should look like Figure 5.12.

File	Code	Data		
▽ **Group 1**	**3K**	**818**	•	⊟
NewPlaySound.c	212	8	•	▶
NewPlaySound.rsrc	n/a	n/a		▶
InterfaceLib	0	0		▶
MWCRuntime.Lib	3492	810		▶
NewPlaySound68K	n/a	n/a		▶
5 file(s)	**3K**	**818**		

Figure 5.12 *The fat binary project after adding the 68K version of the NewPlaySound application.*

What does the PPC compiler do when it's building an application and it encounters a different application in the list of project window files? It simply copies the application's resource fork into the PowerPC application during linking. Recall that the executable code of a 68K application lies in CODE resources in the application's resource fork. So adding the 68K application to the project window allows the 68K executable code to become a part of the fat binary application.

Now that the 68K application has been added to the project, remove the NewPlaySound.rsrc resource file by clicking on its name and selecting **Remove Files** from the Project menu. You can do this because the 68K application holds the snd resource found in this file. Remember, the 68K application was built from a project that included this resource file.

N O T E

Your own projects may be much more involved than the NewPlaySound example, and they may not have an identical set of resources for both 68K and PPC projects. For example, while both projects may share a common resource file, the PPC project may go on to use its own additional resource file that holds some resources used only by the PPC version of the application. In such instances, only remove the common resource file from the project.

Your project window should now look like Figure 5.13.

File	Code	Data		
▽ **Group 1**	**3K**	**818**	•	▾
NewPlaySound.c	212	8	•	▶
InterfaceLib	0	0		▶
MWCRuntime.Lib	3492	810		▶
NewPlaySound68K	n/a	n/a		▶
4 file(s)	**3K**	**818**		

NewPlaySoundPPC.µ

Figure 5.13 *The fat binary project after removing the common resource file NewPlaySound.rsrc.*

Build the Fat Binary Application

If your host computer is a PowerPC-based Mac, select **Run** from the Project menu to build the fat binary. If you're working from a 680x0-based Mac, the **Run** command will be dim; use the **Make** menu item instead. Regardless of which menu item you use, the result will be the same—a fat binary version of NewPlaySound!

If you're fortunate enough to have access to both a 68K Mac and a PowerPC-based Macintosh, try running the fat binary on both machines to verify that on a 68K Mac the program sounds the phone twice, while on a PowerPC-based Mac the program only rings it once.

Examining the Programs with a Resource Editor

Now that you have an honest-to-goodness fat app of your own, you can take a look inside it to see if this chapter's discussions of CODE resources, cfrg resources, and data forks hold true.

Using your resource editor, first open the PPC and 68K versions of the NewPlaySound program. Make sure to open the programs themselves, not the project resource files. Don't open the fat application just yet. Your screen should hold the windows shown in Figure 5.14.

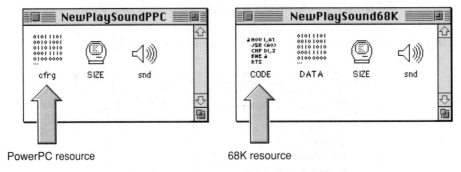

PowerPC resource   68K resource

Figure 5.14 *The PPC version of NewPlaySound contains a cfrg resource,*
while the 68K version holds CODE resources.

In Figure 5.14 you can see that the PPC version of the program has a cfrg resource, as any PowerPC-only application should. This resource was added to the program by the MW C/C++ PPC compiler. Also notice that there are no CODE resources in the PPC version of the program, while there are in the 68K version.

Next, open the fat binary application. In Figure 5.15, notice that the fat binary holds the resources from the 68K version of the program, as well as the cfrg resource that was added by the compiler.

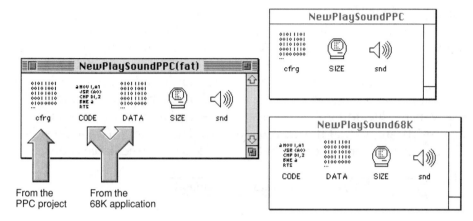

Figure 5.15 *The fat binary holds all of the resources found in both the 68K and PPC versions of a program.*

The executable code for a 68K application is held in the application's CODE resources. The application's data fork is generally empty. Figure 5.16 shows the Get Info window for the 68K version of NewPlaySound. Here you can see that the application's data fork is in fact empty.

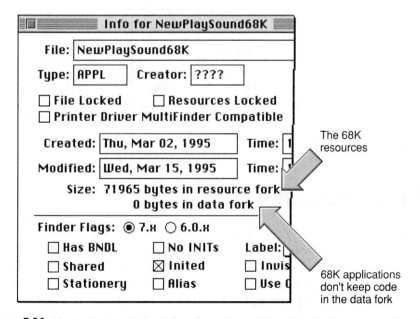

Figure 5.16 *The ResEdit Get Info window shows that a 68K application has an empty data fork.*

Fat applications have two sets of executable code—one in the program's CODE resources, the other in the program's data fork. Figure 5.17 illustrates this for the fat version of NewPlaySound. In the figure, you can see that the fat binary version of this program has a resource fork that's a little larger than the 68K version of the program (see Figure 5.16 to make the comparison). The fat version holds all of the resources found in the 68K version, including the CODE resources—and a cfrg resource. Further, Figure 5.17 shows that the fat version has a data fork with data. This data is the native PowerPC version of the NewPlaySound executable code.

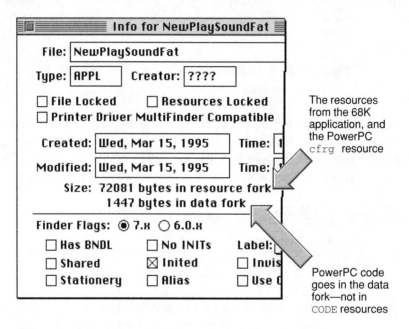

The resources from the 68K application, and the PowerPC cfrg resource

PowerPC code goes in the data fork—not in CODE resources

Figure 5.17 *The ResEdit Get Info window shows that a PPC application has data in its data fork.*

Chapter Summary

Making a fat binary version of one of your applications gives that application the "best of both worlds." A fat binary application is capable of running on both 680x0-based Macs and PowerPC-based Macintoshes. And, when running on a PowerPC-based Mac, the program will run in fast, native PowerPC mode.

You create a fat binary by first making a project for both the MW C/C++ 68K compiler and the MW C/C++ PPC compiler. After building and testing both versions of the program, it's time to create the fat application. Make a copy of the PPC project and add the 68K application. Then remove the resource file from the project. Build the application, and you're all set; you'll have a fat application!

Chapter 6

Getting Started with PowerPlant

PowerPlant is not a compiler—it's not any type of application. It's an application framework. That means it's a set of C++ classes that are used in conjunction with your own C++ object-oriented code. These classes—written by Metrowerks programmers—provide a great deal of the interface functionality common to all Mac applications.

If your CodeWarrior project includes the source code files that hold the PowerPlant classes, you'll find that you won't have to write any code for displaying a menu bar—no calls to the Toolbox routines `GetNewMBar()`, `SetMenuBar()`, `AddResMenu()`, and `DrawMenuBar()`. PowerPlant takes care of all that. You'll also be able to omit much of the menu-handling code found in typical Mac projects; PowerPlant knows how to handle the standard menu items. You won't write any code for handling selections from the Apple menu; PowerPlant handles this menu for you. You also won't write any code for handling menu selections made with command-key equivalents. Again, PowerPlant code does this for you. Menu-handling tasks aren't the only ones handled by PowerPlant; the list goes on and on.

PowerPlant supplies the code that takes care of tasks common to most Mac programs. By incorporating PowerPlant source code into your CodeWarrior projects, you'll spend less time writing interface code. That allows you to devote your programming efforts to the parts of your project that will make your application different from existing programs.

The Example Application

To compile the source code found in the PowerPlant files, you'll rely on either the 68K or the PPC version of the Metrowerks C/C++ compiler. This entire chapter is devoted to the development of a simple Mac application named PPIntro68K. As the program's name suggests, it will be developed using PowerPlant and the MW C/C++ 68K compiler. This compiler was chosen for three reasons. First, while many Metrowerks owners have both the 68K and the PPC compilers, some have just the 68K version. By using the 68K compiler in the walkthrough of this chapter, all Metrowerks owners will benefit. The second reason for using the MW C/C++ 68K compiler is because programs generated by the 68K compiler will run on either a 680x0-based Macintosh or a Power Mac, which will please all Mac owners. Finally, users of the 68K compiler and users of the PPC compiler will benefit equally from the discussions in this chapter; the same PowerPlant classes work with both compilers.

So as not to upset the speed-hungry Power Mac owners, this chapter will end with a section that describes how the PPIntro68K example can be easily turned into an MW C/C++ PPC project.

What the PPIntro68K Example Does

When you run PPIntro68K, your screen will look like the one shown in Figure 6.1. A menu bar with three menus will appear, and a single empty window will open. The window can be moved, resized, and closed.

Figure 6.1 *The PPIntro68K program displays a window and menu bar.*

Figure 6.2 shows the items you'll find in the three menus used by PPIntro68K. The Apple menu allows the user to select the **About** menu item or any of the items found in the user's Apple Menu Items folder. The File menu simply lets the user quit the application. Because PPIntro68K displays only an empty window, the items in the Edit menu are disabled.

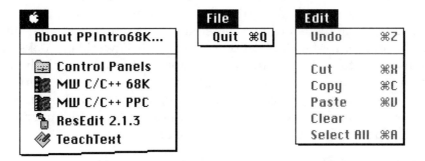

Figure 6.2 *The menus of the PPIntro68K program.*

The next few pages discuss—and show—the PPIntro68K source code I've written. You'll want to note that I've included no code to handle a mouse click in a menu and no code to handle a menu selection such as the Apple menu **About** item or the File menu **Quit** item. Yet the program readily handles these menu choices. The trick to this, of course, lies in the code that makes up the PowerPlant source code files.

The Example Source Code Listing

The PPIntro68K example, like most Macintosh applications, displays a menu bar with menus. Again, like most Mac programs, PPIntro68K opens a window that the user can drag, close, and resize. Because these features are all tasks that are basic to the Mac interface, one would hope that the source code necessary to carry out these tasks would be a part of the application framework used to create the program. And indeed they are—as you'll see from the PPIntro68K source code listing later.

The PPIntro68K.µ project consists of several source files, but only one that I've written. The rest contain the source code that *is* the PowerPlant application framework. My source code initializes the Toolbox, starts up the application, and opens a window. After that, it's up to the PowerPlant source code to handle the user's actions as menus are dropped and the window is moved.

Following is the listing for CPPIntroApp.cp. This file, and a very small header file that CPPIntroApp.cp uses, are the only ones I've created. Most of the code in CPPIntroApp.cp won't look familiar to you, but don't worry about that. The remainder of this chapter will cover the basic concepts of working with the PowerPlant application framework, and in doing so will describe the specifics of this listing. The CPPIntroApp.cp file is included here only to let you see what a source code listing for a Mac application created with PowerPlant looks like. It's also here to make you feel a little more comfortable with the idea that once you understand how PowerPlant works, it will speed up your development time. The fact that this listing, which consists of just over a dozen lines of code, is all the code you need to write to implement a simple Mac interface should convince you of that.

```
// ==============================================================
//                                          constant definitions

const ResIDT   WIND_display = 500;
```

```
// ==========================================================
//                                                  main()

void  main( void )
{
   UQDGlobals::InitializeToolbox( &qd );

   CPPIntroApp theApp;
   theApp.Run();
}


// ==========================================================
//                         CPPIntroApp class constructor

CPPIntroApp :: CPPIntroApp()
{
   URegistrar::RegisterClass( 'wind',
            (ClassCreatorFunc)LWindow::CreateWindowStream );

   mDisplayWindow = LWindow::CreateWindow( WIND_display, this );

   mDisplayWindow->Show();
}
```

The PowerPlant Project

An application created using PowerPlant starts out just as an application created by traditional means does—as a Metrowerks CodeWarrior project. To start developing a PowerPlant application you can launch either the MW C/C++ 68K or MW C/C++ PPC compiler and then select **New Project** from the File menu. Or, to save the effort of adding PowerPlant files to a new project, you could copy an existing PowerPlant project.

The PPIntro68K Example Project Folder

This chapter's PPIntro68K PowerPlant example project can be found in a folder named PP Intro ƒ. In that folder, as in most of my PowerPlant project folders, you'll find five files (they're shown in Figure 6.3). The type of only one of these five files, the PPIntro.PPob file, will be new to you. This file holds a PPob resource, a PowerPlant resource that defines a window in greater detail than a WIND resource does.

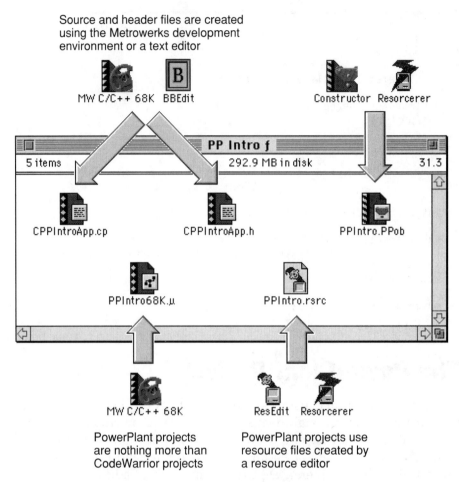

Figure 6.3 *Several different development tools can be used to create the files used in a PowerPlant project.*

The Project and PowerPlant Classes

Looking back at Figure 6.3 you'll notice that there isn't much to indicate that the contents of the PP Intro f folder are PowerPlant-related. Remember, though, that PowerPlant is not an application; it's a collection of classes. The definitions of these classes are held in files in the PowerPlant Library f found on the full-featured Metrowerks CodeWarrior CD. Figure 6.4 shows some of the many folders within the PowerPlant Library f, as well as a few of the files found in one of the library folders.

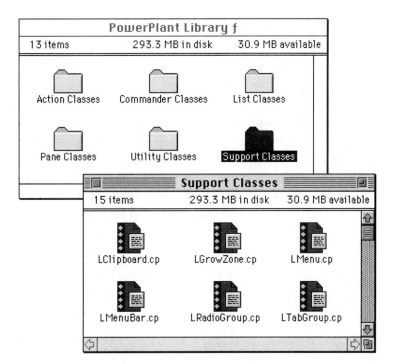

Figure 6.4 *A few of the files that hold PowerPlant source code.*

Double-clicking on the PPIntro68K.µ project file will give you a better idea of how the contents of a project that uses PowerPlant differs from a project that doesn't. Figure 6.5 shows this project file.

File	Code	Data	📄	🔥	
▽ **Application**	0	0			▣
CPPIntroApp.cp	0	0		•	▣
▽ **Resources**	0	0			▣
PPIntro.PPob	0	0			▣
PPIntro.rsrc	0	0			▣
▽ **Libraries**	0	0			▣
CPlusPlus.lib	0	0			▣
PPLibrary68K	0	0			▣
MacOS.lib	0	0			▣
AEObjectSupportLib.o.lib	0	0			▣
7 file(s)	**0**	**0**			

Figure 6.5 *The project window of a CodeWarrior project that uses a PowerPlant precompiled library.*

PowerPlant projects contain more source code than is evident from the PPIntro68K.μ project. In this project you'll see a library named PPLibrary68K. This prebuilt PowerPlant library contains the code found in 40 individual source code files. These source files are all from the PowerPlant Library ƒ shown in Figure 6.4. You don't have to use the PPLibrary68K library in a PowerPlant project. Instead, you can add the individual PowerPlant files and arrange them into segments as you see fit. In Figure 6.6 you can see two versions of a project. Each version holds the same code. The project on the left has seven segments devoted to holding individual PowerPlant source code files, files that will need to be compiled. The project on the right uses the already-compiled PPLibrary68K library in place of the individual PowerPlant files.

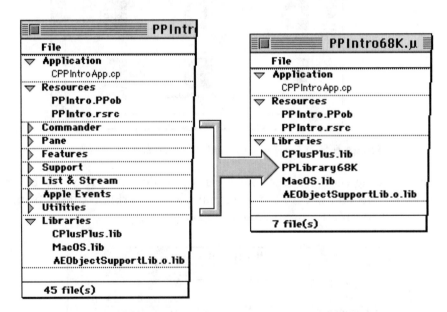

Figure 6.6 *A precompiled library can be used in place of individual PowerPlant source code files.*

To emphasize the idea that a project that uses the PowerPlant source files is the same as one that uses the PPLibrary68K PowerPlant library, two separate versions of the PPIntro68K project are included on the CD with this book. Figure 6.7 shows the project that includes the source files. In this figure you can see that the Support segment holds five PowerPlant files; other segments hold still more PowerPlant files. If you build an application using each project, you'll find that the result is two identical programs.

File	Code	Data	📄	🐛
▽ **Application**	0	0		▾
CPPIntroApp.cp	0	0	•	▸
▽ **Resources**	0	0		▾
PPIntro.PPob	0	0		▸
PPIntro.rsrc	0	0		▸
▷ **Commander**	0	0		▾
▷ **Pane**	0	0		▾
▷ **Features**	0	0		▾
▽ **Support**	0	0		▾
LClipboard.cp	0	0	•	▸
LGrowZone.cp	0	0	•	▸
LMenu.cp	0	0	•	▸
LMenuBar.cp	0	0	•	▸
UDesktop.cp	0	0	•	▸
▷ **List & Stream**	0	0		▾
▷ **Apple Events**	0	0		▾
▷ **Utilities**	0	0		▾
▽ **Libraries**	0	0		▾
CPlusPlus.lib	0	0		▸
MacOS.lib	0	0		▸
AEObjectSupportLib.o.lib	0	0		▸
45 file(s)	0	0		

Window title: PPIntro68KnoLib.μ

Figure 6.7 *The project window of a CodeWarrior project that uses PowerPlant source code files.*

For copyright reasons, the numerous individual files that make up the PowerPlant application framework have *not* been included on the CD that accompanies this book. Instead, one precompiled library named PPLibrary68K is in its place. Only owners of the full version of **CodeWarrior** will be able to compile PPIntro68KnoLib.μ. Readers who haven't yet purchased CodeWarrior from Metrowerks will have to take my word for it when I say that both PPIntro68K.μ and PPIntro68KnoLib.μ generate the same application!

PowerPlant Resources

A Mac application that is built using PowerPlant classes includes resources of the types you're already familiar with and a couple of new types.

The Project Resource File

Figure 6.8 shows the resource file for this chapter's PPIntro68K example project, as viewed in ResEdit. Figure 6.9 shows the same resource file when opened using Resorcerer. Like other Metrowerks projects, a PowerPlant project's resource file can be created and edited using any resource editor, including *ResEdit* and *Resorcerer*. All of the resources in the PPIntro.rsrc file should be recognizable, except for the Mcmd resource and, perhaps, the aedt resource.

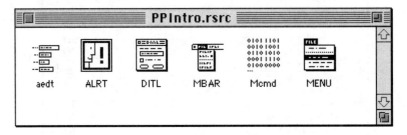

Figure 6.8 *The PPIntro68K project's resource file, as viewed in ResEdit.*

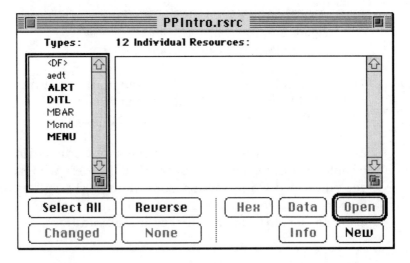

Figure 6.9 *The PPIntro68K project's resource file, as viewed in Resorcerer.*

An aedt resource is an Apple Event Description Table. This is a custom resource used by PowerPlant to help in the support of Apple events.

PowerPlant classes heavily rely on Apple events, so you'll always want your project's resource file to include the three aedt resources pictured in Figure 6.10. To do this you can simply copy aedt resources 128, 129, and 130 from any PowerPlant resource file and paste them in your own project's resource file.

ID	Size	Name
128	48	"Required Suite"
129	156	"Core Suite"
130	204	"Misc Standards"

aedts from PPIntro.rsrc

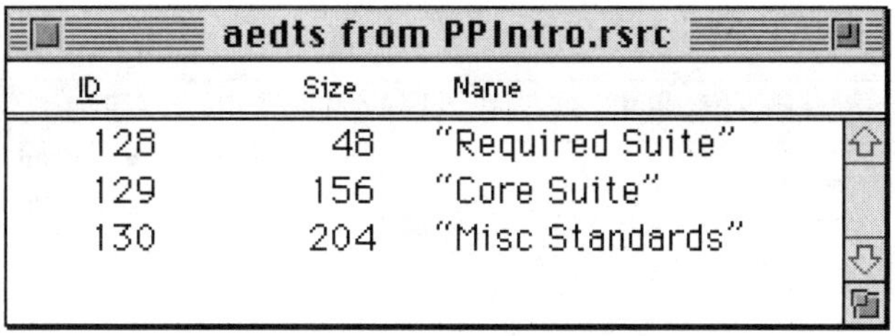

Figure 6.10 *All PowerPlant projects should include the three aedt resources pictured here.*

PowerPlant's use of aedt resources is internal. This means that although you'll need to include the three aedt resources shown in Figure 6.10 in your own projects, you won't need to be concerned with their usage.

N O T E

For the curious, here's a little background information on the aedt resource. The Macintosh Toolbox uses two 32-bit numbers when working with a single Apple event. In PowerPlant, this two-number system is inconvenient. So Metrowerks uses an aedt resource to create a single 32-bit number that points to the two numbers used by a particular Apple event.

N O T E

The Mcmd resources, along with the MENU resources, help PowerPlant classes determine which menu items appear in each menu. The Mcmd resource type and how PowerPlant works with menus are discussed in Chapter 7.

The one ALRT and one DITL resource are used for the PPIntro68K program's About alert box; ResEdit views of them are shown, respectively, in Figures 6.11 and 6.12. The three MENU resources define the items in the program's three menus, while the MBAR resource tells the program the IDs and menu bar display order of the MENU resources. Figures 6.13 and 6.14 show the PPIntro68K project's menu-related resources as viewed in ResEdit. If you use Resorcerer, you can open the `PPIntro.rsrc` file and verify that the ALRT, DITL, MENU, and MBAR resources appear as they do in any of your nonapplication framework projects.

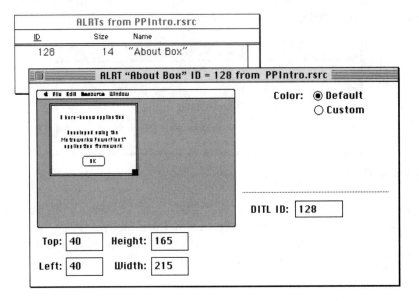

Figure 6.11 *The ALRT resource from the PPIntro68K project's resource file.*

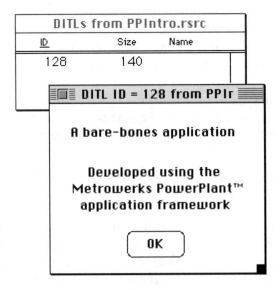

Figure 6.12 *The DITL resource from the PPIntro68K project's resource file.*

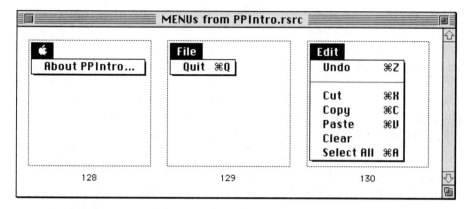

Figure 6.13 *The MENU resources from the PPIntro68K project's resource file.*

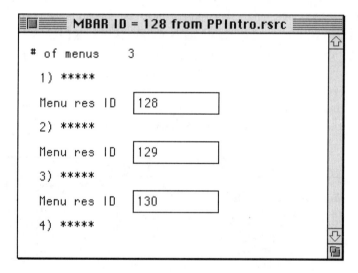

Figure 6.14 *The MBAR resource from the PPIntro68K project's resource file.*

The PowerPlant PPob Resource

While a traditional Mac program can use a WIND resource to adequately describe a window, a program created using PowerPlant requires more information in its window descriptions. Enter the PowerPlant PPob resource. Embedded within a PPob resource is a WIND resource and other information descriptive of a window. Specifically, the PPob resource contains information about a window's *pane* or panes.

The PowerPlant framework supports the concept of window panes. In short, a *pane* is a drawing area within a window. This simple definition makes a pane sound much like a port, a Macintosh programming idea you're already familiar with. There is a substantial difference between the two, however. While a window has a single port associated with it, a PowerPlant window can contain one, two, or many panes. These individual drawing areas can be stationary or resizable and movable. Chapter 8 describes panes in much greater detail.

Since the PPob resource type isn't common to applications other than those created using the Metrowerks compilers, ResEdit provides no resource editor that makes PPob creation and editing easy. That's why the Metrowerks Constructor exists. Constructor makes working with PPob resources simple. If you use the powerful resource editor Resorcerer to create your standard Mac resources, you can use it rather than Constructor to work with the PPob resource. Using Constructor and Resorcerer to create PPob resources are covered in Chapters 8.

If you create a PPob resource using Constructor, you'll save the resource in its own file. That means that you'll have two resource files to add to your PowerPlant project: the ResEdit or Resorcerer file that holds the project's standard resources, and the resource file generated by Constructor. Figure 6.15 shows these two files in the PPIntro68K project.

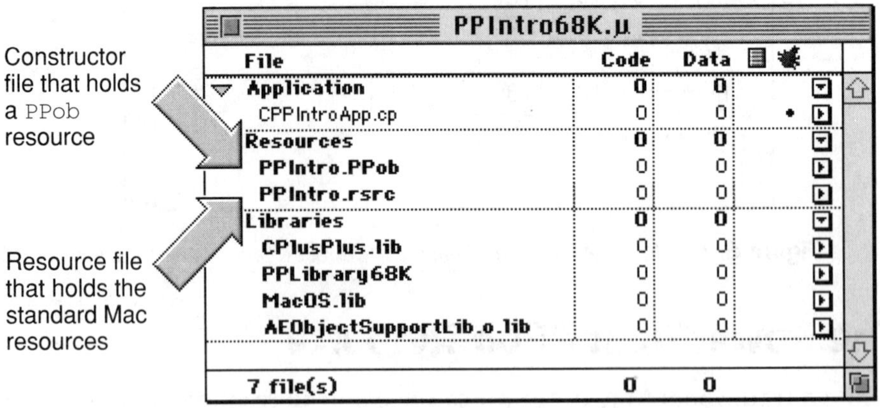

Constructor file that holds a PPob resource

Resource file that holds the standard Mac resources

Figure 6.15 *If you use Constructor to build a PPob resource, you'll have two resource files in your PowerPlant project.*

PowerPlant Classes

The numerous classes that make up the PowerPlant application framework can be found in files in the PowerPlant Library ƒ. If you own the Metrowerks CodeWarrior CD, you'll find this folder in the Metrowerks C/C++ ƒ folder. Within the PowerPlant Library ƒ folder are several folders, each used to hold the files that make up a family of classes. Figure 6.16 illustrates the class folder hierarchy. This figure shows the files found in the Commander family.

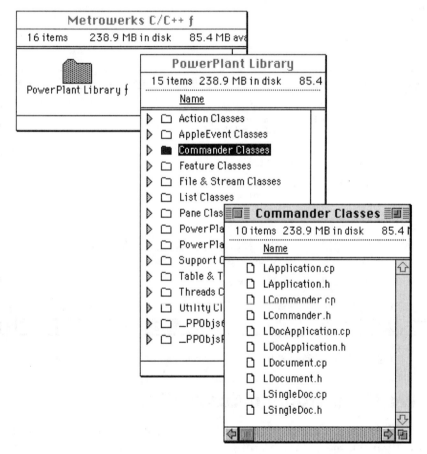

Figure 6.16 *PowerPlant is a collection of dozens of files that hold class definitions.*

In Figure 6.16 you'll note that each PowerPlant class has two files associated with it—a header file and a source code file. Each PowerPlant class uses a header file to define the class and a source code file to define the member functions of that class. Figures 6.17 and 6.18 provide an example. Figure 6.17 shows a part of the LApplication.h header file. This file defines the LApplication class. Figure 6.18 shows a little of the LApplication.cp source code file. In this figure you can see that the Run() function, a member function of the LApplication class, is defined in the source code file.

The LApplication class is
defined in the LApplication.h
header file

```
                            LApplication.h

class   LApplication  :   public LCommander,
                          public LModelObject {
public:
                      LApplication();
        virtual       ~LApplication();

        EProgramState GetState();
        void          SetSleepTime(const Int32 inSleepTime);

        virtual void  Run();

        virtual void  ProcessNextEvent();
        virtual void  DispatchEvent(const EventRecord &inMacEvent);
        virtual void  UseIdleTime(const EventRecord &inMacEvent);

        virtual void  ShowAboutBox();

        virtual Boolean ObeyCommand(CommandT inCommand, void* ioParam);

Line: 12
```

Figure 6.17 *A PowerPlant header file holds one or more class definitions.*

PowerPlant Naming Conventions

PowerPlant uses a naming convention that makes it easy to recognize PowerPlant classes, data members, member functions, and constants. For classes, you'll see that each begins with either "L," "U," or "C." A class that begins with an "L," like LApplication, is a PowerPlant library class. Figure 6.19 highlights this fact.

Run() is one of the LApplication
member functions, so it's listing is
found in the LApplication.cp file

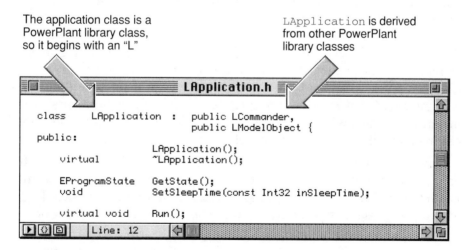

```
                        LApplication.cp

void
LApplication::Run()
{
    ::InitCursor();

    mState = programState_ProcessingEvents;

    while (mState != programState_Quitting) {
        Try_ {
            ProcessNextEvent();|
        }

        Catch_(inErr) {
            SignalPStr_("\pException caught in LApplication::Run");
        } EndCatch_
    }
}

                      Line: 148
```

Figure 6.18 *A PowerPlant source code file holds member function definitions.*

The application class is a
PowerPlant library class,
so it begins with an "L"

LApplication is derived
from other PowerPlant
library classes

```
                        LApplication.h

class     LApplication  :   public LCommander,
                            public LModelObject {
public:
                     LApplication();
    virtual          ~LApplication();

    EProgramState    GetState();
    void             SetSleepTime(const Int32 inSleepTime);

    virtual void     Run();

                      Line: 12
```

Figure 6.19 *PowerPlant library classes begin with the letter "L."*

Classes that begin with a "U" are PowerPlant utility classes. This type
of class, while important, is used more infrequently than a library class.

A utility class also has no dependencies on other PowerPlant classes. An example of a utility class is UQDGlobals.

NOTE

You'll encounter the UQDGlobals class later in this chapter. This class defines a member function named InitializeToolbox().

Your PowerPlant projects will define a class (or classes) of its own. To make it obvious that a class is an application-defined class and not a part of the PowerPlant application framework, you should begin the class name with a "C." This chapter's PPIntro68K.µ project does that for the one class the application defines, CPPIntroApp.

All variables found in PowerPlant code follow the PowerPlant variable naming convention. Class data members will begin with the letter "m." The PPIntro68K project uses a variable named mDisplayWindow. This variable is a data member of the application-defined class CPPIntroApp class. You'll see a listing and explanation of this class a little later in this chapter.

PowerPlant variables that are used as function parameters will begin with "in," "out," or "io." The first is for variables used as input to the function—variables that hold values to be used in the function to which they are passed. The second is used for output—variables that will have their values set by the function for use outside the function. Figure 6.20 shows the header for a function named FindCommandStatus(). This function is a PowerPlant class member function used when working with menus. From the figure you can see that the function's first parameter, inCommand, will be used by FindCommandStatus(). The four other parameters will have their values set by FindCommandStatus().

Local variables begin with "the" and use an uppercase letter for each word break. Three examples are: theCount, theWindow, and theGrandTotal. To generalize, all PowerPlant variable names begin with a lowercase letter and use an uppercase letter for a word break.

For integral values, PowerPlant uses a few of its own data types. These PowerPlant-defined data type names clearly indicate the bit (and thus byte) size of each type. The most common types are the Int8 (equivalent to a char), Int16 (equivalent to a short), and Int32 (equivalent to the long).

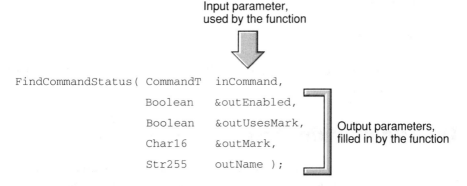

Figure 6.20 *PowerPlant function parameters follow a naming convention that indicates the use of each parameter.*

Related to these integer types are a few other types that are merely synonyms for the PowerPlant-defined types. The CommandT type and the MessageT type—both used in the defining of constants—are the same as the Int32 type. You'll see more of these types in other PowerPlant chapters. The ResIDT type is the same as the Int16 type. This data type is used in defining resource ID constants. For example, your code used in a PowerPlant project might define a constant that represents the resource ID of a WIND resource. Here that constant is named WIND_display:

```
const  ResIDT  WIND_display = 500;
```

Because the ResIDT type is the same as the Int16 type, the above example is the same as this constant definition:

```
const  Int16  WIND_display = 500;
```

Since an Int16 is defined to be a short, the above two definitions are also the same as this constant definition:

```
const  short  WIND_display = 500;
```

While variable names use uppercase characters to denote word breaks, as in theTotalScore, constants contain an underscore for the first break and uppercase for subsequent word breaks:

```
const  ResIDT  ALRT_aboutBox = 128;
```

This difference—the inclusion of an underscore—is simply to highlight the fact that something like ALRT_aboutBox is a constant and not a variable. Finally, when a constant is used as a resource ID (as WIND_display and ALRT_aboutBox are), it should begin with the four characters that make up the resource type (as, obviously, WIND_display and ALRT_aboutBox do).

The LApplication Class

The PowerPlant application framework consists of dozens of classes. Your PowerPlant project will make use of a few, or perhaps many, of these classes. *All* PowerPlant projects, however, will use the LApplication class.

The LApplication class contains about three dozen member functions. Member functions such as EventMouseDown() and EventUpdate() provide a hint that LApplication takes care of event handling. The LApplication member function ObeyCommandStatus() tells you that the application class also handles menu item selections (menu items are also known as commands).

The application class is, obviously, a powerful class. In fact, it is the class that coordinates and manages the flow of control of a program created with PowerPlant. When an event occurs, it is the application class that determines which member function should handle that event. That member function may in turn invoke other member functions belonging to other classes.

Any PowerPlant project *must* define a class derived from the LApplication class. As a refresher, here's the format for the definition of a derived class in C++:

```
class keyword    derivedClassName  :  public keyword    baseClassName
```

As noted earlier, classes that you define in a project that uses PowerPlant should have names that begin with a "C." For the LApplication derived class, the remainder of the class name is typically the project name (less the "68K" or "PPC" suffix) followed by "App." For the PPIntro68K project, the class derived from LApplication would thus be named CPPIntroApp. Here's the class definition:

```
class CPPIntroApp : public LApplication
{
   public:
      CPPIntroApp( void );

   protected:
      LWindow  *mDisplayWindow;
};
```

From this definition you can see that the PPIntro68K version of the class derived from the LApplication class contains one member function (a constructor) and one data member (a pointer to a window object). This, of course, is in addition to the numerous member functions and data members inherited from the LApplication base class.

 The LWindow class and window objects are discussed later in this chapter and in greater detail in Chapter 8.

NOTE

One of the first things a PowerPlant program needs to do is define an instance, or object, of the application class:

```
CPPIntroApp theApp;
```

Figure 6.21 shows that the above line of code creates an object that consists of the data members and the dozens of class member functions (a few of which are named in the figure) inherited from the LApplication class, as well as the single data member and single member function defined by the CPPIntroApp class.

With an object created, any of its class member functions can be invoked. As mentioned, the LApplication class consists of about three dozen member functions. At the top of the program the LApplication member function to call is Run():

```
theApp.Run();
```

The LApplication member function Run() sets the cursor to the arrow, sets the LApplication data member mState to a constant value, and then enters a while loop. From the PowerPlant LApplication.cp source code file, here's the definition of the Run() member function:

```
LApplication::Run()
{
   InitCursor();

   mState = programState_ProcessingEvents;

   while (mState != programState_Quitting)
   {
      Try_
      {
         ProcessNextEvent();
      }

      Catch_(inErr)
      {
         SignalPStr_("\pException caught in LApplication::Run");
      } EndCatch_
   }
}
```

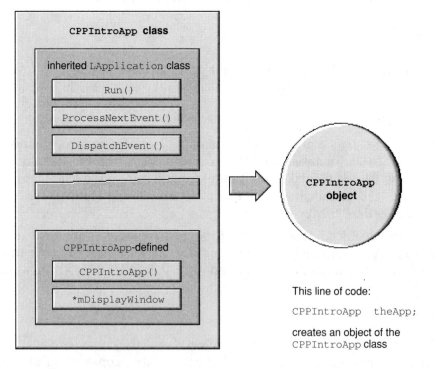

Figure 6.21 *The application object consists of application-defined member functions and data members, as well as all of the LApplication member functions and data members.*

Setting the data member mState to the PowerPlant-defined constant programState_ProcessingEvents means that the while loop test will pass and the loop body will execute. This loop will repeatedly execute until mState is set to the constant programState_Quitting elsewhere in PowerPlant code.

You can verify that mState is an LApplication data member by examining the definition of the LApplication class in the LApplication.h header file. Or, because you know PowerPlant's naming convention (listed earlier in this chapter), you can just assume it's a data member because it begins with an "m."

The Run() while loop acts as the application's main event loop—something you're used to writing yourself. If you look at the main() routine of the PPIntro68K example, you'll see that there is no application-defined main event loop:

```
void  main( void )
{
    UQDGlobals::InitializeToolbox( &qd );

    CPPIntroApp theApp;
    theApp.Run();
}
```

The call to InitializeToolbox() does just what you'd think. The syntax for invoking this routine is discussed later in this chapter.

From C++ you should recall that one class member function can invoke another member function of that same class. The LApplication member function Run() does just this. At the center of the while loop is a call to a routine named ProcessNextEvent(). Like the Run() routine itself, this function is an LApplication member function. ProcessNextEvent() calls the Toolbox routine WaitNextEvent()—just as the main event loop does in any program you've written in the past. ProcessNextEvent() then takes the event information and passes it to another LApplication member function—DispatchEvent().

NOTE You'll notice that while I highlighted what the LApplication member function ProcessNextEvent() does, I didn't show its listing. Keep in mind that while it never hurts to know what's going on in a PowerPlant class, it isn't necessary to know everything about each class. As you begin to make the adjustment to working with an application framework, don't attempt to determine exactly *how* a class handles things. Instead, take the easier route of learning *what* the class handles. Eventually, as you work with PowerPlant more and more, you'll become familiar with its intricacies.

DispatchEvent() serves as nothing more than a branching station. It compares the event type to the Apple-defined event constants (also called event codes) and, based on this comparison, invokes the appropriate PowerPlant routine to handle the event. Mac programs that you've created in the past no doubt have a routine much like DispatchEvent(). The difference will be in the number of event types handled. While your own application probably handled just a few types (mouseDown, keyDown, and updateEvt are the most notable), the PowerPlant DispatchEvent() function must be able to take care of any event type you want your application to be able to handle. Because DispatchEvent() should remind you of code you've written in the past, it warrants a listing here:

```
LApplication::DispatchEvent( const EventRecord& inMacEvent)
{
    switch ( inMacEvent.what )
    {
        case mouseDown:
            AdjustCursor( inMacEvent );
            EventMouseDown( inMacEvent );
            break;

        case mouseUp:
            EventMouseUp( inMacEvent );
            break;

        case keyDown:
            EventKeyDown( inMacEvent );
            break;

        case autoKey:
```

```
                EventAutoKey( inMacEvent );
                break;

        case keyUp:
                EventKeyUp( inMacEvent );
                break;

        case diskEvt:
                EventDisk( inMacEvent );
                break;

        case updateEvt:
                EventUpdate( inMacEvent );
                break;

        case activateEvt:
                EventActivate( inMacEvent );
                break;

        case osEvt:
                EventOS( inMacEvent );
                break;

        case kHighLevelEvent:
                EventHighLevel( inMacEvent );
                break;

        default:
                UseIdleTime( inMacEvent );
                break;
    }
}
```

You've seen quite a bit of the LApplication class, so it's time for a summary. All Metrowerks projects that use PowerPlant must define a class derived from the PowerPlant LApplication class. The derived class will, of course, inherit all of the LApplication class and will include application-specific data members and member functions. More detail of the application-specific parts of this important class will be provided later in this chapter. Next, create an object of this derived class. Then call the object's Run() member function to kick off the program. The Run() function consists of a loop that serves as the application's main event loop. Figure 6.22 illustrates what goes on when the LApplication Run() member function is invoked.

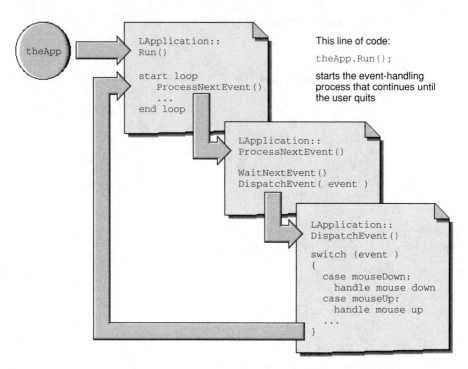

Figure 6.22 *When the application object invokes Run(), the event loop is entered.*

The LWindow Class

The PowerPlant LWindow class exists so that your application can work with windows in much the same way as you're used to. In a PowerPlant project, you'll work with a pointer to an LWindow class object instead of the WindowPtr you're used to working with in nonapplication framework projects.

The LWindow class consists of more than 50 member functions. And, because the LWindow class is itself derived from other PowerPlant classes (two of which, LPane and LView, are discussed in Chapter 8), the number of member functions that can be accessed by an LWindow object is actually far greater.

If you look through the class definition of LWindow in the LWindow.h header file, you'll see that many of the member functions—such as CreateWindow(), Show(), and DoClose()—are analogous to Toolbox routines that work with the `WindowPtr` data type. Since you'll be working with an object of the `LWindow` class, you'll use the `LWindow` member functions and not their Toolbox counterparts. For example, to create and display a window, you'll use the `LWindow` member functions `CreateWindow()` and `Show()`—not the Toolbox routines `GetNewWindow()` and `ShowWindow()`.

PowerPlant Classes and Static Member Functions

From your experience programming in C++ you should recall that the member functions of a class can usually only be accessed through an object, as shown in Figure 6.23. In this figure, a class named `UQDGlobals` holds one data member and four member functions. If the `InitializeToolbox()` member function is to be accessed, there must first be a `UQDGlobals` object. In Figure 6.23 that object is named `QDobject`.

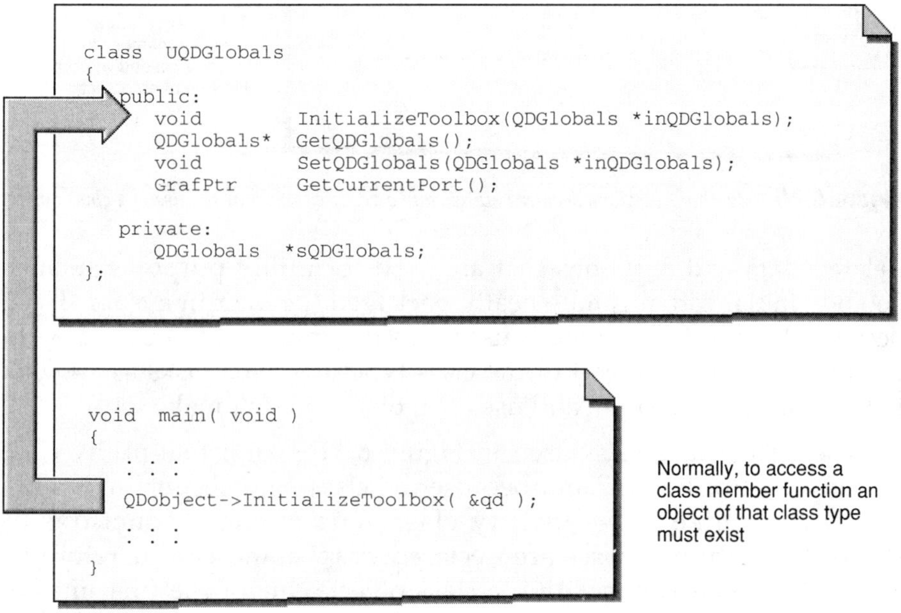

```
class UQDGlobals
{
   public:
      void        InitializeToolbox(QDGlobals *inQDGlobals);
      QDGlobals*  GetQDGlobals();
      void        SetQDGlobals(QDGlobals *inQDGlobals);
      GrafPtr     GetCurrentPort();

   private:
      QDGlobals  *sQDGlobals;
};
```

```
void main( void )
{
   : : :
   QDobject->InitializeToolbox( &qd );
   : : :
}
```

Normally, to access a class member function an object of that class type must exist

Figure 6.23 *A class member function is accessed through an object of that class type.*

In contrast to Figure 6.23, the snippet in Figure 6.24 shows that if a class member function is declared static, that function can be accessed without the use of an object. Instead, the class name is listed, followed by the scope resolution operator (::). Finally, the member function name is given.

```
class  UQDGlobals
{
public:
    static void        InitializeToolbox(QDGlobals *inQDGlobals);
    static QDGlobals*  GetQDGlobals();
    static void        SetQDGlobals(QDGlobals *inQDGlobals);
    static GrafPtr     GetCurrentPort();

private:
    static QDGlobals  *sQDGlobals;
};
```

```
void  main( void )
{
    : : :
    UQDGlobals::InitializeToolbox( &qd );
    : : :

}
```

The static keyword allows a member function to be accessed without the use of an object

Figure 6.24 *Member functions declared static can be accessed without the use of a class object.*

Related data and functions that are used for utility purposes such as Toolbox initialization can be neatly packaged together in a class. Then, because the static keyword is used, this information can be used without first creating an object of the class type. For such tasks as Toolbox initialization, the creation and use of an object doesn't make sense.

The UQDGlobals class used in Figure 6.24 is an actual utility class that is a part of PowerPlant. Because the class name begins with "U," you'll recognize it as a utility class. The member functions of PowerPlant utility classes are declared static and can therefore be invoked without first creating a class object. One of the first lines of code you'll encounter in a source file that uses PowerPlant is the call shown in Figure 6.24:

```
UQDGlobals::InitializeToolbox( &qd );
```

Now that you've seen the above line of code, you've read an explanation of all three lines of code that make up the `main()` function of this chapter's `PPIntro68K` example:

```
void  main( void )
{
    UQDGlobals::InitializeToolbox( &qd );

    CPPIntroApp theApp;
    theApp.Run();
}
```

PowerPlant Classes and the Toolbox

Since thousands of Toolbox routines exist to make life easier for Mac programmers, it makes sense that an application framework, which exists to make life easier still, uses the Toolbox.

If you examine code found in PowerPlant source code files, you'll see the names of many Toolbox calls with which you're familiar. The `UQDGlobals` class, for example, has a member function named `InitializeToolbox()`. Here's a look at the definition of that routine:

```
void  UQDGlobals :: InitializeToolbox( QDGlobals *inQDGlobals )
{
    sQDGlobals = inQDGlobals;

    ::InitGraf( (Ptr) &sQDGlobals->thePort );
    ::InitFonts();
    ::InitWindows();
    ::InitMenus();
    ::TEInit();
    ::InitDialogs( nil );
}
```

`InitializeToolbox()` makes calls to six Toolbox functions—the same functions you've called in Toolbox initialization routines for applications you've written in the past. The difference here is that in PowerPlant a Toolbox call is prefaced by the scope resolution operator. In C++, *function overloading* allows a single program to contain more than one version of a function. The scope resolution operator is used to make sure that the Toolbox version of a function is used—in case PowerPlant (or you) intentionally (or accidentally) define a routine with the same name.

The code you write will contain calls to Toolbox routines. When you make these calls, you should precede each with the scope resolution operator to make it immediately obvious that the function being invoked is a Toolbox routine.

Source Code and the PowerPlant Project

The PowerPlant application framework consists of thousands of lines of source code that will save you hours of effort. But you'll still need to write *some* code of your own.

The #pragma once Directive and Include Files

When a source code file uses a #include directive, the contents of the header file named after the #include are added to the source file. If two source files include the same header file, the contents of the header file will be added to both source files. This redundant work by the compiler can be avoided by making use of the #pragma once directive.

Using the #pragma once directive on a file tells the compiler to include the file's contents in only one source file, no matter how many source files attempt to include it. Figure 6.25 shows an example of the use of the #pragma once directive on a trivial Metrowerks project. In this figure the header file TestHeader.h uses #pragma once. Both of the project's source files, TestUtility.cp and Test.cp, use the #include directive to include this one header file. Because of the use of the #pragma once directive, however, only one of the two files (the first one compiled) will actually include the contents of TestHeader.h. In the figure it's assumed that TestUtility.cp gets compiled before Test.cp. Because TestHeader.h does nothing more than define a symbol, there's no need to have this definition repeated in more than one source code file.

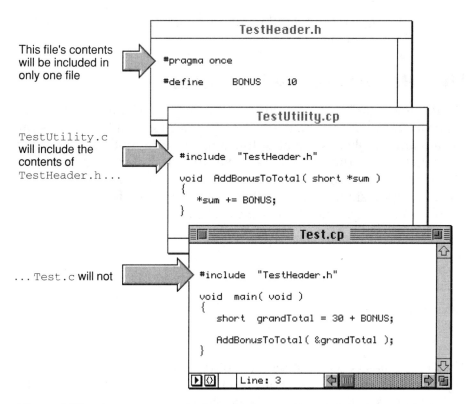

This file's contents will be included in only one file

```
TestHeader.h

#pragma once

#define     BONUS     10
```

`TestUtility.c` will include the contents of `TestHeader.h` . . .

```
TestUtility.cp

#include   "TestHeader.h"

void  AddBonusToTotal( short *sum )
{
    *sum += BONUS;
}
```

. . . `Test.c` will not

```
Test.cp

#include   "TestHeader.h"

void  main( void )
{
    short  grandTotal = 30 + BONUS;

    AddBonusToTotal( &grandTotal );
}

Line: 3
```

Figure 6.25 *The #pragma once directive tells the compiler to include a header file one time.*

N O T E

If the point is simply to prevent the inclusion of `TestHeader.h` in the `Test.cp` file, why not just skip the #include directive in `Test.cp`? In a small project like the one shown in this example, that would be the route to take. In a larger project—one that perhaps consists of a dozen or more files, it becomes difficult to keep track of which file includes which headers. By simply including all necessary header files in each source file and then using the #pragma once directive on each file, you let the compiler keep track of things. As each file is compiled, the compiler will know whether a header file should be included.

As you look through the PowerPlant example projects included on the Metrowerks CD, you'll notice the liberal use of the #pragma once directive.

To avoid putting the compiler through extra paces, you'll want to follow Metrowerks' lead in this area.

The LApplication Derived Class

As discussed earlier in this chapter, every PowerPlant project must define a class derived from the LApplication class. While this class can contain any number of member functions, it should at least contain a constructor. For the PPIntro68K example, the class derived from LApplication is named CPPIntroApp, and it contains a constructor function and a single data member. You'll find the definition for the CPPIntroApp class in the CPPIntroApp.h header file.

```
class  CPPIntroApp : public LApplication
{
   public:
      CPPIntroApp();

   protected:
      LWindow  *mDisplayWindow;
};
```

The CPPIntroApp class data member mDisplayWindow is a pointer to an object of the LWindow class. For the PPIntro68K program, this pointer will keep track of the application's one window.

The purpose of the constructor function will be to take care of initialization matters, such as opening a display window.

The CPPIntroApp Class Constructor

The class that your application derives from the LApplication class is the driving force of your application. When an object of that class is created, that object's constructor function gets executed. For the PPIntro68K program, this is the line that invokes CPPIntroApp():

```
CPPIntroApp theApp;
```

Here's a look at the CPPIntroApp constructor:

```
CPPIntroApp :: CPPIntroApp()
{
```

```
URegistrar::RegisterClass( 'wind',
            (ClassCreatorFunc)LWindow::CreateWindowStream );

mDisplayWindow = LWindow::CreateWindow( WIND_display, this );

mDisplayWindow->Show();
}
```

The first line of the constructor function *registers* the PowerPlant LWindow class. Any of your program's objects that are based on a PowerPlant PPob resource must have a one-time registration of the object's class. Since the application constructor member function will execute at the start of your program—and will execute only once—this is the place to take care of the registering of classes.

Each object that is created from a PPob resource has a four-character ID—much as a resource type has a four-character name (such as WIND or DLOG). In PowerPlant, commonly used PPob objects such as windows have predefined character IDs. A window, for example, has wind as its ID. This ID, enclosed in quotes, serves as the first parameter to the RegisterClass() function. The second parameter is the name of the function that will be used by PowerPlant when it comes time to create an object of this type. Again, for commonly used PPob objects, PowerPlant does the work for you. For example, the LWindow class has a member function named CreateWindowStream() that is used to access PPob information when a new window object is created.

NOTE You needn't register every PowerPlant class your project uses—only the ones that make use of PPob resources. For example, you don't call RegisterClass() for the LApplication class, even though the PPIntro68K project uses this class. Classes that use PPob resources are window-related.

Chapter 8 describes the PPob resource in more detail. There you'll see more information on the URegistrar class member function RegisterClass(). For now, just note that the RegisterClass() function is called directly; there is no URegistrar object to invoke it. Recall from earlier in this chapter that if a class member function is declared static (as the URegistrar class member function RegisterClass() is), it can be called either by an object or directly. If it's called directly, as here, use this form:

```
className :: memberFunctionName()
```

The `LWindow` member function `CreateWindow()` creates a window. This window is an instance (object) of the `LWindow` class and is based on information found in a `PPob` resource. When completed, the call to `CreateWindow()` returns a pointer to the new window object. Since the `LWindow` class object doesn't exist *before* the call to `CreateWindow()` (it is the end result of the call to `CreateWindow()` and thus exists *after* the call), use the scope resolution operator to call the member function directly:

```
mDisplayWindow = LWindow::CreateWindow( WIND_display, this );
```

The first parameter to `CreateWindow()` is the ID of the `WIND` resource that holds information about this window. `WIND_display` is a constant (following the PowerPlant naming convention described earlier in this chapter) that is defined elsewhere in the program:

```
const ResIDT  WIND_display = 500;
```

If you're paying close attention, you'll recall that earlier I stated that a `PPob` resource defines a window. It does. A `PPob` resource consists of more than one part. One of those parts is a `WIND` resource, the same `WIND` resource type with which you're familiar .

N O T E

Once an `LWindow` object exists you can access any of its member functions through the object. The constructor function does that when it invokes the `Show()` member function to display the window:

```
mDisplayWindow->Show();
```

If you programmed in C without the use of an application framework, a very loose translation of the above task might be found in this snippet:

N O T E

```
#define    WIND_ID         500

WindowPtr  theDisplayWindow;

theDisplayWindow = GetNewWindow( WIND_ID, nil, (WindowPtr)-1L );

ShowWindow( theDisplayWindow );
```

Since `CPPIntroApp()` is a constructor for the `CPPIntroApp` class, it gets invoked automatically when a `CPPIntroApp` object is created. The `CPPIntroApp` constructor function is thus referring to the `CPPIntroApp` object. In this example, that object is named `theApp`. Notice in the constructor function that the C++ keyword `this` is used. It refers to the object in question: `theApp`. Also notice the use of `mDisplayWindow`. This variable is the lone data member of the `CPPIntroApp` class. Its value (the `LWindow` object it points to) is a part of `theApp`. Figure 6.26 provides emphasis regarding the `CPPIntroApp` constructor function.

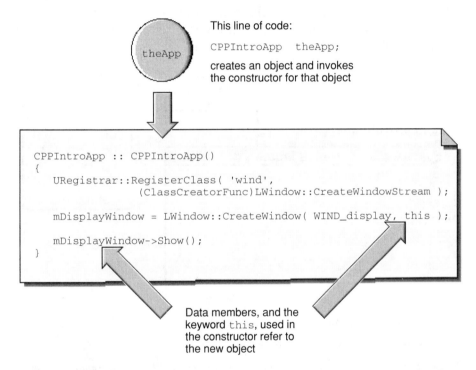

Figure 6.26 *Creating a new application object invokes that object's class constructor.*

What's Left?

What's left after the application object is created, its constructor is invoked, and the application's `Run()` member function is called? For the `PPIntro68K` program, that's it. Once you compile and run `PPIntro68K`, you'll see that you can drag the window about the screen, use its grow box to change its size, and click its go away box to close it. And all without writing a single line of window-handling code. You'll also notice that the menu bar will be properly drawn at the top of the screen—without PPIntro68K making calls to Toolbox routines like SetMenuBar(), AddResMenu(), and DrawMenuBar(). You'll be able drop any of the menus in the menu bar, and you'll be able to select any of the enabled items. And of course, the CPPIntroApp.cp file holds no menu-handling code.

Figure 6.27 shows the one window and three menus you'll see when you run PPIntro68K. Selecting any of the Apple menu items, as well as the **Quit** item from the File menu, will give the expected results. Because there's nothing to edit, the Edit menu items are dim. In the next chapter you'll see how to enable menu items.

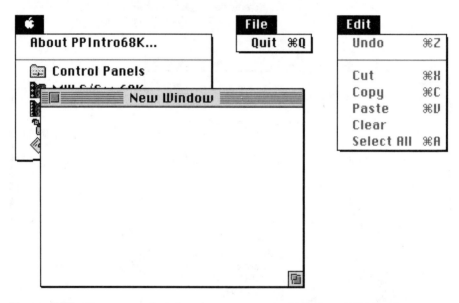

Figure 6.27 *The menus and window that are present in the PPIntro68K example program.*

The PPIntroApp.h Header File Source Code Listing

A PowerPlant project usually keeps class definitions in a header file and the class member function definitions in another file. The PPIntro68K project defines the CPPIntroApp class in a header file named CPPIntroApp.h—the contents of which are shown below.

Because the `CPPIntroApp` class is derived from the PowerPlant `LApplication` class, the `LApplication.h` header file is included:

```
#include <LApplication.h>
```

The compiler must also be made aware of one other class before the `CPPIntroApp` class can be defined. The `mDisplayWindow` data member is to be a pointer to an object of the `LWindow` class. While it isn't necessary to include the entire contents of the PowerPlant `LWindow.h` file in the `CPPIntroApp.h` file, it is necessary to make the compiler aware of the fact that `LWindow` is used as a data type. In C++ you use the `class` keyword in a forward reference to tell the compiler that `LWindow` is indeed a valid data type. Then, if the `CPPIntroApp.h` file is compiled before the compiler encounters the `LWindow` definition, no error will be reported.

```
class  LWindow;
```

Here's the complete listing for the `PPIntro68K` project's `CPPIntroApp.h` header file.

```
// ================================================
//                          application class definition

#pragma once

#include <LApplication.h>

class  LWindow;

class  CPPIntroApp : public LApplication
{
    public:
        CPPIntroApp();

    protected:
        LWindow   *mDisplayWindow;
};
```

The PPIntroApp.cp Source Code Listing

This chapter has covered each line of code in the `CPPIntroApp.cp` file, with the exception of the `#include` files. As you work with PowerPlant more and more, you'll become familiar with which PowerPlant classes your project is using and in which header files those classes are defined. For the PPIntro68K project, there are four header files that should be included:

CPPIntroApp.h	defines the CPPIntroApp class
LWindow.h	defines the LWindow
UDrawingState.h	defines the UQDGlobals class
URegistrar.h	is necessary for registering window-related classes

Earlier in this chapter you saw the PowerPlant naming convention as it applies to resource-related constants. The data type should be ResIDT (which is the size of the short data type). Because the constant represents a resource ID, its name should begin with the four characters of that type. After that, the name needs an underscore and then any characters that add insight into what the resource is used for. Here's how the PPIntroApp.cp file defines the resource ID of the program's one WIND resource:

```
const ResIDT   WIND_display = 500;
```

To end this introduction to PowerPlant, the listing for the PPIntro68K project's CPPIntroApp.cp source file follows.

```
// ==============================================================
//                                           include header files

#include "CPPIntroApp.h"
#include <LWindow.h>
#include <UDrawingState.h>
#include <URegistrar.h>


// ==============================================================
//                                           constant definitions

const ResIDT   WIND_display = 500;


// ==============================================================
//                                                         main()

void  main( void )
```

```
{
    UQDGlobals::InitializeToolbox( &qd );

    CPPIntroApp theApp;
    theApp.Run();
}


// ========================================================
//                              CPPIntroApp class constructor

CPPIntroApp :: CPPIntroApp()
{
    URegistrar::RegisterClass( 'wind',
                (ClassCreatorFunc)LWindow::CreateWindowStream );

    mDisplayWindow = LWindow::CreateWindow( WIND_display, this );

    mDisplayWindow->Show();
}
```

PowerPlant and the MW C/C++ PPC Compiler

If you want to generate a native application—one that takes advantage of the speed of a PowerPC-based Macintosh, you'll need to use the Metrowerks MW C/C++ PPC compiler rather than the MW C/C++ 68K compiler. If you're afraid that what you've learned so far may go to waste, don't be. All the information about PowerPlant to this point still applies. The only thing you'll need to do differently is to create a PPC project rather than a 68K one. Figure 6.28 shows the project used to create a native version of the PPIntro program.

From Figure 6.28 you can see that the PPC project uses the same source code file and same resource files as the 68K project. The difference between the projects is found in the precompiled libraries that each uses. All of the libraries (and the Startup.c and runtime.o files) shown in Figure 6.28 have been included on the CD with this book. If you need to locate any of these files, you can find them by searching the CD from the Finder (by selecting **Find** from the File menu).

If you have a Power Mac, run the MW C/C++ PPC compiler and open the PPIntroPPC.µ project that is included on the CD that came with this book. Select **Make** from the Project menu and you'll have a native version of the PPIntro program in the same folder as the 680x0 version.

PPIntroPPC.μ				
File	**Code**	**Data**	▤	🐾
▽ **Application**	0	0	• ▾	
CPPIntroApp.cp	0	0	• ▶	
▽ **Resources**	0	0	▾	
PPIntro.PPob	n/a	n/a	▶	
PPIntro.rsrc	n/a	n/a	▶	
▽ **Libraries**	0	0	• ▾	
Startup.c	0	0	• ▶	
runtime.o	0	0	▶	
InterfaceLib	0	0	▶	
ObjectSupportLib	0	0	▶	
MWCSupportLib	0	0	▶	
PowerPlantLib	0	0	▶	
9 file(s)	0	0		

Figure 6.28 *The project window for the PowerPC version of the PPIntro project.*

N O T E

If you don't have a Power Mac, you can still create a native version of the PPIntro program. Just run MW C/C++ PPC from your 680x0-based Mac, open the PPIntroPPC.μ project, and then select **Make** from the Project menu. You'll find that you now have a PPIntroPPC application on your hard drive. Remember, though, that this application is PowerPC-only—you will not be able to run it from your 680x0-based Macintosh.

Chapter Summary

PowerPlant is an application framework. An *application framework* is simply a set of C++ classes that contain the code that handles many of the more mundane tasks common to all Macintosh programs. The PowerPlant classes will take care of tasks such as menu handling and window updating, dragging, and resizing.

To use PowerPlant you add PowerPlant source code files to your CodeWarrior project. Then you write additional C++ code to implement the features unique to your program. A second way to add the functionality of PowerPlant to your project is to add one of the precompiled PowerPlant libraries to your project rather than the individual PowerPlant source code files. The disadvantage to this approach is that debugging your PowerPlant project is harder because the debugger can't access the PowerPlant source code.

One of the most important of the many PowerPlant classes is the LApplication class. This class oversees the flow of control that takes place in a program. Every CodeWarrior project that uses PowerPlant must create an application-defined class that is derived from LApplication.

The main() routine of a project that uses PowerPlant should create an object from the derived application class. This act will initiate the object's constructor function. This function will perform initializations and, perhaps, perform some task such as the creation and opening of an empty window. Next, the Run() member function should be invoked to start the application's event loop.

Chapter 7

Menus and PowerPlant

An application framework will not reduce the total amount of code in an application you write, but it will reduce the amount of code *you* have to write. The handling of menus is one area where PowerPlant does just that. With PowerPlant files in your project, you'll be able to forget about most of the menu-related Toolbox functions you've used so often.

A menu selection, whether **Quit**, **Save**, or an application-specific item, always acts on something. What that "something" is varies depending on the menu item. The **Quit** menu item (or command) acts on the application itself. The **Save** command acts on a document. An application-specific menu item (such as **Draw Circle**) might act on the active window. In any case, there will always be a *target* object that receives the action of the command. In this chapter you'll see how PowerPlant keeps track of the target object and how PowerPlant knows which target should receive the action of a menu item selection.

The previous chapter mentioned but didn't describe in detail three resource types that are particular to PowerPlant projects—the Mcmd, the aedt, and the PPob resources. This chapter covers the first of these three types, the Mcmd, which is the menu command resource.

Menus, Resources, and PowerPlant

CodeWarrior projects that use PowerPlant need to include an MBAR resource and MENU resources as do projects that don't use PowerPlant. Additionally, PowerPlant projects must also include resources of the type Mcmd.

The PPIntro68K Program

The PPIntro68K program in Chapter 6 has the menu and menu items shown in Figure 7.1.

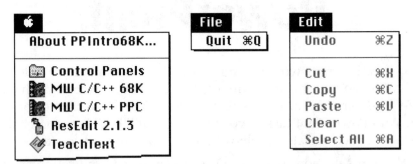

Figure 7.1 *The menus and menu items found in the PPIntro68K program.*

In this section you'll see the menu-related resources that are needed to add the menus shown in Figure 7.1 to a PowerPlant project.

Adding the MENU and MBAR Resources

In the previous chapter you saw that programs developed using PowerPlant use the same MENU and MBAR resources used by a program developed using a traditional compiler. What wasn't mentioned in the last chapter is that PowerPlant requires that some of these resources have certain specific IDs. The Apple, File, and Edit menus, which Apple calls the standard menus (and which Apple suggests should appear in all Macintosh programs), must have these ID numbers:

- The Apple menu must have an ID of 128.
- The File menu must have an ID of 129.
- The Edit menu must have an ID of 130.

Also, the MBAR resource that defines which MENU resources will appear in the application's menu bar must have an ID of 128.

Because PowerPlant handles much of the functionality of the standard menus, the PowerPlant code must make some assumptions about these menus, such as their resource IDs. Looking at the MENU resources in the resource file of the PPIntro68K example in Chapter 6, you can see that the PowerPlant MENU resource ID numbering convention was followed. Figure 7.2 shows a ResEdit view of the menu.

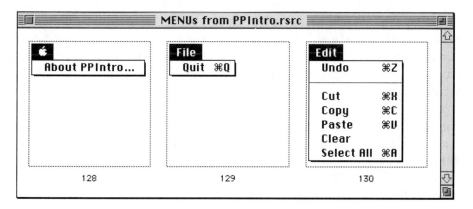

Figure 7.2 *The MENU resources for the PPIntro68K project.*

Menu Items and the Mcmd Resource

In a Macintosh project that doesn't use an application framework, you typically add a #define directive to a source code file (or header file) for each menu item that will appear in the program's menus. Figure 7.3 gives an example using the standard Edit menu.

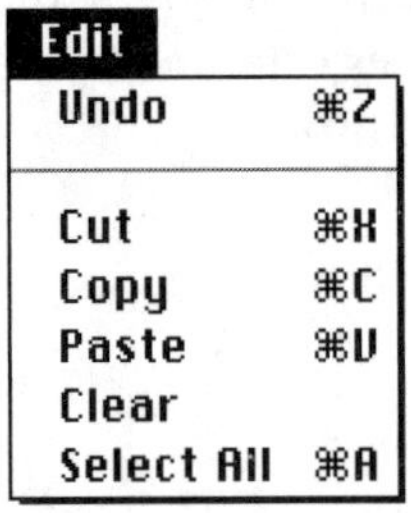

Edit				
Undo	⌘Z	#define	UNDO_ITEM	1
Cut	⌘H	#define	CUT_ITEM	3
Copy	⌘C	#define	COPY_ITEM	4
Paste	⌘U	#define	PASTE_ITEM	5
Clear		#define	CLEAR_ITEM	6
Select All	⌘A	#define	SELECT_ALL_ITEM	7

Figure 7.3 *Macintosh programs usually define constants for each menu item.*

When your program's event loop determined that a mouseDown event was menu related, it would make a call to the Toolbox routine MenuSelect() in order to determine which menu, and which menu item, was selected. The menu item number would then be compared to the item constants (like the ones in Figure 7.3) that were defined using the #define directive. After that, your code would take the proper action necessary to handle the menu choice.

The preceding scheme works fine for a program written *without* the aid of an application framework. An application framework, however, exists to eliminate your need to write the code common to all Macintosh programs, including much of an application's menu handling code. In an application framework like PowerPlant, a class and its member functions are meant to handle a programming task without the programmer making major alterations to the code. Making changes to class definitions and member function code each time you write a program defeats the purpose of PowerPlant. That's why defining menu item constants that specify exactly where in a menu a menu item appears is counterproductive. If at a later time you make program changes that involve rearranging menu items, changes will have to also be made in your source code.

To eliminate the need to define as a constant the menu position of each menu item, PowerPlant obtains menu item numbers by relying on resources rather than source code constants. If each MENU resource has a corresponding resource of a different type (and with the same ID as the MENU), it's a simple matter for a PowerPlant class member function to read in menu item information for each menu. Specifically, the PowerPlant LMenu class has a member function named ReadCommandNumber() that handles this task. The resource that ReadCommandNumber() looks for is the Mcmd resource—a resource type specific to PowerPlant.

 As always, it isn't necessary, but you're free to browse through the code of a PowerPlant class member function. In fact, you don't even have to remember that ReadCommandNumber() is the name of the member function that gets menu item numbers from resources. Having to figure out exactly how each class member function works isn't important.

N O T E

When you add a MENU resource to your project's resource file, you'll also add an Mcmd resource. The Mcmd resource will have the same resource ID as the MENU resource—that's how the PowerPlant code knows which Mcmd holds information about a MENU. Each Mcmd resource holds a *command number* for each menu item in a MENU. Figure 7.4 illustrates this for the PPIntro68K example.

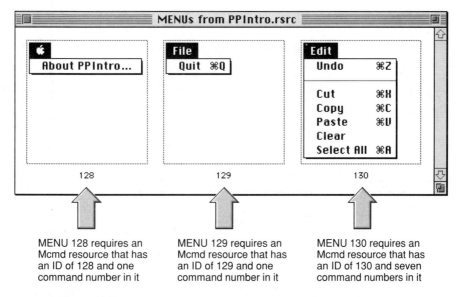

Figure 7.4 *Each MENU resource has a corresponding Mcmd resource.*

For any one program, each command number is unique; that is, no two menus in a single program share any of the same command numbers. Because the Apple, File, and Edit menus hold many of the same items from program to program, Metrowerks was able to define constants to represent many of these menu items. The PowerPlant header file PP_Messages.h lists the predefined command numbers, as well as other constants. Table 7.1 lists the command number constants as well.

 The exception to the scheme of using a unique number for each command is the dashed divider line. This menu item always has a command number of 0 regardless of how many times it appears.

N O T E

Table 7.1 *PowerPlant Command Number Constants.*

Dashed line 'Mcmd' constant (all menus)

cmd_Nothing	=	0

 menu 'Mcmd' constant

cmd_About	=	1

File menu 'Mcmd' constants

cmd_New	=	2
cmd_Open	=	3
cmd_Close	=	4
cmd_Save	=	5
cmd_SaveAs	=	6
cmd_Revert	=	7
cmd_PageSetup	=	8
cmd_Print	=	9
cmd_Quit	=	10

Edit menu 'Mcmd' constants

cmd_Undo	=	11
cmd_Cut	=	12
cmd_Copy	=	13
cmd_Paste	=	14
cmd_Clear	=	15
cmd_SelectAll	=	16

N O T E

The PowerPlant menu command number constants are only useful for the standard menus. Your application will of course also include menu items that are specific to your application. For simplicity, the PPIntro68K example doesn't use any application-specific menu items. An example of how to add a new menu and new menu items appears later in this chapter.

Table 7.1 helps you to easily find the command numbers that will be needed for the menu items in the three menus of the PPIntro68K example program. Figure 7.5 shows the command numbers that would be entered into the three Mcmd resources. The constant names are shown in parentheses.

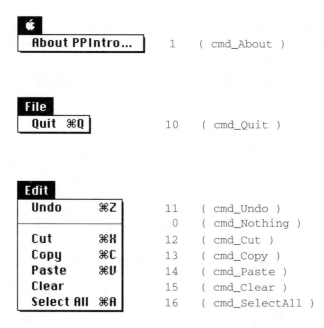

Figure 7.5 *The command number constants for the menu items in the PPIntro68K program.*

N O T E

As you'll see later in this chapter, the command name (such as cmd_Quit) will be used in your application source code, while the command number (such as 10) will be used in the Mcmd resource.

PowerPlant uses a few resource types that aren't common to other Mac applications. As you've just read, the Mcmd is one of them. To make editing resources of these new types easier, Metrowerks has included TMPL resources for each. Without these templates, you'd have to edit PowerPlant resources using the hex editor in ResEdit or Resorcerer— definitely not an easy task. With these templates, PowerPlant resources such as the Mcmd can be opened in an easy-to-edit format.

If you use Resorcerer as your resource editor, read the next section. If you're a ResEdit user, skip the following section and move on to "The Mcmd Resource and ResEdit" section.

The Mcmd Resource and Resorcerer

If you're a Resorcerer user, copy the file named PowerPlant Resorcerer TMPLs into the Private Templates folder in your Resorcerer folder (if you don't have a Private Templates folder, create a new untitled folder and give it this name). Refer to Figure 7.6. The PowerPlant Resorcerer TMPLs file can be found on this book's CD. If you own the full version of Metrowerks CodeWarrior, you'll find it on that CD as well.

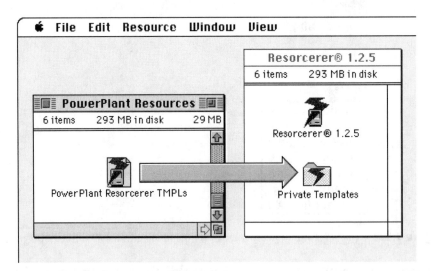

Figure 7.6 *Resorcerer users should make sure the PowerPlant Resorcerer TMPLs file is in the Private Templates folder.*

The Chapter 6 folder has a folder named PP Intro ƒ. It contains a Resorcerer resource file named PPIntro.rsrc. It holds the resources for the PPIntro68K program, including the menu-related MBAR, MENU, and Mcmd resources. If you'd like to get a little practice working with Mcmd resources, create a new, empty `Resorcerer` file in a scratch folder. The next several pages will describe how to add the three `PPIntro68K` `Mcmd` resources to this file.

With an open `Resorcerer` file, select **New Resource** from the Resource menu. `Resorcerer`'s New Resource dialog box, pictured in Figure 7.7, will open. Scroll to `Mcmd` and click on it.

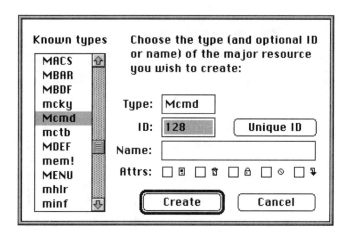

Figure 7.7 *Resorcerer's New Resource dialog box, with the Mcmd type selected.*

After clicking the **Create** button, `Resorcerer` creates a new `Mcmd` resource, gives it an ID of 128, and opens the `Mcmd` editor. Initially the `Mcmd` has no items in it. Click the **New** button to add an item. Figure 7.8 shows that `Resorcerer` gives new items a value of 0.

Figure 7.8 *Adding a new command number to an Mcmd resource.*

You can change the value of the new item to any of the PowerPlant-defined Mcmd constants—they're listed in the arrow pop-up menu that's located to the left of the new item. Figure 7.9 shows that the menu item is being given the value represented by the constant cmd_About.

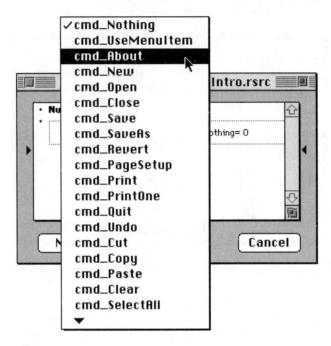

Figure 7.9 *Changing the command number of an item in an Mcmd resource.*

In Figure 7.10 you can see that the menu item now has a value of 1. Recall from Table 7.1 that cmd_About is a constant that represents the number 1. Figure 7.11 shows the relationship between a MENU resource, an Mcmd resource, and the command number constants.

The Apple menu of the PPIntro68K program has just this single **About** item, so the Mcmd resource for MENU **128** is complete. You can save the changed resource and click in the close box of the Mcmd editor.

Next, give the Mcmd a descriptive name by selecting **Resource Info** from the Resource menu. Type the name "Apple" in the Name field, as shown in Figure 7.12. This name will be displayed in Resorcerer, but won't be used by the application that uses the resource. Save the file and close the resource information dialog box.

Figure 7.10 *The Mcmd resource with one menu command number.*

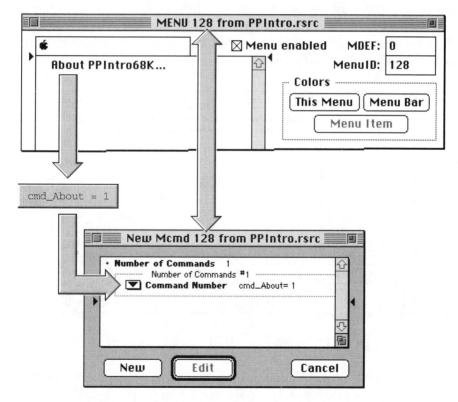

Figure 7.11 *The Mcmd resource ID matches the ID of a MENU resource,
and its command numbers correspond to menu items.*

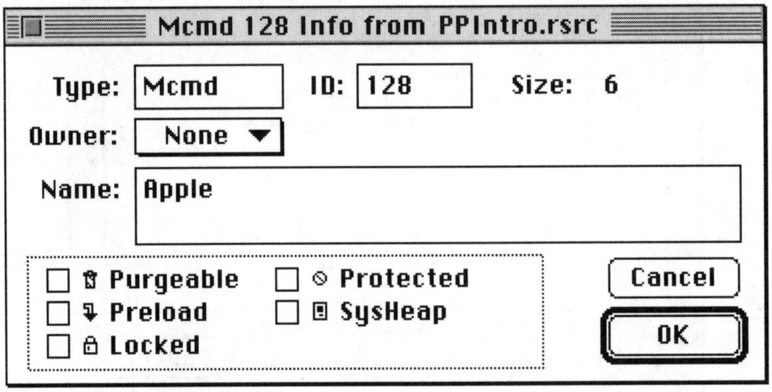

Figure 7.12 *Naming the Mcmd resource.*

Now create the Mcmd for the File menu. Click the **New** button in the File window—as is being done in Figure 7.13. **Resorcerer** will create a new **Mcmd** resource with an ID of 129. You can click on the **Info** button in the File window to give this new resource the name "File."

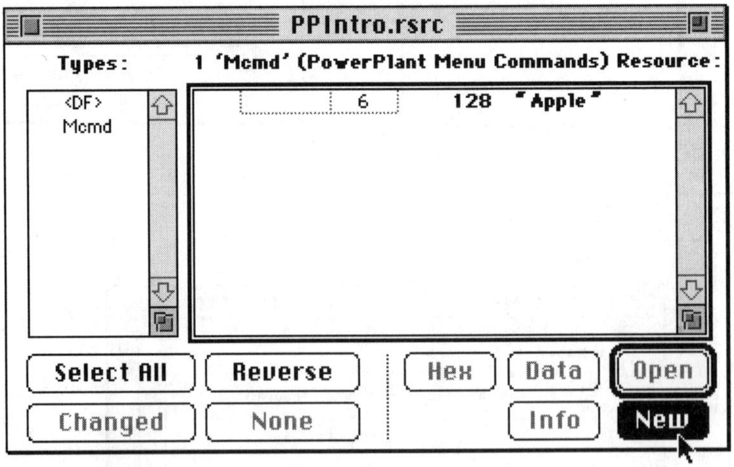

Figure 7.13 *Adding a new Mcmd resource to a resource file.*

Click the **New** button to add an item. Like the PPIntro68K example's Apple menu, the File menu has only one menu item—here it's the **Quit** item. PowerPlant defines cmd_Quit to have a value of 10, so that's the command number to enter in the File menu's Mcmd resource. If you didn't remember that a **Quit** menu item should have an Mcmd command number of 10 (or you didn't care to look it up), simply use the pop-up menu to select cmd_Quit, as was done for the **About** menu item in the Apple menu. Figure 7.14 shows the Mcmd resource for the File menu.

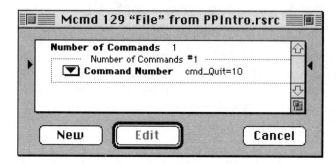

Figure 7.14 *The Mcmd resource for the PPIntro68K File menu.*

Next, create an Mcmd resource for the Edit menu. Again click the New button in the File window, as shown back in Figure 7.13. Then click the **New** button in the Mcmd editor and use the pop-up menu to add the **Undo** menu command number. Insert each of the Edit menu's seven command numbers in this way. Figure 7.15 shows the Mcmd resource that is used for the PPIntro68K Edit menu.

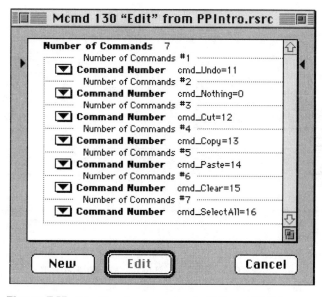

Figure 7.15 *The Mcmd resource for the PPIntro68K Edit menu.*

Note that the IDs of the three Mcmd resources match the IDs of the three MENU resources.

The Mcmd Resource and ResEdit

If you're a Resorcerer user, skip this section since it covers the material you just read, from a ResEdit-user point of view. If you use ResEdit, launch ResEdit now. Then open the PowerPlant ResEdit TMPLs file that's found on this book's CD. If you own the complete version of Metrowerks CodeWarrior, you'll notice that this file also appears on that CD.; either version will work. Next, open the ResEdit Preferences file that's found in the Preferences folder in the System Folder of your Mac's hard drive. Click once on the **TMPL** icon in the PowerPlant ResEdit TMPLs file and select **Copy** from the Edit menu. Now click on the ResEdit Preferences file and then select **Paste** from the Edit menu, as shown in Figure 7.16. You've just copied all of the PowerPlant templates to the ResEdit Preferences file.

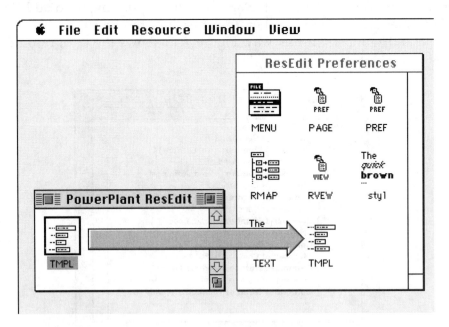

Figure 7.16 *ResEdit users should make sure the TMPL resources from the PowerPlant ResEdit file are copied to the ResEdit Preferences file.*

The PP Intro ƒ folder on the included CD contains a Resorcerer resource file named PPIntro.rsrc. It holds the resources, including the menu-related MBAR, MENU, and Mcmd resources, for the PPIntro68K program. If you use ResEdit rather than Resorcerer, you can open and work with this file by launching ResEdit and then selecting the **Open** menu item in the File menu. If you'd like to get a little practice working with Mcmd resources, you can instead create a new, empty ResEdit file in a scratch folder. The next several pages will describe how to add the three PPIntro68K Mcmd resources to this file.

With a ResEdit file open, select **Create New Resource** from the Resource menu. In the Select New Type dialog box (shown in Figure 7.17), scroll down to the Mcmd resource. Any resource that appears in this list has an editor associated with it. Before adding the PowerPlant TMPL resources to the ResEdit Preferences file, the Mcmd resource would not have appeared in this list. Now, ResEdit knows about this new template and will use it whenever you add a new Mcmd resource to any ResEdit file. After clicking on the Mcmd resource in the list, click the **OK** button.

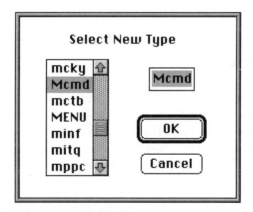

Figure 7.17 *ResEdit's Select New Type dialog box, with the Mcmd type selected.*

You'll see that a new Mcmd resource editing window has opened. ResEdit has given this resource an ID of 128, as it does with most new resources. Since the MENU resource for the Apple menu has an ID of 128—and because the Mcmd resource is paired by ID with a MENU resource—this Mcmd resource should be used to hold the command numbers of the Apple menu items.

Click once on the row of asterisks, then select **Insert New Field(s)** from the Resource menu. In the edit box that appears, type in the number 1. Recall from Table 7.1 that the number 1 is always used for the **About** menu item in the Apple menu. Because there's only one item in the Apple menu, the Mcmd resource for the Apple menu will have only one command number in it. Figure 7.18 shows the completed Mcmd 128 resource. Figure 7.19 shows the relationship between a MENU resource, an Mcmd resource, and the command number constants.

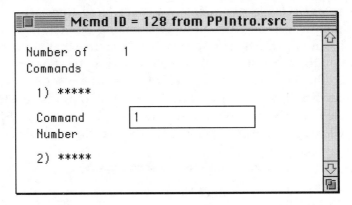

Figure 7.18 *The Mcmd resource with one menu command number.*

Next, select **Get Resource Info** from the Resource menu. Give this resource the name "Apple" so that you'll be able to quickly identify this Mcmd resource from the others that you'll be creating. This name will be displayed in ResEdit but won't be used by the application that uses the resource. Figure 7.20 shows the ResEdit Get Resource Info dialog box.

Now create the Mcmd for the File menu. Again select **Create New Resource** from the Resource menu. Use the Get Resource Info dialog box to give the Mcmd resource the name "File." If the Mcmd doesn't have an ID of 129 (to match the File MENU resource ID), give it that ID now. The File menu for the PPIntro68K example has just a single menu item—the **Quit** item. PowerPlant defines cmd_Quit to have a value of 10, so that's the command number to enter in the File menu's Mcmd resource, as shown in Figure 7.21. Remember to click on the row of asterisks and then select **Insert New Field(s)** from the Resource menu to add an edit text box to the Mcmd editor.

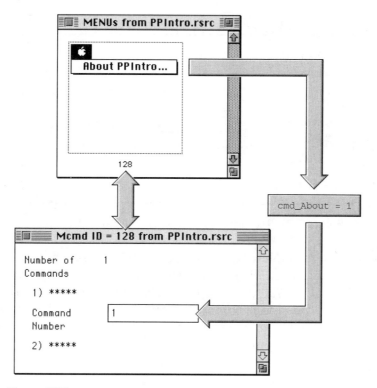

Figure 7.19 *The Mcmd resource ID matches the ID of a MENU resource, and its command numbers correspond to menu items.*

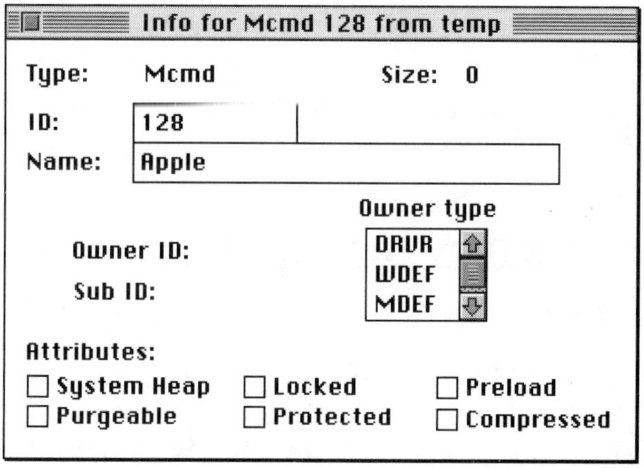

Figure 7.20 *Naming the Mcmd resource.*

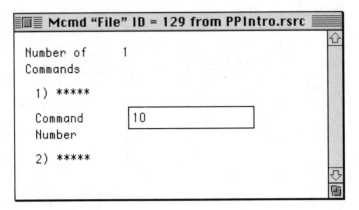

Figure 7.21 *The Mcmd resource for the PPIntro68K File menu.*

Finally, select **Create New Resource** from the Resource menu to add the Mcmd resource for the Edit menu. Using the Get Resource Info dialog box, give it an ID of 130 (like the Edit MENU resource has) and the name "Edit." Insert the seven command numbers shown below in this resource. Figure 7.22 shows a part of the Mcmd resource that is used for the PPIntro68K Edit menu.

```
cmd_Undo       =    11
cmd_Nothing    =     0
cmd_Cut        =    12
cmd_Copy       =    13
cmd_Paste      =    14
cmd_Clear      =    15
cmd_SelectAll  =    16
```

Note that the IDs of the three Mcmd resources match the IDs of the three MENU resources.

Adding Application-Specific Menu Items

Applications usually have more than just the three standard menus (Apple, File, and Edit), and more than just the standard menu commands found in those menus. To interact with any of these items, PowerPlant needs additional information—information that you will supply.

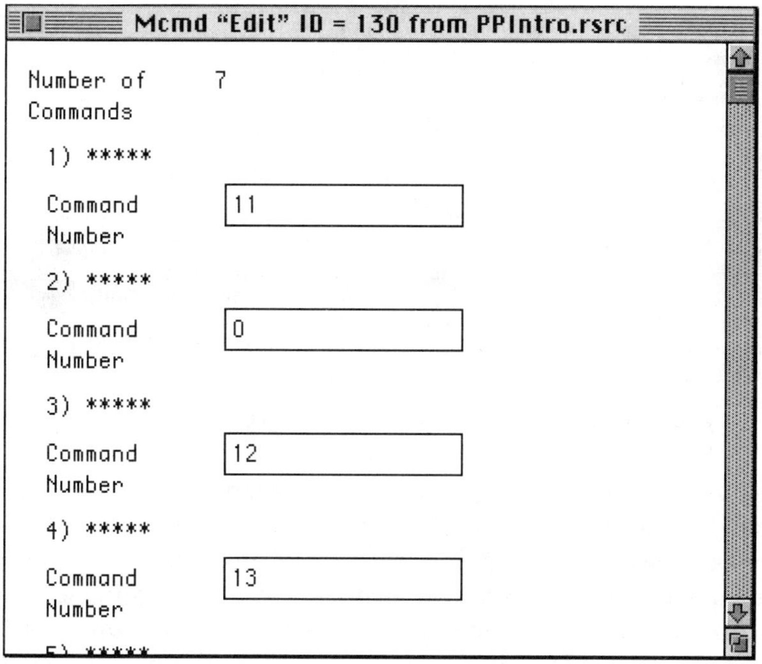

Figure 7.22 *The Mcmd resource for the PPIntro68K Edit menu.*

Command Numbers and Application Menus

For application-specific menu items, you'll provide your own command numbers. These numbers should be *outside* the PowerPlant reserved range of -999 to 999. While negative values in the -1000 to -65535 range can be used as command numbers, you'll want to stick with the 1000 to 65535 positive range. That's because a command number that is negative results in a menu item that can't have its appearance altered.

Adding Resources for a New Menu

Each application-specific menu will require a new MENU resource, and a mention in the MBAR resource. This is the same as you would do for a menu addition using any programming environment. In this chapter you'll add a Draw menu to the PPIntro68K in program Chapter 6 to create a new program named PPMenu68K. Figure 7.23 shows a ResEdit view of the MENU resource you'll be creating.

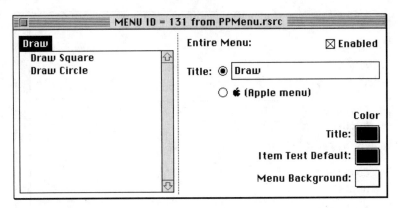

Figure 7.23 *The MENU resource for the PPMenu68K Draw menu.*

The addition of a new MENU resource requires the addition of a new Mcmd resource. Because I've given the new MENU resource an ID of 131, the new Mcmd resource will also have this ID. And because the MENU resource has two menu items in it, the Mcmd resource will have two command numbers. These command numbers can each have any value in the range of 1000 to 65535, as mentioned a few pages back. Figure 7.24 shows this new Mcmd in ResEdit, while Figure 7.25 shows the same resource in Resorcerer.

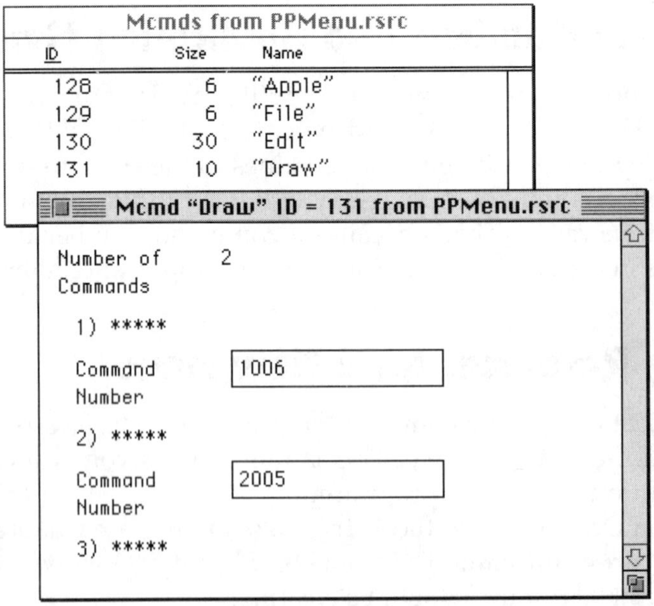

Figure 7.24 *The Mcmd resource for the PPMenu68K Draw menu, as viewed in ResEdit.*

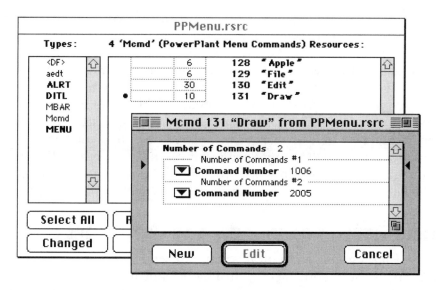

Figure 7.25 *The Mcmd resource for the PPMenu68K Draw menu, as viewed in Resorcerer.*

Adding a MENU and Mcmd resource for a new menu is the first step to letting PowerPlant in on your intentions. After that, you'll need to add some code to a project's source code file.

Menus, Commands, and Commanders

When the user makes a menu selection, PowerPlant sends a command to one of the objects in the application. The object that receives this command is referred to as a *commander*. Understanding this relationship between menus, commands, and commanders is an important part of programming with PowerPlant.

Defining Menu Item Constants

For standard menu items such as **Quit, Copy**, and **Cut**, your source code need not include definitions of the menu item command numbers—they're already defined in the PP_Messages.h header file. For menu items that are specific to your application, though, you'll need to add constant definitions:

```
const  CommandT   cmd_DrawSquare  =  1006;
const  CommandT   cmd_DrawCircle  =  2005;
```

Earlier in this chapter you read that one of the advantages of using PowerPlant was that you wouldn't have to make changes to your project's source code if you rearranged menu items. To stress this point, I've intentionally given the two menu command numbers values that do not give any indication of the order in which the items appear in the Draw menu (or even that they appear in the same menu). In the PPMenu68K example, the **Draw Square** item appears as the first menu item and **Draw Circle** appears as the second item. If I switched the two items around in the MENU and Mcmd resources and then rebuilt the application, the program would work properly, without changes being made to the values of the cmd_DrawSquare and cmd_DrawCircle constants.

Menu Items, Commands, and the Target

Macintosh programs are typically menu driven. It is a menu command that brings about some action. In PowerPlant nomenclature a menu choice (whether invoked by a menu selection or command key) is called a *command*. To carry out a command, the command must be directed at an object.

When a menu item is selected, the command is directed at the *target* object. Application frameworks, including PowerPlant, are typically based on object-oriented programming. A PowerPlant-created program consists of at least one, and usually many more, objects. All PowerPlant programs consist of the application object—the object created from the class derived from LApplication. The previous chapter's PPIntro68K program named that object theApp:

```
CPPIntroApp theApp;
```

Once the preceding line of code executes, the CPPIntroApp class constructor member function is invoked and a second object is created—an LWindow object:

```
mDisplayWindow = LWindow::CreateWindow( WIND_display, this );

mDisplayWindow->Show();
```

From the preceding code you can see that PPIntro68K consists of two objects. When a menu command (such as **Quit**) is made in PPIntro68K, it will be directed at the window—the target object. The window is the target object because it is active. If the user closes the window by clicking in the window's close box, the application object will become the active object, and thus the target object. With the window closed, the same menu item selection (such as **Quit**) that was previously directed at the window object will now be directed at the application object.

Figure 7.26 shows a look at the screen for three scenarios in a hypothetical Mac program. Assuming the same menu item is selected, each of the three screens will have a different target object. In the top view, the application object, which is the only object at this point in the running of the program, will be the recipient, or target, of a menu command. In the middle view, the window will be the target—it's active. In the bottom screen, the edit text item object with the I-beam will be the target—it's now the active object.

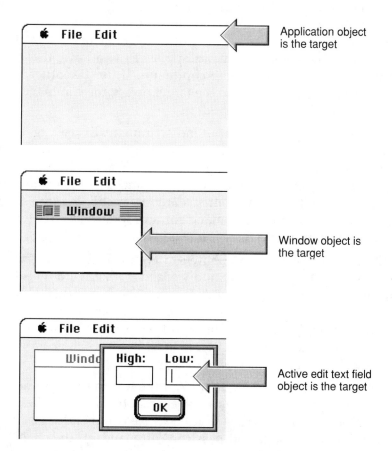

Figure 7.26 *The target object in an application changes as the program executes.*

Commands and the Chain of Command

While some menu items are useful to more than one object type, a menu item doesn't typically have a use to every object in a program. For example, the **Copy** menu item in the Edit menu may work for either an active edit text item object or an active picture object, but won't make sense for a window object or application object. As a second example, the **Quit** menu item from the File menu is meaningless to all objects except the application object. Regardless of this, each and every menu command is always directed at the object that is the target at the time the menu selection is made. What happens next, however, depends on whether the command can be used by that object.

If a menu command applies to the target object, the target object will handle the command. Consider the case of a program that has a window open and active when the user selects **Close** from the File menu. Because the **Close** command applies to windows, the window object will be able to handle the command. If, on the other hand, a menu command doesn't apply to the target object, the command will be passed to a different object for handling.

The passing of a command isn't indiscriminate. Every target resides at the bottom of a *chain of command*, and commands are always considered to be passed upwards along the chain. The application itself is always the top object in the chain. Windows and documents lie beneath the application, and window contents are lower still. Figure 7.27 gives an example of the chain of command for a program that has two open windows—one empty, and one with text in it.

If the user of the program shown in Figure 7.27 selects the **Close** menu item while the leftmost window is active, that window is the target and will handle the command. Figure 7.28 shows this. If the user instead selects the **Quit** menu item while the leftmost window is active, the command again starts at the window. Since a window is only responsible for window-related commands, it passes the command up the chain to the application, as shown in Figure 7.29.

Again referring back to Figure 7.27, if the text in the rightmost window is active (perhaps the text is an object that the user can click on and edit), then the text is the target. Since a **Close** command doesn't apply to the text, the text object will pass the command up the chain to the window object. Here the **Close** command applies, and the window will handle the command by closing itself.

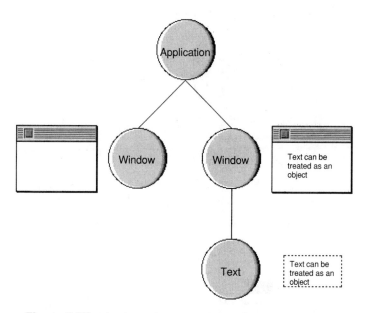

Figure 7.27 *The chain of command for a simple Mac application.*

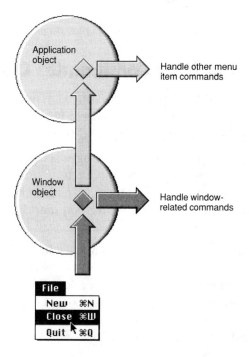

Figure 7.28 *A window as the target object can handle a **Close** menu item.*

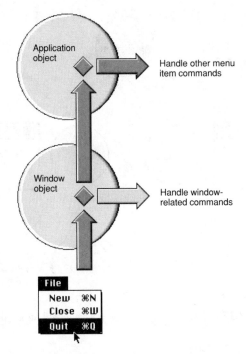

Figure 7.29 *A window as the target object passes a* **Quit** *command up the chain of command.*

The Target and the LCommander Class

A target object—an object that is capable of handling a **menu** command—is referred to as a *commander* object. That's because the class of which the target is an instance of is derived from the LCommander class.

A program's chain of command changes as the program runs. As windows and dialog boxes open, become active, inactive, and close, the chain of command changes. The LCommander class keeps track of these changes. It is also responsible for routing commands to the appropriate object in the chain.

In C++, multiple inheritance allows a class to be derived from more than one base class. PowerPlant makes extensive use of multiple inheritance, as the following lines of code from a few PowerPlant header files show. These definitions show which classes the LApplication, LWindow, and LEditField classes are derived from. You've already worked with LApplication and LWindow in the PPIntro68K example in Chapter 6. The LEditField class is used to add an edit text field to a window.

```
class   LApplication : public  LCommander,
                       public  LModelObject

class   LWindow       : public  LView,
                        public  LCommander,
                        public  LModelObject

class   LEditField    : public  LPane,
                        public  LCommander,
                        public  LPeriodical,
                        public  LUndoer
```

While the preceding three classes are each derived from a different set of base classes, they have one commonality: The LCommander class is one of the base classes. That means that an object of any one of these classes (and numerous other PowerPlant classes) can be a target; it can be a commander that resides in the chain of command. There it can handle a menu command or pass it upwards in the chain.

ObeyCommand() and the Chain of Command

Before describing exactly how the PowerPlant chain of command operates, it's time for a quick diversion. If you haven't used an application framework before, you'll appreciate this example—it has nothing to do with frameworks or PowerPlant. From object-oriented programming, you know that a derived class inherits the member functions of the class on which it is based. You also know that a derived class can override member functions of the base class. Figure 7.30 shows a base class named Vehicle and a class named Automobile that is derived from Vehicle. Note that both classes have a member function named WriteInfo().

When a derived class overrides a base class member function, as the Automobile class overrides WriteInfo(), it is the derived class version of the member function that gets invoked by a derived class object. In the following snippet the Automobile::WriteInfo() function gets invoked:

```
Automobile  *theObject;

theObject = new Automobile;
theObject->WriteInfo( 2 );
```

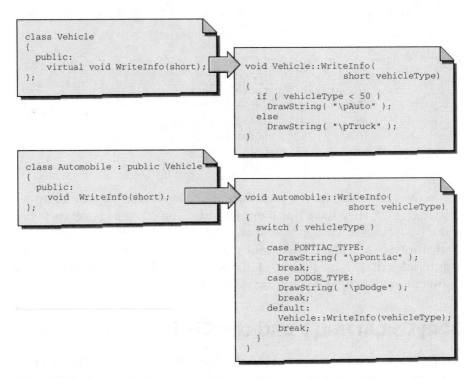

```
class Vehicle
{
  public:
    virtual void WriteInfo(short);
};
```

```
void Vehicle::WriteInfo(
                    short vehicleType)
{
  if ( vehicleType < 50 )
    DrawString( "\pAuto" );
  else
    DrawString( "\pTruck" );
}
```

```
class Automobile : public Vehicle
{
  public:
    void  WriteInfo(short);
};
```

```
void Automobile::WriteInfo(
                    short vehicleType)
{
  switch ( vehicleType )
  {
    case PONTIAC_TYPE:
      DrawString( "\pPontiac" );
      break;
    case DODGE_TYPE:
      DrawString( "\pDodge" );
      break;
    default:
      Vehicle::WriteInfo(vehicleType);
      break;
  }
}
```

Figure 7.30 *In C++ both a base class and a derived class may have identically named functions.*

N O T E

Recall that in C++ if a base class member function is to be made available for overriding by a derived class, the base class member function must be declared using the virtual keyword.

When a derived class overrides a member function, the base class version of the function is still accessible to the derived class. To differentiate between the two versions of the function, however, the base class name must be included in the call to the base class version. In Figure 7.31 you can see that the derived class version of WriteInfo() uses this technique to invoke the base class version of the function with the same name.

A closer examination of the derived class version of WriteInfo() shows that the function examines vehicleType to see if its value matches any of the auto types that WriteInfo() recognizes, namely, Pontiac

or Dodge. If the passed-in value does match, WriteInfo() handles
things by printing out the vehicle type. If the passed-in value doesn't
match, WriteInfo() defers the handling of things to the base class version of WriteInfo(). Here is the code that does that:

```
default:
   Vehicle::WriteInfo(vehicleType);
   break;
```

```
void Vehicle::WriteInfo(short vehicleType)
{
  if ( vehicleType < 50 )
    DrawString( "\pAuto" );
  else
    DrawString( "\pTruck" );
}
```

```
void Automobile::WriteInfo(short vehicleType)
{
  switch ( vehicleType )
  {
    case PONTIAC_TYPE:
      DrawString( "\pPontiac" );
      break;
    case DODGE_TYPE:
      DrawString( "\pDodge" );
      break;
    default:
      Vehicle::WriteInfo(vehicleType);
      break;
  }
}
```

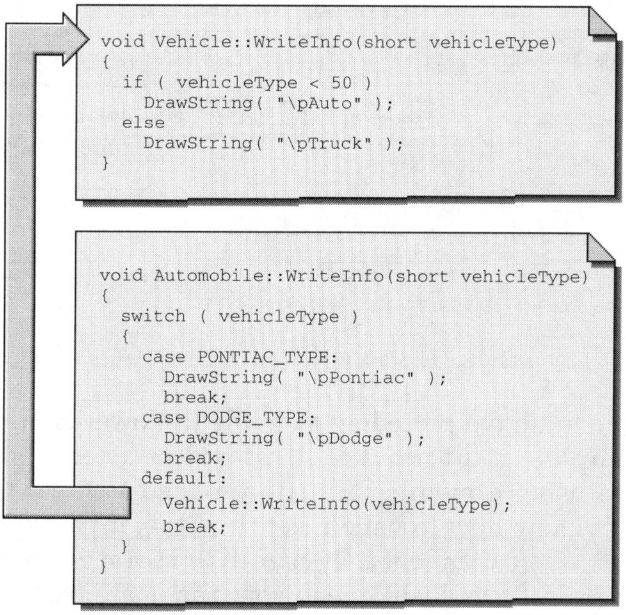

Figure 7.31 *A derived class version of a function may invoke
the base class version of the same function.*

In essence, the Automobile class version of WriteInfo() function takes
first crack at handling vehicleType. If the Automobile class version of
WriteInfo() can't handle the information in vehicleType, it passes
control up to the base class version of WriteInfo(). We'll assume this
program defines vehicle types in the 0 to 49 range to be different car
types, and vehicle types greater than 49 to be different truck types. The
base class version of WriteInfo() simply checks the value of
vehicleType and writes out a generic vehicle type string ("Auto" or
"Truck") based on this value. Figure 7.32 shows this.

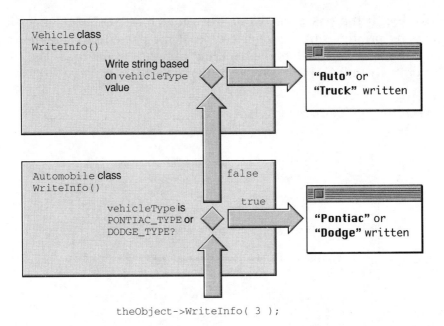

```
theObject->WriteInfo( 3 );
```

Figure 7.32 *Information not handled by the derived class is passed up to the base class.*

Now it's time to tie the preceding example to PowerPlant. In the preceding example an Automobile class object attempts to handle vehicleType using a member function named WriteInfo(). If the object doesn't know how to handle vehicleType, it passes it up to the Vehicle class, where the identically named WriteInfo() member function handles it. In PowerPlant, menu commands are passed about just as the vehicleType parameter is. In PowerPlant, this menu command parameter is named inCommand.

Like the vehicle example, PowerPlant uses identically named member functions to handle a command. In the vehicle example this routine was named WriteInfo(). In PowerPlant, this routine will always be named ObeyCommand().

When the Automobile class member function WriteInfo() can't handle a vehicle command, it relinquishes control to the Vehicle class version of the WriteInfo() function. In PowerPlant, if an object's ObeyCommand() function can't handle a menu command, it too let's another class handle the command. In a simple PowerPlant program, the target object attempts to handle a menu command. If a window object—based on the `LWindow` class—is the target, it will try to handle the command. If the `LWindow` class `ObeyCommand()` member function has no provision for handling the particular type of menu command selected, the command will be passed up the chain of command to the application object. The application object—based on the `LApplication` class—will then handle the command using its own version of `ObeyCommand()`. Table 7.2 summarizes how my own trivial vehicle example compares to a simple PowerPlant program.

Table 7.2 *The Vehicle example is analogous to the PowerPlant way of handling menu commands*

	Vehicle example	PowerPlant program
Command that gets passed	`vehicleType`	`inCommand` (a menu command)
Functions that handle command	`WriteInfo()`	`ObeyCommand()`
Classes that handle command (chain of command)	`Automobile -> Vehicle`	`LWindow -> LApplication`

Overriding ObeyCommand()

Every class that is derived from the `LCommander` class must override the `ObeyCommand()` member function. Since (as you saw earlier) several PowerPlant classes, including `LApplication` and `LWindow`, are derived from `LCommander`, the code that makes up PowerPlant includes several versions of the `ObeyCommand()` function.

NOTE

Control objects, such as buttons, are the exception to the previous statement. They don't use the chain of command, and they don't have an `ObeyCommand()` member function.

Any of your own application-defined classes that are derived from LCommander should also override ObeyCommand(). In the previous chapter you learned that all PowerPlant programs define a class derived from the LApplication class. Since LApplication is itself derived from LCommander, then the application-defined class too should override ObeyCommand(). The last chapter's CPPIntroApp class, shown as follows, *doesn't* do this.

```
class  CPPIntroApp : public LApplication
{
   public:
      CPPIntroApp();

   protected:
      LWindow   *mDisplayWindow;
};
```

Because the CPPIntroApp class doesn't override ObeyCommand(), the application object is capable of handling only standard menu commands that PowerPlant knows of—menu items such as **About** and **Quit**. When the PPIntro68K program receives one of these commands, and a window isn't open, the application itself is the target. The LCommander class (the overseer of commands) will first check to see if the application object, based on the CPPIntroApp class, has an ObeyCommand() function. The CPPIntroApp class doesn't, so the command is sent up the chain of command to the class CPPIntroApp is derived from—LApplication. LApplication *does* have an ObeyCommand() function, so this is the routine that attempts to, and does, handle the command.

For an application to handle anything but the most common menu commands, its class must include an ObeyCommand() member function. Then, when a menu command is issued and the application object receives it, the application object can handle it. The **New** menu item is one example. The **New** menu item in the File menu usually means that a new window should be created. But what kind of window? That's an application-specific issue, so PowerPlant can't handle this menu item on its own. Its handling will be governed by the ObeyCommand() function defined in the class derived from LApplication. Figure 7.33 shows the sequence of ObeyCommand() functions in the chain of command for a simple PowerPlant program that implements a **New** command.

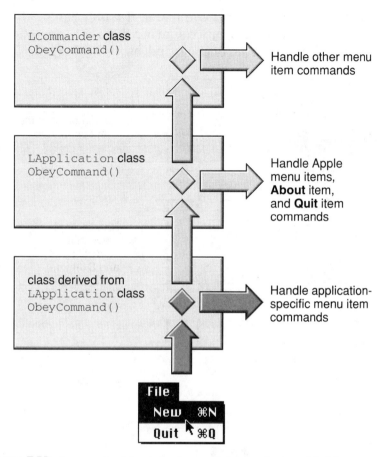

Figure 7.33 *An example of the chain of command for a selection of the **New** menu item.*

In Figure 7.33 you see that because a project's application class is derived from the LApplication class, it is the LApplication class version of ObeyCommand() that handles menu commands that the derived class can't handle. Further, if the LApplication class can't handle the command, it is up to the class that LApplication is derived from— LCommander —to handle the command.

Because PowerPlant knows how to handle standard menu commands, any ObeyCommand() function you write shouldn't also attempt to handle these same items. While the application-defined ObeyCommand()

will handle the File menu's **New** command, it won't handle the same menu's **Quit** command. Instead, any command that isn't application-specific should be sent up the chain of command, as shown in Figure 7.34.

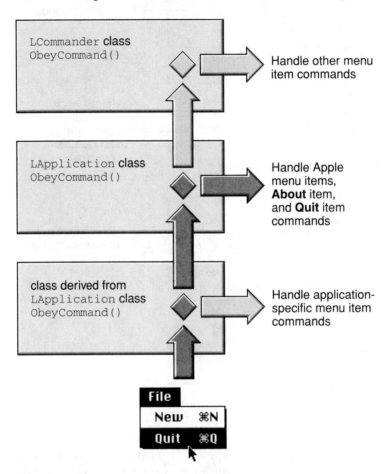

Figure 7.34 *An example of the chain of command for a selection of the **Quit** menu item.*

A Look at the ObeyCommand() Member Function

When writing the LApplication-derived class that's required for each PowerPlant project, include an ObeyCommand() member function. The prototype for the ObeyCommand() function will always be the same:

```
virtual Boolean  ObeyCommand( CommandT  inCommand,
                             void*      ioParam );
```

To allow ObeyCommand() to be overridden by other classes, it must be a virtual function. The return type for ObeyCommand() is Boolean so that the function can report as to whether or not the command it received was handled.

ObeyCommand() requires two parameters. The first, inCommand, is the menu command that is to be handled. The second is a pointer to any extra application-specific information that ObeyCommand() might require. In many versions of ObeyCommand() this second parameter is ignored.

The LApplication-derived class that's found in this chapter's PPMenu68K example overrides ObeyCommand(). Here's a look at that class.

```
class  CPPMenuApp : public LApplication
{
   public:
                      CPPMenuApp();

      virtual Boolean  ObeyCommand( CommandT  inCommand,
                                   void*      ioParam );

      virtual void     FindCommandStatus( CommandT  inCommand,
                                Boolean   &outEnabled,
                                Boolean   &outUsesMark,
                                Char16    &outMark,
                                Str255    outName );
   protected:
      LWindow  *mDisplayWindow;
};
```

As you can see, the CPPMenuApp class also overrides a second LApplication function: FindCommandStatus(). You'll read about this member function later in this chapter.

N O T E

As a reminder, the application class derived from LApplication is used in main() to create the application object:

```
CPPMenuApp theApp;
theApp.Run();
```

After including the prototype of ObeyCommand() in your class definition, write the ObeyCommand() function. When you do, it will always be written with the following three points in mind:

1. A switch statement should be used to examine the inCommand parameter.

2. A case section should be included for each application-specific menu item that the class is to be capable of handling.

3. The switch statement's default section should be used to invoke the base class version of ObeyCommand().

For the PPMenu68K program, here's how the ObeyCommand() function looks for the CPPMenuApp class:

```
Boolean CPPMenuApp :: ObeyCommand( CommandT   inCommand,
                                   void       *ioParam )
{
   Boolean  cmdHandled = true;
   Rect     theRect;

   switch ( inCommand )
   {
      case cmd_DrawSquare:
         ::SetRect( &theRect, 10, 10, 100, 100 );
         ::FrameRect( &theRect );
         break;

      case cmd_DrawCircle:
         ::SetRect( &theRect, 30, 30, 130, 130 );
         ::FrameOval( &theRect );
         break;

      default:
         cmdHandled = LApplication::ObeyCommand( inCommand, ioParam
   );
         break;
   }

   return cmdHandled;
}
```

From the preceding class definition you can see that the PPMenu68K application will be able to handle two application-specific menu items.

The first, **Draw Square**, does just that—it draws a square in the active window. The second, **Draw Circle**, draws a circle. Both menu commands are implemented using calls to QuickDraw Toolbox routines. As discussed in Chapter 6, the scope resolution operator (::) is used to make it clear to anyone reading the code that SetRect(), FrameRect(), and FrameOval() are Toolbox routines.

 Since menu commands that perform drawing always apply to a window, it would make more sense to have these two commands handled by an ObeyCommand() routine written for a window class derived from LWindow. In Chapter 8 that's exactly what we'll do.

N O T E

Earlier in this chapter you saw that for an application-specific menu command, a constant with the value of the menu's command number should be defined in the source code. For its two application-specific menu items, the PPMenu68K program uses command numbers 1006 and 2005 for Mcmd command numbers. Figure 7.35 serves to remind you where these values come from by showing a ResEdit and a Resorcerer view of the Mcmd resource that holds these two command numbers.

Here are the two constants you'll find at the top of the source code:

```
const  CommandT   cmd_DrawSquare  =  1006;
const  CommandT   cmd_DrawCircle  =  2005;
```

The constants are then used in the switch statement in ObeyCommand():

```
case cmd_DrawSquare:
  // draw a square

case cmd_DrawCircle:
  // draw a circle
```

If a menu selection other than one of the two application-specific menu items is made, the PPMenuApp class version of ObeyCommand() uses the default section of the switch statement to invoke a different version of ObeyCommand()—the version found in the LApplication base class:

```
default:
  cmdHandled = LApplication::ObeyCommand( inCommand, ioParam );
  break;
```

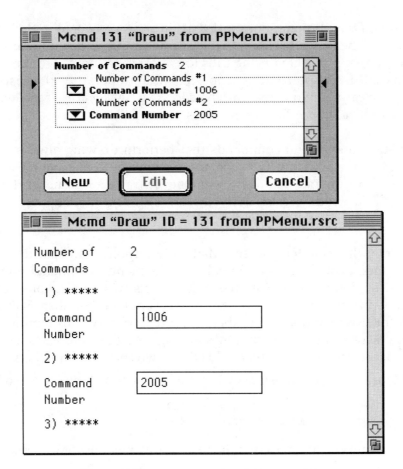

Figure 7.35 *Resorcerer and ResEdit views of the Mcmd resource for the PPMenu68K Draw menu.*

LApplication is a PowerPlant class, so you won't have to write its version of ObeyCommand()—it already exists. You'll find the LApplication version of ObeyCommand() in the PowerPlant file LApplication.cp. Listed as follows is a part of that function.

```
Boolean  LApplication :: ObeyCommand( CommandT  inCommand,
                                      void      *ioParam )
{
   Boolean  cmdHandled = true;

   ResIDT   theMenuID;
   Int16    theMenuItem;
```

```
   if ( IsSyntheticCommand( inCommand, theMenuID, theMenuItem ) )
   {
      ...
      // menu command is from a synthetic menu, handle here
      ...
   }
   else
   {
      switch ( inCommand )
      {
         case cmd_About:
            ShowAboutBox();
            break;

         case cmd_Quit:
            SendAEQuit();
            break;

         default:
            cmdHandled = LCommander::ObeyCommand( inCommand, ioParam );
            break;
      }
   }
   return cmdHandled;
}
```

The first part of the LApplication version of ObeyCommand() handles synthetic menu commands. For menus that hold a variable number of menu items, such as the Apple menu and a Font menu, PowerPlant uses a concept called *synthetic menu commands*. These are menu command numbers that are determined at runtime—not in Mcmd resources.

 Examples in this book won't use synthetic menus, except for the Apple menu, which holds a variable number of Apple menu items. If you think your application requires other menus of this type, and you're an owner of the full version of Metrowerks CodeWarrior, you'll find synthetic menu commands thoroughly described in the *PowerPlant Manual* document on the CodeWarrior CD.

N O T E

If a menu command isn't a synthetic command (and most won't be), the LApplication version of ObeyCommand() follows the pattern discussed earlier. A switch statement examines the menu command, and case sections handle the commands the class is familiar with. For LApplication, that means there is a `case` section to handle the **About** and **Quit** menu items. The actual handling of these two menu items is performed by other PowerPlant functions, namely, `ShowAboutBox()` and `SendAEQuit()`. For any other menu item, a different version of `ObeyCommand()` must be called. The `LApplication` class is derived from the `LCommander` class, so it's the `LCommander` version of `ObeyCommand()` that gets invoked here:

```
case cmd_About:
   ShowAboutBox();
   break;

case cmd_Quit:
   SendAEQuit();
   break;

default:
   cmdHandled = LCommander::ObeyCommand( inCommand, ioParam );
   break;
```

These last few pages have shown how a menu command can work its way up the chain of command from the `LApplication`-derived class to the `LApplication` class and finally to the `LCommander` class. Depending on what objects are on the screen when a menu item is selected by the user, an application can of course have a different chain of command. What's important to keep in mind is that PowerPlant already includes many of the `ObeyCommand()` member functions—you're responsible for writing only the versions that accompany your own application-defined derived classes.

Overriding FindCommandStatus()

As a program runs, menu items may need to be updated. A menu item might have a checkmark beside it that gets toggled on and off as the item is selected. Or, a menu item may need to be disabled under certain circumstances. For example, the **Close** item in the File menu should become disabled after the user closes the last open window. PowerPlant eliminates much of the confusion associated with keeping track of the state of menu items through the use of the `FindCommandStatus()` member function.

When the menu bar is clicked on by the user, a PowerPlant routine named `UpdateMenus()` is called. `UpdateMenus()` in turn calls the `LCommander` class member function `FindCommandStatus()` for *every* menu item that has an `Mcmd` resource (only a menu item created on the fly, and thus represented by a synthetic command number, doesn't have a Mcmd resource). `FindCommandStatus()` determines the status of a menu item. That is, it determines the following:

- If the item has a mark
- What that mark is (such as a checkmark)
- Whether the item should be marked at the current point in time
- Whether the menu item should be enabled or disabled at the current point in time

Like `ObeyCommand()`, the `FindCommandStatus()` function can be found in several of the classes in the PowerPlant libraries of code. That is because the `FindCommandStatus()` function, again like `ObeyCommand()`, can be overridden by other classes. Any of your application-defined classes that will be capable of handling menu item selections should override `FindCommandStatus()`, just as they do with `ObeyCommand()`. For the PPMenu68K example, the `CPPMenuApp` class, derived from `LApplication`, handles the **Draw Square** and **Draw Circle** menu items. Therefore this class has both an `ObeyCommand()` and a `FindCommandStatus()` member function. Here's another look at the `CPPMenuApp` class definition:

```
class  CPPMenuApp : public LApplication
{
   public:
                       CPPMenuApp();

      virtual Boolean  ObeyCommand( CommandT  inCommand,
                                    void*     ioParam );

      virtual void     FindCommandStatus( CommandT  inCommand,
                                          Boolean   &outEnabled,
                                          Boolean   &outUsesMark,
                                          Char16    &outMark,
                                          Str255    outName );
   protected:
      LWindow   *mDisplayWindow;
};
```

When UpdateMenus() calls a FindCommandStatus() routine, it passes the command number of the menu item that is to be updated. The FindCommandStatus() function is then responsible for filling in some or all of the other four parameters for use by UpdateMenus(). Figure 7.36 shows the information held in each of the FindCommandStatus() parameters.

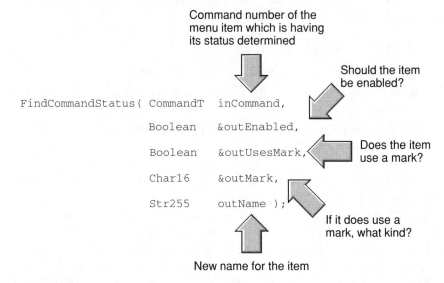

Figure 7.36 *The information held in each of the FindCommandStatus() parameters.*

The FindCommandStatus() routine of an application-defined class should have a switch statement with a case section for each menu command handled by the ObeyCommand() member function of that same class. Within each case section, you'll specify the status of one menu item. Here's the CPPMenuApp class version of FindCommandStatus():

```
void   CPPMenuApp :: FindCommandStatus( CommandT   inCommand,
                                        Boolean    &outEnabled,
                                        Boolean    &outUsesMark,
                                        Char16     &outMark,
                                        Str255     outName )
{
   switch ( inCommand )
   {
      case cmd_DrawSquare:
         outEnabled  = true;
         outUsesMark = false;
         break;
```

```
        case cmd_DrawCircle:
           outEnabled  = true;
           outUsesMark = false;
           break;

        default:
           LApplication::FindCommandStatus( inCommand, outEnabled,
                                            outUsesMark, outMark,
                                            outName );
           break;
    }
}
```

If FindCommandStatus() is passed an inCommand value of cmd_DrawSquare, the routine will set outEnabled to true and outUsesMark to false. This will tell the calling routine that the **Draw Square** menu item should be enabled and should not have any kind of mark beside it. Since this menu item uses no mark, there is no need to give outMark a value. And since the **Draw Square** menu item doesn't have its text changed (the item will always appear as "Draw Square" in the menu), there is no need to assign outName a string value.

If FindCommandStatus() receives an inCommand value of cmd_DrawCircle, outEnabled will again be set to true and outUsesMark will again be set to false. This is because the **Draw Circle** menu item behaves the same as the **Draw Square** menu item: It is always enabled and doesn't use a mark.

Near the end of this chapter, a second menu example (PPMoreMenu68K) will demonstrate using a checkmark with a menu item.

N O T E

Every application-specific menu item that you add to your program should have a case section in both the ObeyCommand() and FindCommandStatus() member functions of an application-defined class. Figure 7.37 shows that the two application-specific menu items in PPMenu68K appear in the ObeyCommand() and FindCommandStatus() routines of the CPPMenuApp class. The ObeyCommand() member function provides for the handling of these menu selections, while the FindCommandStatus() function describes the appearance of the menu items.

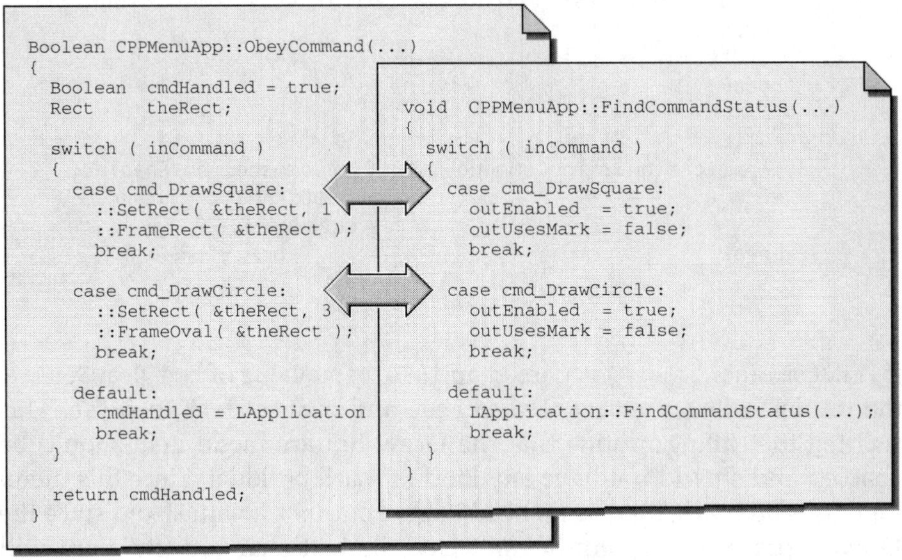

```
Boolean CPPMenuApp::ObeyCommand(...)
{
  Boolean  cmdHandled = true;
  Rect     theRect;

  switch ( inCommand )
  {
    case cmd_DrawSquare:
      ::SetRect( &theRect, 1
      ::FrameRect( &theRect );
      break;

    case cmd_DrawCircle:
      ::SetRect( &theRect, 3
      ::FrameOval( &theRect );
      break;

    default:
      cmdHandled = LApplication
      break;
  }

  return cmdHandled;
}
```

```
void CPPMenuApp::FindCommandStatus(...)
{
  switch ( inCommand )
  {
    case cmd_DrawSquare:
      outEnabled  = true;
      outUsesMark = false;
      break;

    case cmd_DrawCircle:
      outEnabled  = true;
      outUsesMark = false;
      break;

    default:
      LApplication::FindCommandStatus(...);
      break;
  }
}
```

Figure 7.37 *Application-specific menu items should be listed in both the ObeyCommand() and FindCommandStatus() member functions.*

The PPMenu68K Example Application

The PPIntro68K program in Chapter 6 demonstrates the use of menus in an application created using PowerPlant, but only to a limited extent. PPIntro68K only implemented the standard menus found in all Mac programs. Typical Mac applications will also add menus and menu items not common to all other programs. While PowerPlant won't know how to handle selections made from these application-specific menus, it will, as you've seen, allow you to easily add support for your own menu items.

PPMenu68K uses the same three menus that last chapter's PPIntro68K used—the Apple, File, and Edit menus. Also, it implements a Draw menu that holds two menu items. In Figure 7.38 you can see that the **Draw Square** item has already been selected and the **Draw Circle** item is about to be chosen.

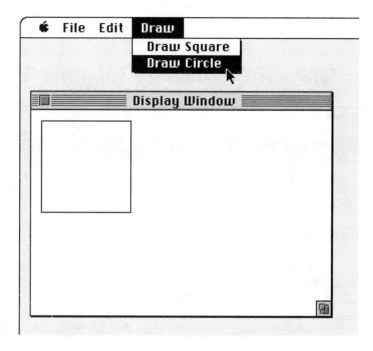

Figure 7.38 *The PPMenu68K program in action.*

The PPMenu68K Project

If you've programmed the Macintosh for any length of time, you no doubt begin a new project by copying an existing one. When creating a new PowerPlant project, save yourself some work and do the same. For this chapter's PPMenu68K.µ project, I copied the PPIntro68K.µ project (see Chapter 6) and renamed it. I also copied the PPIntro.cp source code file and resource files and renamed them.

After opening the copied project with the MW C/C++ 68K compiler, I used the **Add Files** menu item from the Project menu to add the new source code file and resource files. At this point I moved the files to their appropriate segments. My project window then looked like the one shown in Figure 7.39. Finally, I removed the PPIntro files using the **Remove Files** menu item from the Project menu. The final version of the PPMenu68K.μ project looks like the one shown in Figure 7.40.

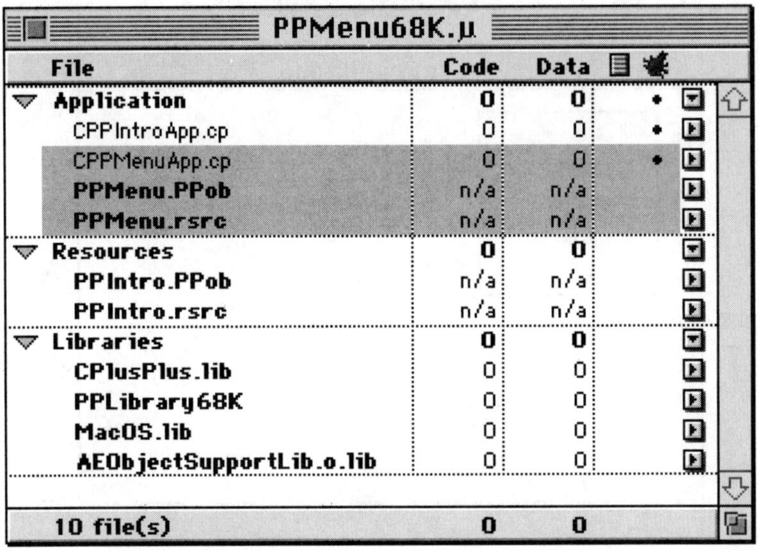

Figure 7.39 *The PPMenu68K project window after adding the appropriate files, and before removing old files.*

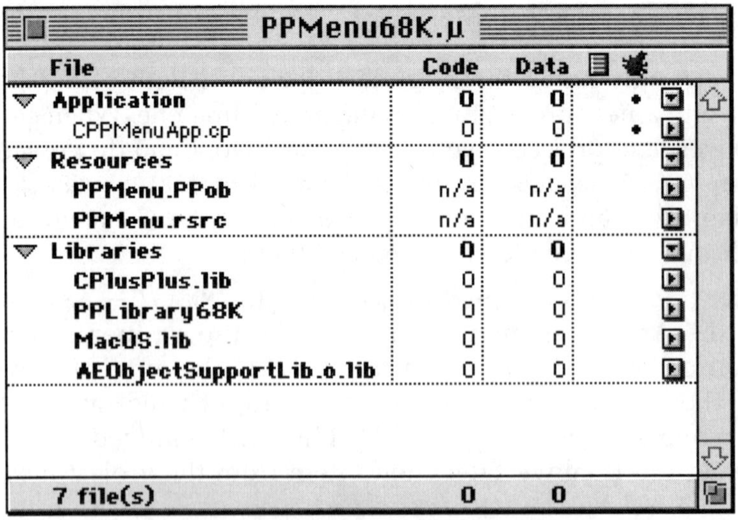

Figure 7.40 *The PPMenu68K project window after removing old files and rearranging the new files.*

N O T E It's a good idea to add the new files before removing the old. If you remove the unwanted files *before* adding the new ones, the Application and Resources segments will be empty and the compiler will remove them. While adding and naming new segments isn't a difficult chore, you might as well avoid it when possible.

Finally, I selected **Preferences** from the Edit menu and clicked on the Project icon in the Preferences dialog box. That gave me the opportunity to fill in the edit box with the information the compiler uses later on when it comes time to name the compiled application. Figure 7.41 shows that I chose the name PPMenu68K for this application.

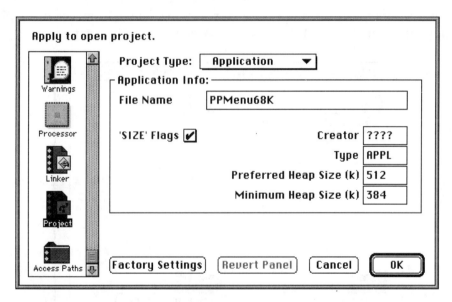

Figure 7.41 *Providing a name for the new application.*

With the project all set up, it's time to get to work on the resources and source code necessary for the PPMenu68K program.

The PPMenu68K Resources

The PPMenu68K project has all of the same resource types that were found in last chapter's PPIntro68K project. Figure 7.42 provides a ResEdit look at the resources you'll find in the PPMenu.rsrc file used in the project.

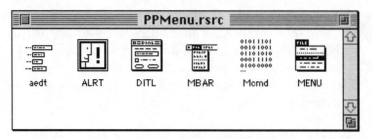

Figure 7.42 *The resources used in the PPMenu68K project.*

PPMenu.rsrc is nothing more than a copy of PPIntro.rsrc with a few additions. First, the text of the item in the MENU resource for the Apple menu (ID 128) was changed to match the name of the program. Then a new MENU resource was added to support the application's Draw menu. Figure 7.43 shows the project's four MENU resources, as viewed from ResEdit.

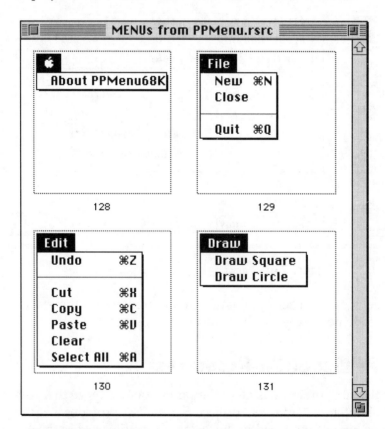

Figure 7.43 *The MENU resources used in the PPMenu68K project.*

To make PowerPlant aware of the new menu items, a new Mcmd resource was added. In Figure 7.44 you can see that the new Mcmd resource has the same ID (131) as the new MENU resource. Figure 7.45 shows the list of Mcmd resources when PPMenu.rsrc is opened with Resorcerer rather than ResEdit.

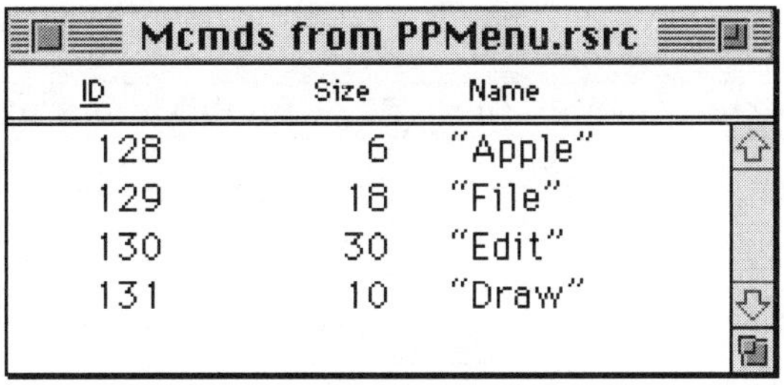

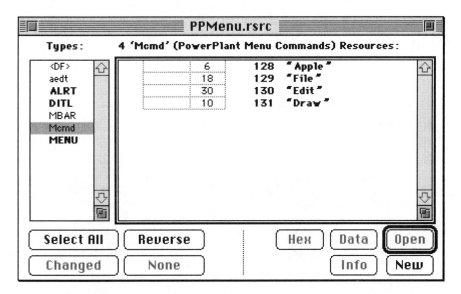

Figure 7.44 *The Mcmd resources used in the PPMenu68K project, as viewed in ResEdit.*

Figure 7.45 *The Mcmd resources used in the PPMenu68K project, as viewed in Resorcerer.*

In this chapter's *Adding Application-Specific Menu Items* section you saw how two command numbers were added to an Mcmd resource. Those command numbers were, in fact, for the two menu items used in the Draw menu of the PPMenu68K example. Figure 7.46 shows these Mcmd 131 command numbers in ResEdit, while Figure 7.47 shows them in Resorcerer.

NOTE

Recall from the *Adding Application-Specific Menu Items* section that the values given to the two command numbers in Mcmd resource 131 were arbitrary. The PowerPlant numbering convention for command numbers for application-specific menu items states that command numbers should be given values greater than 999. Beyond that, the choice is up to you.

```
Mcmd "Draw" ID = 131 from PPMenu.rsrc

Number of        2
Commands

  1) *****

  Command          1006
  Number

  2) *****

  Command          2005
  Number

  3) *****
```

Figure 7.46 *The command numbers for Mcmd resource 131, as viewed in ResEdit.*

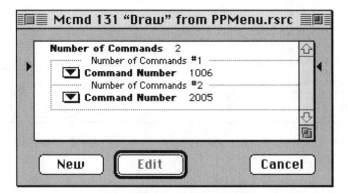

Figure 7.47 *The command numbers for Mcmd resource 131, as viewed in Resorcerer.*

The PPMenuApp.h Header File Source Code Listing

In keeping with the convention of defining classes in separate header files, the PPMenu68K project has a header file (CPPMenuApp.h) that holds the definition for the LApplication-derived CPPMenuApp class. As you saw in the previous chapter, there are a few lines of code that precede the class definition:

■ The #pragma once directive starts off the header file to insure that the contents of this header file are included only once in the PPMenu68K project.

■ The LApplication.h PowerPlant header file is included so that its data members and member functions can be inherited by the class that is derived from it—CPPMenuApp.

■ The LWindow class is used in a forward reference so that the compiler understands the type associated with the mDisplayWindow data member.

The CPPMenuApp.h header file is a copy of the preceding chapter's CPPIntroApp.h file. After changing the class references from CPPIntroApp to CPPMenuApp, I added the ObeyCommand() and FindCommandStatus() member functions, as discussed earlier in this chapter.

```
#pragma once

#include <LApplication.h>

class   LWindow;

class   CPPMenuApp : public LApplication
{
   public:
                    CPPMenuApp();

      virtual Boolean  ObeyCommand( CommandT  inCommand,
                                    void*     ioParam );

      virtual void     FindCommandStatus( CommandT  inCommand,
```

```
                                Boolean    &outEnabled,
                                Boolean    &outUsesMark,
                                Char16     &outMark,
                                Str255     outName );
     protected:
         LWindow  *mDisplayWindow;
};
```

The CPPMenuApp.cp Source Code Listing

The CPPMenuApp.cp file holds the source code for the PPMenu68K program.
You'll find that it follows the same format of the PPIntro68K program:

- Include PowerPlant and application-defined header files that hold definitions of member functions used in the source code file.

- Define constants for the WIND resource and Mcmd command numbers used in the source code.

- Initialize the Toolbox.

- Create the application object and start the application by invoking the object's Run() member function.

- Have the application object's constructor register PPob-based classes and create and show a window.

Also, PPMenu68K includes menu-handling code not found in the preceding chapter's PPIntro68K project. PPMenu68K also does the following:

- Overrides ObeyCommand() to handle menu selections.

- Overrides FindCommandStatus() to inform PowerPlant of the status of menu items.

```
// ==============================================================
//                                          include header files

#include "CPPMenuApp.h"
#include <LWindow.h>
#include <UDrawingState.h>
#include <URegistrar.h>
```

```
// ================================================================
//                                         constant definitions

const  ResIDT      WIND_display    =    500;
const  CommandT    cmd_DrawSquare  =   1006;
const  CommandT    cmd_DrawCircle  =   2005;


// ================================================================
//                                                        main()

void  main( void )
{
   UQDGlobals::InitializeToolbox( &qd );

   CPPMenuApp theApp;
   theApp.Run();
}


// ================================================================
//                               CPPMenuApp class constructor

CPPMenuApp :: CPPMenuApp()
{
   URegistrar::RegisterClass( 'wind',
            (ClassCreatorFunc)LWindow::CreateWindowStream );

   mDisplayWindow = LWindow::CreateWindow( WIND_display, this );
   mDisplayWindow->Show();
}


// ================================================================
//                       Override LApplication::ObeyCommand()

Boolean CPPMenuApp :: ObeyCommand( CommandT  inCommand,
                                   void      *ioParam )
{
   Boolean   cmdHandled = true;
   Rect      theRect;

   switch ( inCommand )
   {
      case cmd_DrawSquare:
         ::SetRect( &theRect, 10, 10, 100, 100 );
```

```
         ::FrameRect( &theRect );
         break;

      case cmd_DrawCircle:
         ::SetRect( &theRect, 30, 30, 130, 130 );
         ::FrameOval( &theRect );
         break;

      default:
         cmdHandled = LApplication::ObeyCommand( inCommand, ioParam );
         break;
   }

   return cmdHandled;
}


// ============================================================
//                 Override LApplication::FindCommandStatus()

void   CPPMenuApp :: FindCommandStatus( CommandT   inCommand,
                                        Boolean    &outEnabled,
                                        Boolean    &outUsesMark,
                                        Char16     &outMark,
                                        Str255     outName )
{
   switch ( inCommand )
   {
      case cmd_DrawSquare:
         outEnabled  = true;
         outUsesMark = false;
         break;

      case cmd_DrawCircle:
         outEnabled  = true;
         outUsesMark = false;
         break;

      default:
         LApplication::FindCommandStatus( inCommand, outEnabled,
                                          outUsesMark, outMark,
                                          outName );
         break;
   }
}
```

NOTE

After successfully compiling and running PPMenu68K, try making a few changes to ObeyCommand(). If you question the use of Toolbox calls in a PowerPlant project, try changing the code under the cmd_DrawSquare case label. Alter the values of the parameters to FrameRect(). Or, change the calls to the drawing routines. Substitute the call to FrameRect() with a call to the Toolbox function FrameRoundRect(). To draw a line rather than a square, replace the SetRect() and FrameRect() calls with calls to the Toolbox routines MoveTo() and Line().

PPMenu and the MW C/C++ PPC Compiler

If you want to make a native version of PPMenu, copy the preceding chapter's PPIntroPPC.μ project and rename it PPMenuPPC.μ. Then follow the same steps used to create this chapter's PPMenu68K.μ project. You'll use the same source code file and the same resource files as the PPMenu68K.μ project uses, so your project's Application and Resources segments will look identical for both projects. Figure 7.48 shows the PowerPC version of the PPMenu project window.

File	Code	Data	目	🕯
▽ **Application**	**0**	**0**	•	⊡
CPPMenuApp.cp	0	0	•	▶
▽ **Resources**	**0**	**0**		⊡
PPMenu.PPob	n/a	n/a		▶
PPMenu.rsrc	n/a	n/a		▶
▽ **Libraries**	**0**	**0**	•	⊡
Startup.c	0	0	•	▶
runtime.o	0	0		▶
InterfaceLib	0	0		▶
ObjectSupportLib	0	0		▶
MWCSupportLib	0	0		▶
PowerPlantLib	0	0		▶
9 file(s)	**0**	**0**		

PPMenuPPC.μ

Figure 7.48 *The PowerPC version of the PPMenu project.*

Adding to the PPMenu68K Example

Now that you've got a solid working knowledge of how menus work in PowerPlant, adding a menu item to a menu in an existing project should be a simple task—and it is!

The PPMenu68K example has just a single menu item in its File menu—the **Quit** item. The PPMoreMenu68K program that you'll find on the included CD adds two new menu items to the File menu: a **Window Visible** item and a dashed line. When the program runs, a single window will be displayed. At that time the **Window Visible** item will have a checkmark by it. Selecting this item will hide the window and uncheck this menu item. Figure 7.49 shows how this new menu item functions.

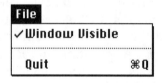

When checked, window is visible.
Now select this item to hide window.

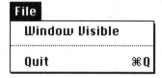

When unchecked, window is hidden.
Now select this item to show window.

Figure 7.49 *The menu item added to the PPMenu68K project, and how it functions.*

PPMoreMenu68K shows how to add menu items to a menu, how to implement a mark by a menu item, and how to hide and show a window.

The PPMoreMenu68K Project

The PPMoreMenu68K.µ project was created using the same method you saw earlier in this chapter: An existing project was copied and renamed. Since the PPMoreMenu68K program is almost identical to the PPMenu68K program, it was the PPMenu68K.µ project that was copied. That project's source code file and resource file were also copied and renamed. Then they were added to the project in place of the old source code file and resource files; Figure 7.50 shows the result.

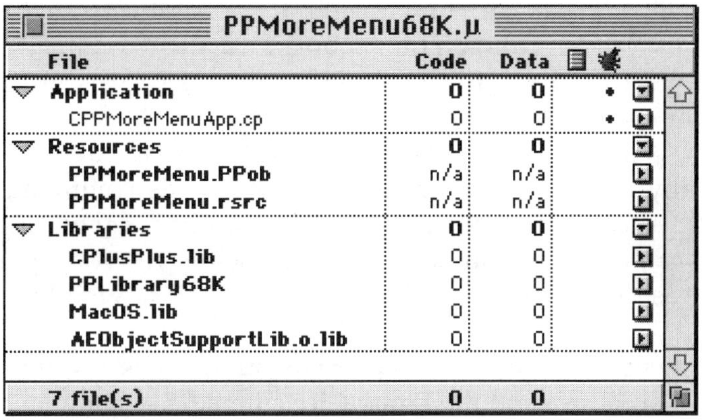

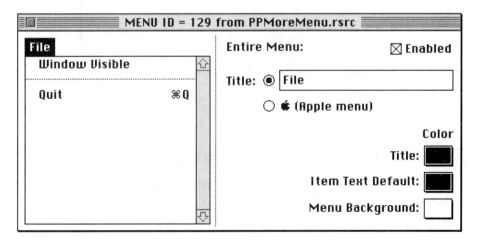

Figure 7.50 *The PPMoreMenu68K project window.*

Adding the New Menu-Related Resources

In a PowerPlant project the addition of a new menu items requires a change to a MENU resource and the corresponding Mcmd resource. Figure 7.51 shows MENU resource 129 after it has been altered in ResEdit. Resorcerer users will see the same three menu items in the Resorcerer MENU editor.

Figure 7.51 *The new items in the File MENU resource.*

Because MENU 129 has three menu items, its Mcmd resource will need three command numbers. The second and third menu items—the dashed line and the **Quit** item—should be represented by the PowerPlant constants cmd_Nothing (0) and cmd_Quit (10). The first menu item, **Window Visible**, is an application-specific item and as such can have any unused value greater than 999 as its command number. Figure 7.52 shows the Mcmd 129 resource in Resorcerer. Figure 7.53 shows the same resource in ResEdit. In these figures you can see that I chose 3000 as the command number for the **Window Visible** item.

Recall that the **Draw Square** menu item has a command number of 1006 and the **Draw Circle** item has a command number of 2005. These are the only two command numbers greater than 999 that the **Window Visible** menu item can't use.

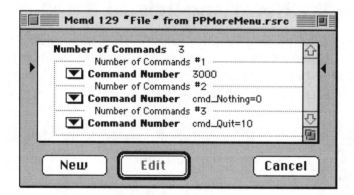

Figure 7.52 *The new menu command numbers in the File Mcmd resource, as viewed in Resorcerer.*

Adding the New Menu-Related Source Code

Each application-specific menu item should have its own constant defined in the source code. Since I'm starting with the PPMenu68K source code, I'll need to add just one constant to the two that already exist. I've shown the new code in bold type as follows. Note that the constant has the same value as the command number in the Mcmd 129 resource.

```
const  CommandT  cmd_DrawSquare      =  1006;
const  CommandT  cmd_DrawCircle      =  2005;
const  CommandT  cmd_HideShowWindow  =  3000;
```

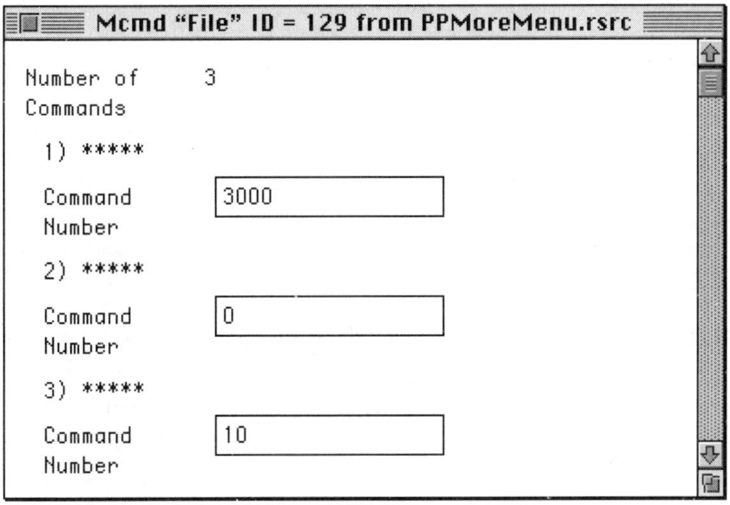

Figure 7.53 *The new menu command numbers in the File Mcmd resource, as viewed in ResEdit.*

Each application-specific menu item needs a case section in an ObeyCommand() and FindCommandStatus() routine. In the code that follows, you can see how the ObeyCommand() function from PPMenu68K has been changed to include the ability to handle this new menu item. Here again I've shown the new code in a larger type.

```
Boolean CPPMoreMenuApp :: ObeyCommand( CommandT   inCommand,
                                       void       *ioParam )
{
   Boolean   cmdHandled = true;
   Rect      theRect;

   switch ( inCommand )
   {
      case cmd_HideShowWindow:
         if ( mDisplayWindow->IsVisible() )
            mDisplayWindow->Hide();
         else
            mDisplayWindow->Show();
         break;

      case cmd_DrawSquare:
         ::SetRect( &theRect, 10, 10, 100, 100 );
         ::FrameRect( &theRect );
         break;

      case cmd_DrawCircle:
```

```
        ::SetRect( &theRect, 30, 30, 130, 130 );
        ::FrameOval( &theRect );
        break;

    default:
        cmdHandled = LApplication::ObeyCommand( inCommand, ioParam );
        break;
    }

    return cmdHandled;
}
```

When the user selects **Window Visible** from the File menu, Obey
Command() responds by having the program's window object invoke
IsVisible(). If the window object that invokes this function is visible,
IsVisible() returns true and ObeyCommand() hides the window. If the
window is already hidden, IsVisible() returns false and
ObeyCommand() shows the window.

N O T E

But how is one to *know* that a PowerPlant function exists to
check the visibility of a window? And how does one know
the exact function name and parameters? The same way I
did—by having the entire staff of Metrowerks at your disposal as you write a CodeWarrior book! Seriously though,
while Metrowerks technical personnel were very helpful in
writing this book, I didn't need them here. Instead, I opened
a few PowerPlant header files and scrolled through them. In
particular, I looked through LWindows.h, LView.h, and
LPane.h.

A window is an object of the LWindow class, so it makes sense to
look through LWindows.h. The LWindow class is derived from
the LView class, which in turn is derived from the LPane class.
So it also makes sense to look at the header files that hold the
definitions of these classes as well. And what was I looking *for*
in these files? Interestingly named member functions. When I
came across the IsVisible() routine in LPane.h, I knew I had
found what I needed. When you need to perform some programming task, you should do the same. Don't immediately
set about writing your own function. Instead, explore the
PowerPlant header files. The more you become familiar with
them, the easier it becomes to use PowerPlant.

The `IsVisible()` function, along with the `Show()` and `Hide()` LPane class member functions, make it possible to use the **Window Visible** menu item to toggle the visibility of a window.

Whether or not the window is visible should be quite apparent by looking at the screen; It's either there or it's not. Still, I'll offer the user some additional feedback by displaying a checkmark next to the **Window Visible** menu item when the window really is visible. While this feature might not be of great benefit to a user of the program, it will allow me to demonstrate how to give a menu item a mark beside it.

After adding a new `case` section to `ObeyCommand()`, I'll add a `case` section to `FindCommandStatus()`. In the following snippet you can see how `FindCommandStatus()` has been changed from the `PPMenu68K` version. Once again I've shown the new code in larger type.

```
void  CPPMoreMenuApp :: FindCommandStatus( CommandT  inCommand,
                                           Boolean   &outEnabled,
                                           Boolean   &outUsesMark,
                                           Char16    &outMark,
                                           Str255    outName )
{
   switch ( inCommand )
   {
      case cmd_HideShowWindow:
         outEnabled  = true;
         outUsesMark = true;
         if ( mDisplayWindow->IsVisible() )
            outMark = checkMark;
         else
            outMark = noMark;
         break;

      case cmd_DrawSquare:
         outEnabled  = true;
         outUsesMark = false;
         break;

      case cmd_DrawCircle:
         outEnabled  = true;
         outUsesMark = false;
         break;

      default:
         LApplication::FindCommandStatus( inCommand, outEnabled,
                                          outUsesMark, outMark,
```

```
    outName );
        break;
    }
}
```

The **Window Visible** menu item will be enabled, so outEnabled is
assigned a value of true. Unlike the other two application-specific
menu items, **Draw Square** and **Draw Circle**, the **Window Visible** menu
item will have a mark. So outUsesmark is set to true. After that, I've
again used the IsVisible() function:

```
case cmd_HideShowWindow:
    outEnabled = true;
    outUsesMark = true;
    if ( mDisplayWindow->IsVisible() )
        outMark = checkMark;
    else
        outMark = noMark;
    break;
```

If IsVisible() returns true, the window is currently visible and the
Window Visible menu item should have a checkmark beside it, so
outMark is set to the Apple constant checkMark. If IsVisible() returns
false, the window is hidden and the menu item should have no mark
next to it, so outMark is set to noMark.

 The most common marks for a menu item are a checkmark, a
diamond, the command key symbol, and, of course, no mark
at all. Apple's universal header files define checkMark,
diamondMark, commandMark, and noMark for these different
N O T E types of menu item marks.

After compiling and running PPMoreMenu68K, try making some simple
changes to the source code listing and then rerunning it. Change the
outMark variable under the cmd_HideShowWindow case label in
FindCommandStatus() from checkMark to diamondMark; or, try altering
the code under the cmd_DrawSquare case label in FindCommandStatus()
so that a checkmark appears next to the **Draw Square** menu item under
certain conditions. If you want to add another menu item to a menu,
make sure you remember to do the following:

- Change the MENU resource.
- Add a new command number to the Mcmd resource.

- Add a constant that matches the new `Mcmd` command number.
- Use the constant in a case section in `ObeyCommand()`.
- Use the constant in a case section in `FindCommandStatus()`.

PPMoreMenu and the MW C/C++ PPC Compiler

If you're using the Metrowerks PowerPC compiler, follow the same steps used to create this chapter's `PPMenuPPC.µ` project. This time start with the `PPMenuPPC.µ` project and turn it into a project named `PPMoreMenuPPC.µ`. When complete, your project window should look like the one shown in Figure 7.54.

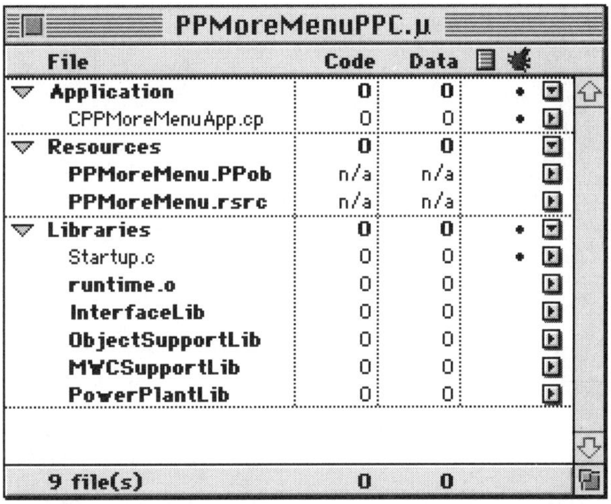

File	Code	Data		
▽ **Application**	0	0	• ▾
CPPMoreMenuApp.cp	0	0	• ▸
▽ **Resources**	0	0	▾
PPMoreMenu.PPob	n/a	n/a	▸
PPMoreMenu.rsrc	n/a	n/a	▸
▽ **Libraries**	0	0	• ▾
Startup.c	0	0	• ▸
runtime.o	0	0	▸
InterfaceLib	0	0	▸
ObjectSupportLib	0	0	▸
MWCSupportLib	0	0	▸
PowerPlantLib	0	0	▸
9 file(s)	0	0	

Figure 7.54 *The PowerPC version of the PPMoreMenu project.*

Chapter Summary

PowerPlant classes greatly reduce the amount of menu-handling code you'll need to write for an application. You will, however, need to create `Mcmd` resources for each MENU resource. That is something you don't need to do when you create an application without PowerPlant.

When the user makes a menu selection, PowerPlant sends a command to one of the objects in the application. The object that receives this command is referred to as a commander, or target. Through the use of the `ObeyCommand()` member function, the target object gets the first opportunity to handle the menu command. If the command doesn't pertain to the target, the target will pass the command up to the next higher object in the chain of command.

To keep track of the current state of each menu item, PowerPlant relies on the `FindCommandStatus()` member function. You can use this routine to tell PowerPlant under what conditions menu items should be enabled or disabled, or checked or unchecked.

Chapter 8

Panes, Constructor, and PowerPlant

An application framework takes care of much of the drudgery of programming. Its job is to handle the tasks common to all programs. Drawing is a big part of any Mac program—it's the graphics and text that are drawn to a window that makes one Mac program different from all other Macintosh applications. Because drawing varies with each program, you might suspect that this is the point where an application framework loses its effectiveness. Not so! Easing the task of drawing, and working with drawn objects, is where PowerPlant really shines.

In a PowerPlant project, you'll rely on panes to serve as areas of a window that hold drawn objects. Each pane will have the ability to draw itself (as in response to an update), and will have other features not found in a traditional Mac programming environment—like the ability to allow the user to drag a pane about a window. In this chapter you'll learn all about panes—the theory behind what they are, the creation of them using the Metrowerks Constructor, and an example program that uses a draggable pane.

Windows, Views, and Panes

Anything that is drawn in a PowerPlant-created program is drawn in a pane.

About PowerPlant Panes

A pane is a rectangle that occupies part or all of a window. A pane is an object that is derived from the PowerPlant LPane class. As one of its many member functions, the LPane class (and thus any class derived from LPane) includes a member function named DrawSelf(). This routine, as you probably have just guessed, draws the contents of the pane.

To create a self-contained drawing area in a window, a program creates a class derived from LPane or LView. The LView class is itself derived from LPane. A class derived directly from the LPane class is a pane, while a class derived from the LView class is a view. Objects derived from either class are drawing areas. The difference is that a view may contain other views or panes, while a pane may not.

If a drawing area is to hold a standard element of the Macintosh interface, such as a button or scroller, the program can create an object derived from one of the many PowerPlant classes, which themselves are derived from the LPane class. For example, the LScroller class is derived from LView (which is derived from LPane) and is used to add a scroll bar *inside* a window. Note that because the LScroller class is derived from LView (rather than directly from LPane), a scroll bar object is a view and as such may contain a view or pane within it. Typically, a scroller object will contain text or a picture object inside it.

A pane doesn't exist on its own; it is always inside something else. Typically, that "something" is a window. Thus a scroll bar in a window would be an `LScroller` object in an `LWindow` object (or objects derived from these classes). So that you realize the "pane connection" here, it's important to take note of the fact that both the `LScroller` and `LWindow` classes are derived from the `LView` class, which, in turn, is derived from the `LPane` class.

You've just read that a view is an object that can hold other views or panes. When a view does hold still another view or pane, it is said to be the superview of the held view or pane. For instance, a window is the superview of a scroll bar that appears in the window. From the scroll bar's perspective, it is considered a *subpane* of the window. This hierarchy doesn't carry on infinitely, of course. At the top is the window, which has no superview. A view that doesn't have a superview is called a *top level container*.

Creating Panes

Panes can be created using `Resorcerer` or the Metrowerks `Constructor`. Because `Constructor` provides a more graphical look at the panes you're creating, I'll describe its use in this chapter.

A pane (or view, or collection of panes and views) can be defined in a `PPob` resource. `Constructor` exists to create `PPob` resources. Using `Constructor` you can easily create a single `PPob` resource that defines a window and all of its views and panes. This collection is referred to as a *containment hierarchy*. Once you're satisfied with the look of a window and its subpanes, you can save the results in a `PPob` resource that's stored in a `Constructor` file. When you create your CodeWarrior project, you'll include this file in your project window. When you write your source code, you'll include code that reads the `PPob` data from the `Constructor` file and then creates an object (or objects) based on this information.

Using Constructor to Gain an Understanding of Panes

One way to explore the relationship of windows, views, and panes is to compare the look of an existing program that was created using the

PowerPlant framework with the PPob resources that are used by that program. You can do this by first running a program and taking note of the contents of one of the program's windows. Then run the Metrowerks Constructor and look at the PPob resource for that same window.

While the details of Constructor won't be covered until later in this chapter, the figures in this section will still provide you with a feel for how windows, views, and panes are used together. After reading this chapter, use the Constructor to explore the resource files of a few PowerPlant-created applications.

The full-featured Metrowerks CodeWarrior CD comes with several example PowerPlant projects. The CD's PowerPlant documentation provides a walk through many of the examples.

N O T E

Later in this chapter you'll see the source code for a PowerPlant-created application that displays a single window. Within the window of the PPDemoPane68K program is a box that can be clicked on and dragged about the window. Figure 8.1 shows that program.

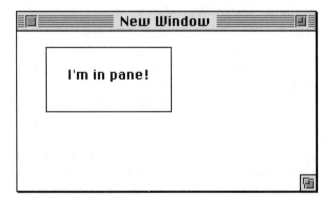

Figure 8.1 *The PPDemoPane program displays a window with a draggable box in it.*

The CodeWarrior project from which this example program was built includes a PPob resource file. When opened with the Constructor, I'm able to get a graphical look at the different pane-related components of the program. When I double-clicked on the large white object shown in Figure 8.2, Constructor told me that this object is a representation of the program's window—an LWindow object with an ID of 500.

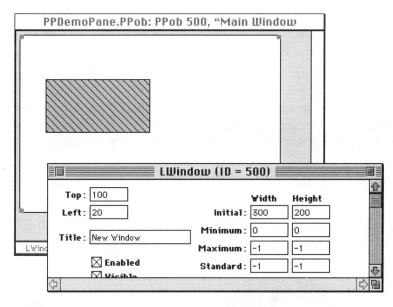

Figure 8.2 *Constructor allows you to view the class type of various objects in a window.*

The only object pictured in the window object in `Constructor` is a hatched rectangle. When I double-clicked on that object, `Constructor` let me know that this rectangle represented an `LPane` object with an ID of 520, as shown in Figure 8.3.

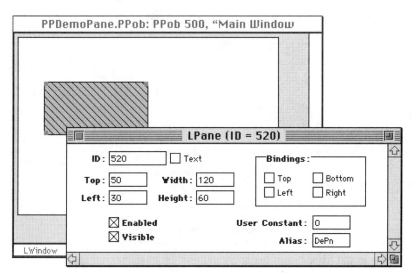

Figure 8.3 *The hatched object in the window object is of the LPane class.*

Figures 8.2 and 8.3 illustrate that the example program that I ran consisted of an `LWindow` object with a single pane object in it. As it turns out, the window's framed rectangle with the text drawn in it is the pane.

As another example, consider the `PaneView` demo—one of the PowerPlant examples found on the CodeWarrior CW5 CD. This program displays a window like the one shown in Figure 8.4. In this figure I've labeled the three objects that are held in this window. Figure 8.5 shows the `PPob` resource for this window, as seen in `Constructor`.

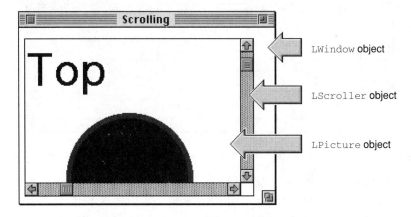

Figure 8.4 *A window with three objects in it.*

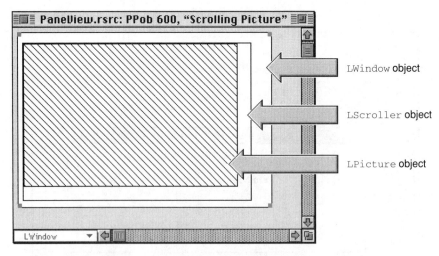

Figure 8.5 *The window of Figure 8.4, as viewed in Constructor.*

Looking at Figures 8.4 and 8.5 it may not be immediately obvious that panes are present in the program's window. If you look at the declarations of the `LWindow`, `LScroller`, and `LPicture` PowerPlant classes, though, you'll see the connection. Each of these three classes is derived from the `LView` class. The `LView` class, in turn, is derived from the `LPane` class. That tells you that all three of these object types will be able to do the things panes can do, such as draw themselves and respond to mouse clicks.

Creating a PPob Resource with Constructor

The PowerPlant examples you've seen to this point have all used a `PPob` resource to define a window, but you've had no exposure to creating one of these PowerPlant-specific resources. Now is the time. You'll find a folder named `PP Intro (from C06)` ƒ in the Chapter 8 example folder on this book's CD. I've copied this folder from the Chapter 6 example folder, but I've left out one file. You'll find that the `PPIntro.PPob` resource file is missing. In this section I'll end the mystery of where PPob files come from by using the Metrowerks `Constructor` to create a new version of the `PPIntro.PPob` file.

> You'll find a copy of `Constructor` on the included CD. This view editing application is undergoing an upgrade—you'll always find the latest version of it on the full-featured CodeWarrior CD.
>
> **N O T E**

Using Constructor to Create a PPob

When you launch `Constructor`, you'll see an opening screen like Figure 8.6. The untitled window that appears on the screen contains a list of resource types that `Constructor` recognizes. In version 2.0 of the ever-evolving `Constructor` program, only one resource type is editable—the view type. A view is the combination of a `WIND` resource and a `PPob` resource. The result is packaged together and is generally referred to as a `PPob` (as I've called it throughout the preceding two chapters).

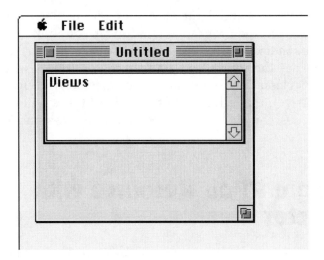

Figure 8.6 *The opening screen of Constructor displays a list that holds the view editor.*

A single Constructor file can contain more than one view, though the file I'll be working on here won't. To see a list of the different views in this file, double-click on **Views** in the window's list. The result is shown in Figure 8.7.

A view corresponds to a PPob resource. Thus Constructor is capable of holding data for more than one PPob. A single PPob resource stores information about one window and all of its subpanes.

N O T E

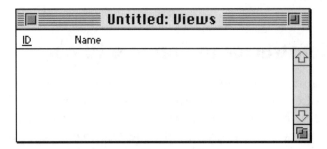

Figure 8.7 *A list that will eventually hold the views, or PPob resources, of a project.*

You'll notice that clicking on Views also opens a large, floating Tools palette. You won't use the Tools palette in this example. The palette is described later in this chapter.

N O T E

Unsurprisingly, there are no views in this new, empty file. To add a view, select **New View** from the Views menu. That will place one new view, with an ID of 128, in the window that holds the list of views (see Figure 8.8).

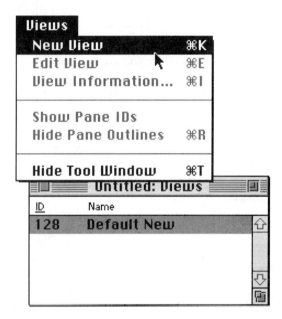

Figure 8.8 *Us the New View menu item to create a new view—a new PPob resource.*

You can change the default ID and name that **Constructor** gives the new view by selecting **View Information** from the Views menu. In Figure 8.9 you can see that I've given this view an ID of 500 and the name "Main Window."

Close the Information window and double-click on the view name in the view list. When you do, a view editor like the one shown in Figure 8.10 will open.

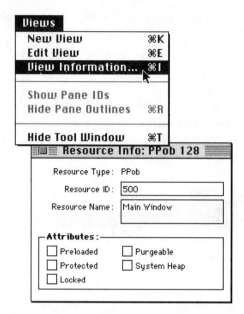

Figure 8.9 *Use the View Information menu item to change the ID and name of a PPob resource.*

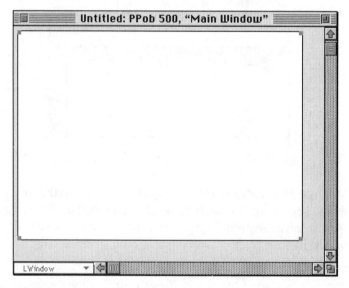

Figure 8.10 *The view editor allows you to add subpanes to a single PPob.*

The large white object in the window represents the boundaries of the window. By double-clicking on this object, you'll be able to edit many of the window's attributes. Figure 8.11 shows the settings I've used to define the window that you see in the PPIntro program.

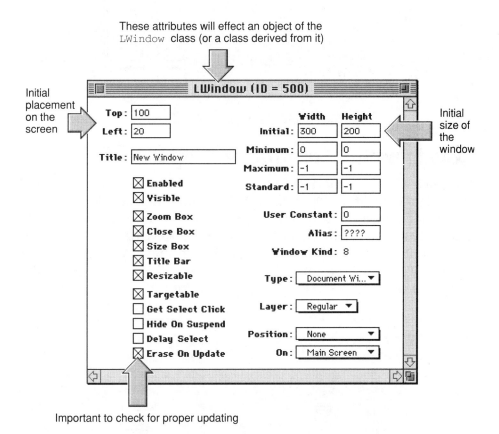

Figure 8.11 *Some of the key attributes of a window.*

That's all there is to creating a simple PPob using Constructor. Later in this chapter I'll return to Constructor to create a PPob that includes a pane in the window. Before quitting Constructor, be certain to select **Save As** from the File menu to save your work to a file. In Figure 8.12 you can see that I've typed in PPIntro.PPob as the file's name.

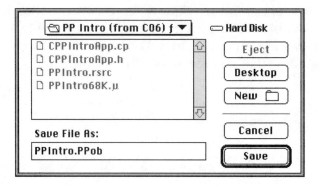

Figure 8.12 *Saving the PPob in a file.*

Examining the Constructor Output

Now, in a resource editor, let's see what the Constructor file looks like. Opening the PPIntro.PPob file with ResEdit, you'll see the resources shown in Figure 8.13. As described earlier, what I've been calling a PPob is actually a PPob resource and a WIND resource. ResEdit isn't capable of editing or viewing a PPob, but you can look at the WIND. Notice in the figure that the WIND information (such as **Top** and **Height**) matches the numbers I used in my session with the Constructor.

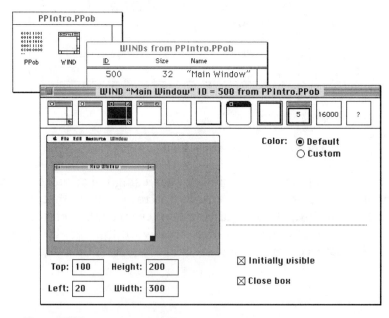

Figure 8.13 *Viewing the Constructor-created PPob resource in ResEdit.*

If you use Resorcerer as your resource editor, you will be able to view and edit PPob resources, though not in as graphical a manner as Constructor allows. Figure 8.14 shows part of the PPob resource created using Constructor.

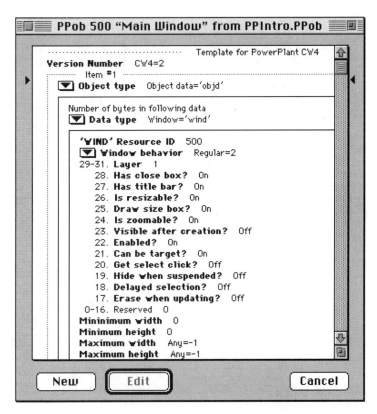

Figure 8.14 *Viewing the Constructor-created PPob resource in Resorcerer.*

A Pane Example

This chapter's PPDemoPane68K program opens a window that holds a single pane in it. It's surrounded by a 1-pixel-wide frame so that you can see the pane. Inside the pane is a string of text. On its own, this is no spectacular feat. The preceding could be achieved without going through the effort of creating a pane—a call to the Toolbox functions FrameRect() and DrawString() would do the trick. To show off the fact that a pane can do more than hold a simple drawing, PPDemoPane68K gives its pane the ability to be dragged about the window. When the

user clicks the mouse button on the frame and drags the mouse, an outline of the pane follows. When the user releases the mouse button, the
pane disappears from its old location and appears at the new location.
The entire pane, including its contents, are moved. Figure 8.15 illustrates this effect.

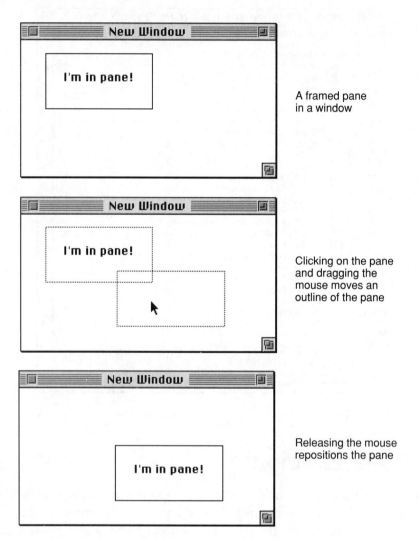

Figure 8.15 *The PPDemoPane68K program opens a
window that holds a pane that can be dragged.*

The user can even drag the pane partially off the window, as shown in Figure 8.16. The program will know not to draw any of the pane outside of the window. When the user drags the pane back onto the window, the pane and its contents will be restored.

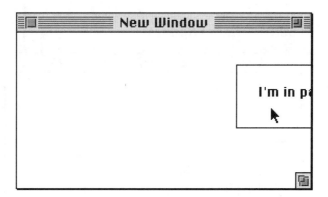

Figure 8.16 *The pane can be dragged beyond the edge of the window.*

Since `PPDemoPane68K` exists to demonstrate panes, the program makes minimal use of menus. In fact, the menus are identical to the ones seen in the first PowerPlant example in this book—the `PPIntro68K` program from Chapter 6. There are just the three standard menus, and only the Apple and File menus have enabled items in them. The File menu contains just a **Quit** item.

Creating the PPob File

You've had some exposure to `Constructor` and the `PPob` resource that `Constructor` creates, so the following pages should be an easy exercise for you. The `PPDemoPane68K` project needs a single `PPob` resource. That resource will hold the information for both the program's one window and the one pane that appears in that window.

The window information in `PPDemoPane.PPob` is identical to that found in the `PPIntro.PPob` file created earlier in this chapter. The file holds a single view; it has an ID of 500 and is named "Main Window." Recall that the ID and name are set with the **View Information** menu item. Figure 8.17 shows this.

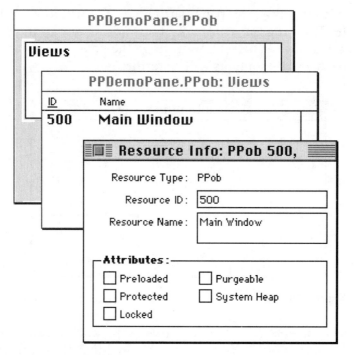

Figure 8.17 *Creating the new PPob resource in Constructor.*

Double-clicking on the window name in the Views list opens the view editor. The object in the editor represents the window that will be represented by an object of the LWindow class. Double-clicking on the object in the view editor allows you to edit the window information. If you compare Figure 8.18 to the figure that displayed the information for the window created in Constructor for the PPIntro program (Figure 8.11), you'll see that I've used all of the same values.

Now comes the new stuff. It's time to add a pane to the window. Move the cursor over the LPane icon at the top of the Tools floating palette and click the mouse button. With the mouse button held down, drag to the window in the view editor—an outline of the LPane icon will follow. This is demonstrated in Figure 8.19.

When you're over the window in the view editor, release the mouse button. You've just added a pane to the window, as shown in Figure 8.20. Don't worry about the pane's size or position in the window; those details can be altered at any time in Constructor.

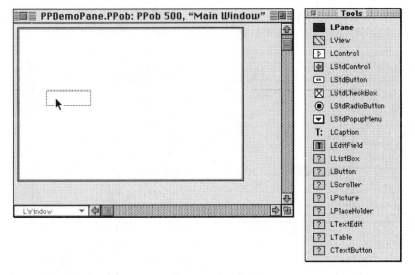

PPDemoPane.PPob: PPob 500, "Main Window"

LWindow (ID = 500)

Top: 100
Left: 20

Title: New Window

	Width	Height
Initial:	300	200
Minimum:	0	0
Maximum:	-1	-1
Standard:	-1	-1

☒ Enabled
☒ Visible
☒ Zoom Box
☒ Close Box
☒ Size Box
☒ Title Bar
☒ Resizable
☒ Targetable
☐ Get Select Click
☐ Hide On Suspend
☐ Delay Select
☒ Erase On Update

User Constant: 0
Alias: ????
Window Kind: 8

Type: Document Wi...▼
Layer: Regular ▼
Position: None ▼
On: Main Screen ▼

LWindow

Figure 8.18 *Editing the attributes of the PPob window.*

PPDemoPane.PPob: PPob 500, "Main Window"

LWindow

Tools
■ LPane
◩ LView
▷ LControl
◈ LStdControl
ᵒᵏ LStdButton
☒ LStdCheckBox
◉ LStdRadioButton
▼ LStdPopupMenu
T: LCaption
T LEditField
? LListBox
? LButton
? LScroller
? LPicture
? LPlaceHolder
? LTextEdit
? LTable
? CTextButton

Figure 8.19 *Using the Tools palette to add a pane to a window.*

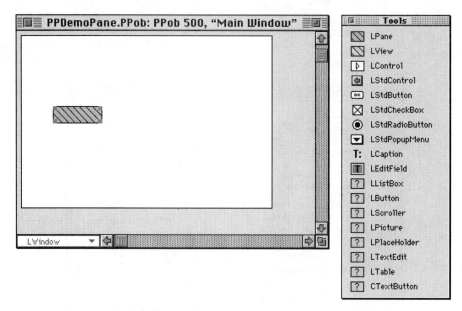

Figure 8.20 *Releasing the mouse button adds the new pane to the window.*

Now double-click on the pane in the window. When you do, you'll see a pane editor like Figure 8.21. Here you can give the pane an ID and set its size and position. I've given the pane an ID in the 500 range to show it's related to the window (which has an ID of 500). While this makes sense, it isn't vital, I could have given the pane a different ID.

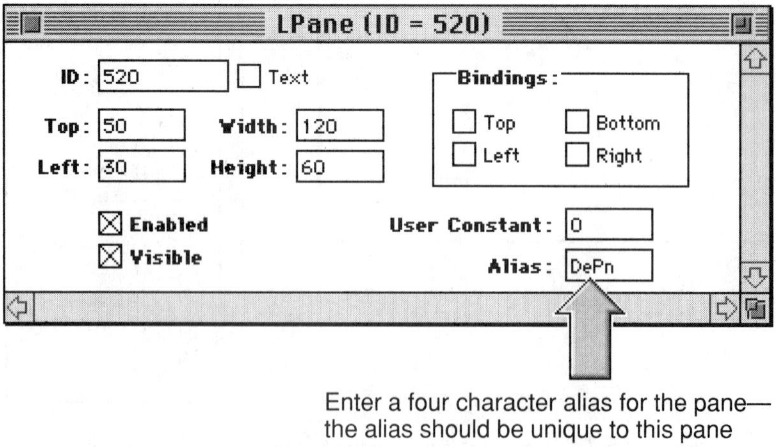

```
┌─────────────────────────────────────────────────────────┐
│ ▓▓▓▓▓▓▓▓▓▓▓▓▓▓▓  LPane (ID = 520)  ▓▓▓▓▓▓▓▓▓▓▓▓▓          │
├─────────────────────────────────────────────────────────┤
│                                                      ⇧   │
│    ID: [520]        ☐ Text     ┌─Bindings:─────────┐     │
│                                │                    │     │
│  Top: [50]    Width: [120]     │ ☐ Top    ☐ Bottom  │     │
│ Left: [30]   Height: [60]      │ ☐ Left   ☐ Right   │     │
│                                └────────────────────┘     │
│         ☒ Enabled          User Constant: [0]             │
│         ☒ Visible                                         │
│                                  Alias: [DePn]       ⇩   │
│ ⇦                                            ⇨  ▦        │
└─────────────────────────────────────────────────────────┘
```

Enter a four character alias for the pane—
the alias should be unique to this pane

Figure 8.21 *Double-clicking on a pane opens a pane editor.*

In Figure 8.21 you can see that I've filled in a four-character *alias* for the pane. This alias will be used in your source code when you register the class that will be associated with this pane. I'll have more to say about this alias a little later in this chapter. For now, it's enough to know that you can use any four characters, provided they aren't all lowercase characters—strings that are all lowercase are reserved by PowerPlant. You can use the four characters to hint at what the alias stands for. I've used DePn to stand for "Demo Pane."

When you're finished adding information in the pane editor, close it. In Figure 8.22 you can see that Constructor enlarged the pane in the window because I increased its size in the pane editor.

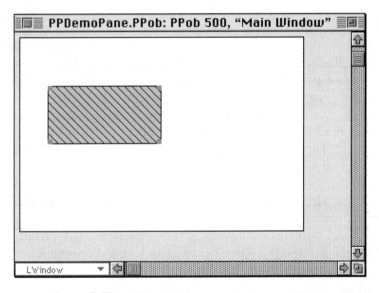

Figure 8.22 *A change of the pane's size in the pane editor will be reflected in the Constructor view editor.*

That's it for adding the pane. If you haven't done so already, save the file by selecting **Save As** from the File menu. Name it PPDemoPane.PPob.

The PPDemoPane68K Project

A program's PowerPlant project typically includes one source code file for each class declared by the program. That source code file in turn includes a header file. The header file declares the class, and the source

Metrowerks CodeWarrior Programming for the Mac

254

code file defines the member functions of that class. The example PowerPlant projects you've seen in this book have followed this convention. Each of my examples has declared a single class (derived from LApplication), and each example has had a single .cp source code file to hold the code for this one class. Each example also has had a single .h header file that was used in an #include directive by that source code file.

You've also seen this pairing of header and source files in the PowerPlant library of classes. Each PowerPlant class is declared in an .h file, while the member functions for that class appear in a .cp file. Examples are LWindow.h/LWindow.cp and LApplication.h/LApplication.cp.

The PPDemoPane example declares two classes, so its project holds two source code files. The first class is the application class that all PowerPlant programs must have. Its class is declared in the CPPDemoPaneApp.h header file, and its member function code appears in CPPDemoPaneApp.cp. The second class is a class used to define a pane object. This class is declared in the header file CTestPane.h, and its member functions are defined in CTestPane.cp. Figure 8.23 shows the two .cp files in the PPDemoPane68K.μ project window.

Recall that the file name for an application-defined class in a PowerPlant project should be the class name. From Figure 8.23 you can surmise that the PPDemoPane68K program has a class named CPPDemoPaneApp and a class named CTestPane.

The PPDemoPane68K Resources

The PPDemoPane68K project holds two resource files. The first, PPDemoPane.PPob, was created in Constructor earlier in this chapter. It holds the PPob resource for the program's one window.

The second file, PPDemoPane.rsrc, holds the standard Macintosh resources such as the MBAR and MENU resources. Figure 8.24 shows the resource file, as viewed in ResEdit. The contents of this resource file are identical to those found in the PPIntro program of Chapter 6. If you need a refresher on any of these resources, refer back to Chapters 6 and 7.

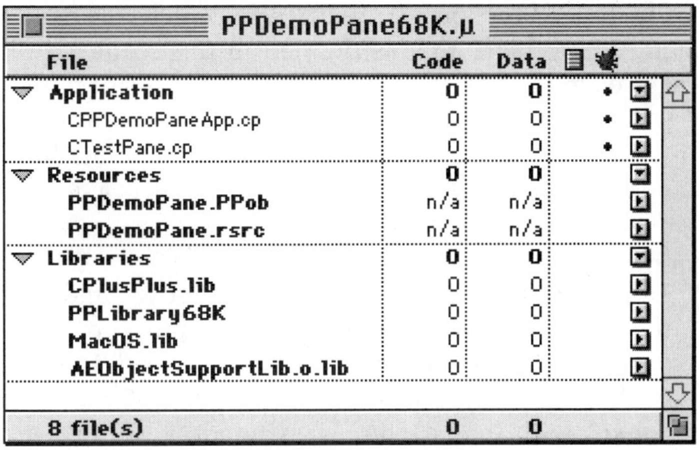

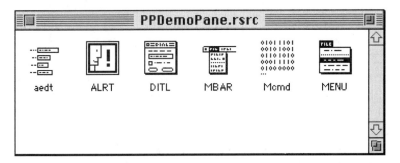

Figure 8.23 *The PPDemoPane68K project window.*

Figure 8.24 *The resources for the PPDemoPane68K project.*

The Pane Class

As an application is represented by an object (derived from the LApplication class), and as a window is represented by an object (of the LWindow class, or a class derived from it), a pane is represented by an object. The pane will be derived from both the LPane and LCommander classes.

The member functions that will be a part of the pane class depend on the functionality that the pane object is to have. The LPane class consists of about 75 member functions, so there's plenty that you can do with a pane. Your application-defined pane class will of course inherit all of these member functions, so your pane object will have access to each of them. Many work fine as defined in the LPane.cp file; others you'll want to override and tailor to the specific needs of your pane. For example, you won't need to override the LPane member functions Show() and Hide(). Another example of an LPane member function that is general enough for use with any pane is ResizeFrame(), which, of course, changes the size of a pane.

NOTE Don't confuse the LPane versions of Show() and Hide() with the LWindow versions used in the Chapter 7 example PPMore MenuApp68K. Remember, different classes can declare functions of the same name. In PPMoreMenuApp68K I used Hide() and Show() with the LWindow class window mDisplayWindow, as shown here:

```
mDisplayWindow->Hide();
```

If you use Hide() with a pane, the LPane class version of the function will be used to hide the pane, not a window.

Other LPane functions not only *should* be overridden, they *must* be overridden. In particular, a class derived from LPane must override the DrawSelf() function. PowerPlant invokes the DrawSelf() function to draw the contents of a pane. Because the contents of a pane are specific to an application, PowerPlant can't possibly know what to draw in a pane. For instance, the PPDemoPane68K program has a pane that has a one-pixel-wide frame drawn along its border, and text that says "I'm in pane!" drawn near its center. This drawing takes place in the overridden version of DrawSelf().

The other function that a class derived from LPane *must* override is ClickSelf(). This function is called by PowerPlant when the user clicks the mouse on a pane. Again, how a program responds to a mouse click on a pane is an application-specific issue. A program may allow the pane to be dragged, may hide the pane, or may perform any number of other actions to the pane. Or, it might ignore the mouse click all together. The PPDemoPane68K program drags its pane in response to a user clicking on it.

Any pane class declared by a program must have its objects built from a *stream*. In C++, a stream is a general term for a flow of data. The class constructor, along with one other function, takes care of this. You'll read more about streams just ahead.

NOTE

Here's an example of an ANSI C++ line of code that uses a stream:

```
cout << "Enter your age: ";
```

If you've ever used `cout` in a C++ program, you've used a stream. `cout` is an object that corresponds to the standard output stream. This stream "flows" data representing text to the monitor. The C++ header file that holds the declaration of cout, `iostream.h`, provides you with a strong hint that `cout` works with streams.

Now that you know a class derived from `LPane` must override `DrawSelf()` and `ClickSelf()`, and needs to have a function or two for the creation of an object from a stream, you should have a pretty good idea of what a minimal application-defined pane class looks like. Here's the pane class declaration from the `PPDemoPane68K` program. Each of the four member functions that are a part of the `CTestPane` class is discussed in this chapter.

```
class  CTestPane : public LPane, public LCommander
{
    public:
        CTestPane( LStream *inStream );
        static  CTestPane*  CreateTestPaneStream( LStream *inStream );

    protected:
        virtual void  DrawSelf();
        virtual void  ClickSelf( const SMouseDownEvent  &inMouseDown );
};
```

NOTE

For simplicity, I've omitted the `ObeyCommand()` and `Find CommandStatus()` member functions from this program's two classes. The only menus and menu items that `PPDemoPane68K` includes are the standard ones that PowerPlant handles without any help from my code.

Registering the Pane

Earlier in this chapter I said that any pane class declared by a program must have its objects built from a stream, and that a stream is a general term for a flow of data. In a PowerPlant program this stream of data is the PPob information that was saved to a file by Constructor.

For every pane class in your program, you need to call Register Class(). This URegistrar class function registers the class. Registering a class consists of pairing the pane's alias with a function used to create an object of this particular pane class. Recall that the alias for a pane was set in Constructor. Here's the call to RegisterClass() for the CTestPane class:

```
URegistrar::RegisterClass( 'DePn',
          (ClassCreatorFunc) CTestPane::CreateTestPaneStream);
```

The two parameters to RegisterClass() are the pane alias and a pointer to the class member function used to create an object of this class type. Figure 8.25 shows where these two parameters come from.

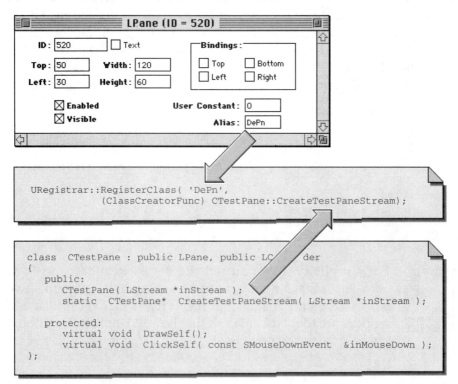

Figure 8.25 *Registering a pane in a PowerPlant project.*

The registering of classes typically takes place in the application's constructor function. Except for this one additional registration, the body of the constructor function for the `CPPDemoPaneApp` class is the same as that of the `CPPIntroApp` class in the Chapter 6 program `PPIntro68K`.

```
CPPDemoPaneApp :: CPPDemoPaneApp()
{
   URegistrar::RegisterClass( 'wind',
             (ClassCreatorFunc) LWindow::CreateWindowStream );
   URegistrar::RegisterClass( 'DePn',
             (ClassCreatorFunc) CTestPane::CreateTestPaneStream);

   mDisplayWindow = LWindow::CreateWindow( WIND_display, this );

   mDisplayWindow->Show();
}
```

In the preceding example the alias `DePn` is paired with the `Create TestPaneStream()` function. When a window that holds a pane of this type is created, PowerPlant will be able to match the pane's alias with the function that creates the pane. A new pane object will be created and placed in the window. The line of code that creates the window is shown above, I'll repeat it here:

```
mDisplayWindow = LWindow::CreateWindow( WIND_display, this );
```

Now let's look at the pane class member function that creates the new pane object:

```
CTestPane*  CTestPane :: CreateTestPaneStream( LStream *inStream )
{
   return ( new CTestPane( inStream ) );
}
```

The above *pane-creation* function accepts a pointer to the `LStream` object that holds the `PPob` data and returns a pointer to the new pane object that gets created. Remember, the pane-creation function is called by PowerPlant from the `CreateWindow()` function—your program doesn't have to call it explicitly. That also means your program does not have to be concerned with the `LStream` class—PowerPlant passes in this parameter. The pane-creation function simply calls the pane class constructor, passing along the stream that holds the `PPob` data to read. The *construct-from-stream* constructor function calls the base class constructor—the constructor for `LPane`.

```
CTestPane :: CTestPane( LStream  *inStream ) : LPane( inStream )
{

}
```

If the registering of a class and the subsequent creation of a class object seem a bit confusing, keep the following points in mind:

- For each pane class, call `RegisterClass()`.
- The first parameter to `RegisterClass()` is the pane's alias, as defined in `Constructor`.
- The second parameter to `RegisterClass()` is a pointer to the class pane-creation function.
- The pane-creation function name follows this format: `Create[class name - leading C]Sream()`. Thus for class `CTestPane`, the function is `CreateTestPaneStream()`.
- The pane-creation function calls the pane's constructor.
- The pane's construct-from-stream constructor calls the `LPane` base class constructor.

Overriding DrawSelf()

When a pane needs updating, PowerPlant will call the pane object's `DrawSelf()` function. That's why your pane class needs to override this `LPane` function. Here's how the `CTestPane` class overrides it:

```
void  CTestPane :: DrawSelf( void )
{
   Rect   frame;

   CalcLocalFrameRect( frame );
   ::FrameRect( &frame );

   ::TextFont( systemFont );
   ::TextSize( 12 );
   ::MoveTo( frame.left + 20, frame.top + 30 );
   ::DrawString( "\pI'm in pane!" );
}
```

The `DrawSelf()` function begins by calling `CalcLocalFrameRect()`. This routine, inherited from the `LPane` class, returns the location of the rectangle that holds the pane. The coordinates are local to the pane's superview. In this program the pane's superview is the window. With the boundaries of the pane known, DrawSelf() can frame the pane with a call to the Toolbox function FrameRect().

 The superview of a pane could be a view. Recall from the first section in this chapter that a window can hold a view, and the view in turn can hold one or more panes.

N O T E

DrawSelf() finishes with Toolbox calls that set up and draw the text inside the pane. TextFont() sets the font to the system font, also known as Chicago. TextSize() sets the font to 12 points. A call to MoveTo() sets drawing to begin 20 pixels from the left edge of the pane and 30 pixels from the top of the pane. A call to DrawString() does the drawing.

Overriding ClickSelf()

When the user clicks on the CTestPane object, PowerPlant calls Click Self(). CTestPane overrides the LPane ClickSelf() member function so that PowerPlant calls the program's version of this function. In this version ClickSelf() responds by dragging the pane as the user drags the mouse. Here's a look at ClickSelf():

```
void  CTestPane :: ClickSelf( const SMouseDownEvent &inMouseDown )
{
   Rect    oldFrame;
   Rect    newFrame;
   Point   oldPoint;
   Point   newPoint;
   Int32   horizChange;
   Int32   vertChange;

   SwitchTarget( this );
   FocusDraw();

   ::PenNormal();
   ::PenPat( &qd.gray );
   ::PenMode( patXor );

   oldPoint = newPoint = inMouseDown.whereLocal;
   CalcLocalFrameRect( oldFrame );
   newFrame = oldFrame;
```

```
while ( ::StillDown() )
{
    ::GetMouse( &newPoint );

    if ( ::EqualPt( newPoint, oldPoint ) == false )
    {
        ::FrameRect( &oldFrame );
        ::OffsetRect( &newFrame, newPoint.h - oldPoint.h,
                      newPoint.v - oldPoint.v );
        ::FrameRect( &newFrame );
        oldPoint = newPoint;
        oldFrame = newFrame;
    }
}

horizChange = newPoint.h - inMouseDown.whereLocal.h;
vertChange  = newPoint.v - inMouseDown.whereLocal.v;
if ( horizChange != 0 || vertChange != 0 )
    MoveBy( horizChange, vertChange, true );

::PenNormal();
}
```

ClickSelf() begins by making the pane the target. When the CTestPane object receives a click, it calls SwitchTarget(this) to make itself the target. Next, ClickSelf() prepares for drawing in the pane by calling FocusDraw(). Because a pane doesn't have its own coordinate system, it relies on that of its superview.

The primary task of ClickSelf() is to track the mouse movements for as long as the user holds down the mouse button. A while loop accomplishes this. The Toolbox function StillDown() is at the center of the while test. Before the loop begins, calls to three Toolbox functions set the pen to a dashed gray so that as the pane is dragged, its outline can be dragged about the window. Then, variables representing the old and new mouse location are set up. Finally, variables representing the old and new pane frame are set.

The while loop body offsets the pane rectangle and surrounds it in a dashed gray frame. The loop body draws only this ghost of a frame, not the pane contents. This occurs only once the user has released the mouse button and ended the while loop. When that happens, the change from the final position of the pane to its starting position is calculated. Then a call to the inherited `LPane` function `MoveBy()` is made. This function moves the pane by wiping it out at its old, original location, and redrawing it at its new location. Of course, `MoveBy()` isn't directly doing the drawing—its the `CTestPane` `DrawSelf()` member function that is being invoked by PowerPlant when `MoveBy()`is called.

The CTestPane.h Header Listing

The declaration of the `CTestPane` class is made in the `CTestPane.h` header file, which is shown here.

```
#pragma once

#include <LPane.h>
#include <LCommander.h>

class  CTestPane : public LPane, public LCommander
{
    public:
        CTestPane( LStream *inStream );

        static  CTestPane*  CreateTestPaneStream( LStream *inStream );

    protected:
        virtual void  DrawSelf();
        virtual void  ClickSelf( const SMouseDownEvent  &inMouseDown );
};
```

The CTestPane.cp Source Code Listing

The `CTestPane.cp` source code file holds the definitions of the `CTest Pane` class member functions. `CreateTestPaneStream()` is invoked by PowerPlant when `CreateWindow()` is called to create a new window. `CreateTestPaneStream()` simply calls the `CTestPane` class constructor to create a new pane object. The `CTestPane` calls the `LPane` constructor to do the work of getting `PPob` information from the stream.

The `DrawSelf()` function gets called by PowerPlant in response to the update of the window. The `ClickSelf()` function is invoked by PowerPlant in reaction to a click of the mouse on the pane.

```
// ============================================================
//                                        include header files

#include "CTestPane.h"


// ============================================================
//           create a CTestPane pane from a PPob resource

CTestPane*  CTestPane :: CreateTestPaneStream( LStream *inStream )
{
   return ( new CTestPane( inStream ) );
}



// ============================================================
//                  the construct-from-stream constructor

CTestPane :: CTestPane( LStream  *inStream ) : LPane( inStream )
{

}



// ============================================================
//                       draw the pane's frame and contents

void  CTestPane :: DrawSelf( void )
{
   Rect   frame;

   CalcLocalFrameRect( frame );
   ::FrameRect( &frame );

   ::TextFont( systemFont );
   ::TextSize( 12 );
   ::MoveTo( frame.left + 20, frame.top + 30 );
   ::DrawString( "\pI'm in pane!" );
}



// ============================================================
//                       respond to a mouse click on the pane

void  CTestPane :: ClickSelf( const SMouseDownEvent &inMouseDown )
{
   Rect    oldFrame;
```

```
Rect    newFrame;
Point   oldPoint;
Point   newPoint;
Int32   horizChange;
Int32   vertChange;

SwitchTarget( this );
FocusDraw();

::PenNormal();
::PenPat( &qd.gray );
::PenMode( patXor );

oldPoint = newPoint = inMouseDown.whereLocal;
CalcLocalFrameRect( oldFrame );
newFrame = oldFrame;

while ( ::StillDown() )
{
    ::GetMouse( &newPoint );

    if ( ::EqualPt( newPoint, oldPoint ) == false )
    {
        ::FrameRect( &oldFrame );
        ::OffsetRect( &newFrame, newPoint.h - oldPoint.h,
                        newPoint.v - oldPoint.v );
        ::FrameRect( &newFrame );
        oldPoint = newPoint;
        oldFrame = newFrame;
    }
}

horizChange = newPoint.h - inMouseDown.whereLocal.h;
vertChange  = newPoint.v - inMouseDown.whereLocal.v;
if ( horizChange != 0 || vertChange != 0 )
    MoveBy( horizChange, vertChange, true );

::PenNormal();
}
```

The CPPDemoPaneApp.h Header Listing

The CPPDemoPaneApp class is the application class required of all
PowerPlant projects. This class consists of a constructor function and a
pointer to a window object.

```
#pragma once

#include <LApplication.h>

class  LWindow;

class  CPPDemoPaneApp : public LApplication
{
   public:
      CPPDemoPaneApp();

   protected:
      LWindow   *mDisplayWindow;
};
```

The CPPDemoPaneApp.cp Source Code Listing

The listing for CPPDemoPaneApp.cp consists of just the main() function
and the constructor for the CPPDemoPaneApp class.

```
// ============================================================
//                                          include header files

#include "CPPDemoPaneApp.h"
#include "CTestPane.h"
#include <LWindow.h>
#include <UDrawingState.h>
#include <URegistrar.h>


// ============================================================
//                                          constant definitions

const ResIDT   WIND_display = 500;


// ============================================================
//                                                        main()

void  main( void )
{
   UQDGlobals::InitializeToolbox( &qd );

   CPPDemoPaneApp theApp;
   theApp.Run();
}
```

```
// ============================================================
//                        CPPDemoPaneApp class constructor

CPPDemoPaneApp :: CPPDemoPaneApp()
{
   URegistrar::RegisterClass( 'wind',
            (ClassCreatorFunc) LWindow::CreateWindowStream );
   URegistrar::RegisterClass( 'DePn',
            (ClassCreatorFunc) CTestPane::CreateTestPaneStream);

   mDisplayWindow = LWindow::CreateWindow( WIND_display, this );

   mDisplayWindow->Show();
}
```

Chapter Summary

In a PowerPlant-created project, it is the pane that holds a drawing. A pane object is derived (directly or indirectly) from the PowerPlant LPane class. A pane serves as a self-contained drawing area that knows how to respond to mouse clicks and how to redraw, or update, itself.

Panes are created using Constructor, the Metrowerks application that is a graphical editor of PPob resources. You'll save a PPob resource in a Constructor file, include that file in a project, and then write source code that reconstructs a pane object from the data held in the Constructor file.

Chapter 9

ZoneRanger and Macintosh Memory

When a Macintosh application launches, the operating system allocates a section of memory devoted to just that application. This section, or partition, includes an application heap, also called a heap or heap zone. In this chapter you'll see just what goes on in the heap—how individual blocks of memory are allocated within this heap, and how pointers and handles in your application are used to access these memory blocks.

ZoneRanger is a Macintosh program that is included on the Metrowerks CodeWarrior CD, and the CD that accompanies this book. This software utility is used as a memory checker. ZoneRanger "spies" on the heap zone of each application that is running on your Macintosh. There are many difficult-to-grasp concepts included in the theory of how an application is stored in memory. ZoneRanger provides a numerical and graphical look at how each running application is using memory. With this information you'll be able to gain a better understanding of Macintosh memory and, in the process, determine how much memory your application uses, how much free space it leaves unused, and how it can make more efficient use of the memory allocated to it.

Macintosh Memory

Gaining an understanding of how an application uses memory is paramount to developing Macintosh applications that are free of bugs. Knowing how a program is stored in RAM also allows you to reserve just the right amount of memory for it—a practice that end users will appreciate.

N O T E
The memory model discussed in this section applies to 680x0-based Macintosh computers. The memory model for PowerPC-based Macs has many similarities, and some differences, to that of the 680x0 model. If you're programming for 680x0-based Macintoshes, all of the information in this section applies. If you're creating fat applications, all of the information again applies. In the unlikely event that your application will be PowerPC-only, read this section to gain a background on Macintosh memory. After reading about ZoneRanger and walking through a 680x0 example later in this chapter, you'll be ready for the last section in this chapter, "ZoneRanger and Native PowerPC Programs." It points out some important differences between 680x0 memory and Power Mac memory. For more Power Mac memory details, refer to *Inside Macintosh: PowerPC System Software* or the M&T book *Programming the PowerPC*.

Memory Overview

When a program is launched, the Macintosh operating system locates a section of free RAM in which to load some or all of the launched application's code. During the entire time that the application is running, the memory that makes up this *application partition* is devoted to that application. When the user quits an application, the partition's memory returns to the pool of free memory and becomes available for use by the next application that is launched.

An application partition consists of four principle sections: an *A5 World*, an *application stack*, an *application heap*, and a section of free memory between the application stack and heap. These four areas of memory can be found in each program that is running. Figure 9.1 illustrates these sections for a Macintosh that has two applications, or *processes*, executing.

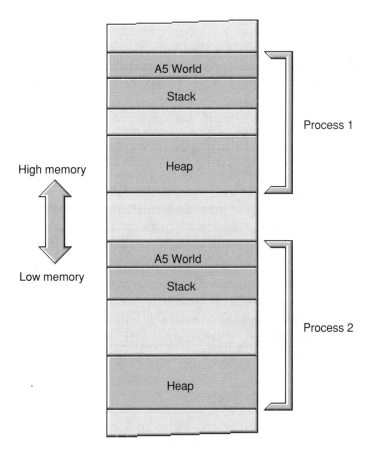

Figure 9.1 *Macintosh RAM with two applications running.*

An application's A5 World is a section of memory that holds that application's global variables. This area of memory is named after the central processing unit register that the operating system uses to keep track of just where this memory section starts—the A5 register.

The A5 World holds the values of an application's global variables. The application stack, on the other hand, holds information local to routines in the program. The stack is primarily used to hold parameters, local variables, and return addresses.

The application heap is used to hold the executable code of an application, as well as data structures created as the result of Toolbox calls. Application-created data also gets stored in the heap.

When a program is launched, the operating system determines the amount of memory that should be devoted to the application's A5 World. Because the number of global variables in an application is fixed, the size of the A5 World will remain constant during the execution of an application. The same is not true of the application stack and the application heap. As functions are called, the size of the stack will grow and shrink as parameters are passed and local variables are created and destroyed. And as an application executes, the size of the heap will also grow and shrink as code and resources get loaded and unloaded.

The free, unallocated memory that lies between the stack and the heap of an application partition is used by both the stack and the heap. The bottom of the stack is fixed in memory, just beneath the A5 World. As the stack becomes larger, it grows downward in memory. As the heap becomes larger, it grows upward in memory, toward the stack (as shown in Figure 9.2).

While the A5 World, the stack, and the heap are all important areas of an application partition, it is the heap area that ZoneRanger tracks. When an application you've built executes, its code will be in the application heap. As your program executes, it will load resource code into the heap. Before looking at ZoneRanger, a little more background information on the heap will be helpful.

The Application Heap

As your application executes, the Memory Manager will allocate and deallocate blocks of memory in the heap. Each block of memory is a

contiguous series of bytes that holds a segment of executable code (a
CODE resource), resource data (such as WIND, MENU, or DLOG data), or
application data (such as the contents of a struct). Each of these blocks
has a size and type, and, possibly, one or more attributes. To keep track
of this information, each block begins with a block header. Figure 9.3
shows a section of memory with a single process (application) executing. Within this example application heap are three blocks of data, each
beginning with a block header.

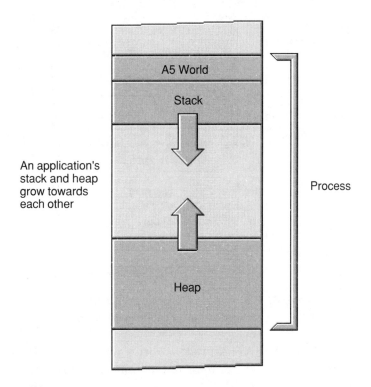

Figure 9.2 *An application's heap and stack grow toward one another.*

Because low memory is pictured at the bottom of Figure 9.3,
the start of a block of memory is at the bottom of the block.

N O T E

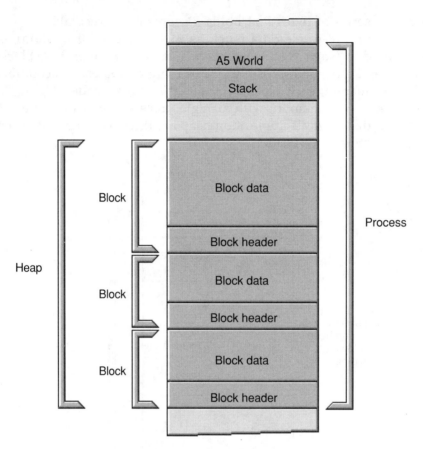

Figure 9.3 *Each block begins with a header that provides descriptive information about the block.*

The size of each block, given in bytes, varies with the block's contents. The type of block can be either relocatable, nonrelocatable, or free.

A relocatable block can be moved about in the heap. The Memory Manager will occasionally move relocatable blocks so that it can make the most efficient use of memory. The contents of a relocatable block are accessed by your program through the use of a handle.

A nonrelocatable block cannot be moved in memory. Whatever memory location a nonrelocatable block is originally placed in is the location at which it will remain until the application terminates.

A free block is exactly as its name implies—an unallocated area of memory that is free to accept data and become a relocatable or nonrelocatable block.

Relocatable Blocks

In addition to the size and type of block, the block header for a relocatable block also lists the block's three *attributes*. A relocatable block can have the attributes of being *locked* or *unlocked*, *purgeable* or *unpurgeable*, *resource data* or *nonresource* data.

If a relocatable block has its locked/unlocked attribute set to **locked**, the block is no longer free to be moved about in memory. A relocatable block may occasionally and temporarily be locked so that the Memory Manager won't move the block while the block's data is being accessed by the application.

If a relocatable block's purgeable/unpurgeable attribute is set to **purgeable**, the Memory Manager is given the freedom to purge, or deallocate, the data in the block. This purging won't happen indiscriminately, however. Only when the Memory Manager cannot find free heap memory to satisfy an application's need to load other data will the Memory Manager purge an existing block.

If a relocatable block has its resource data/nonresource data attribute set to **resource data**, you know that the block holds the data from a resource.

In Figure 9.3 you saw a heap with three blocks in it. There, no gaps of free memory existed between blocks. The more likely scenario is that during the course of loading and unloading relocatable, purgeable blocks, gaps of free memory will develop, as shown in Figure 9.4. To eliminate these blocks of free memory (which are often too small to be of use when loading other blocks), the Memory Manager will periodically perform memory compaction. Memory compaction shuffles relocatable blocks (that are not locked) in an attempt to eliminate as many of the memory gaps as possible.

Your application will always access a relocatable block through a handle. Here's part of a function that uses a local variable to store a picture handle that is returned by the Toolbox function GetPicture():

```
void GetPictureResource( short pictID )
{
    PicHandle thePicture;

    thePicture = GetPicture( pictID );
    ...
}
```

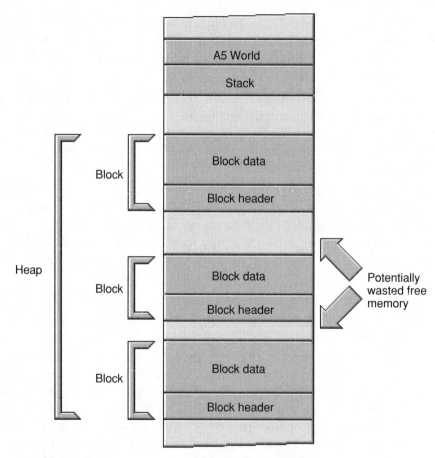

Figure 9.4 *The Memory Manager compacts memory to create one large, free block of memory from other, smaller blocks of free memory.*

While the relocatable block (which holds the PICT resource code) will be in the heap, the handle will be on the stack. That's because in the above snippet the handle is declared to be a local variable.

A handle is a program's means of keeping track of a relocatable block of memory. This is done through *double indirection*—also referred to as *double dereferencing*. A handle holds the address of a master pointer, and the master pointer in turn holds the starting address of the relocatable block. The master pointer is always in the heap and is always fixed—it cannot be relocated. Figure 9.5 shows a stack with three items in it. One of those items is a handle. In the figure you can see that the handle points to the master pointer, while the master pointer points to the relocatable block.

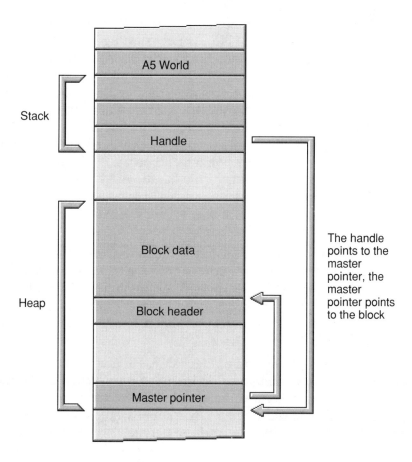

Figure 9.5 *A handle leads to a master pointer which in turn leads to a relocatable block.*

NOTE Because lower addresses are assumed to be at the bottom of Mac memory illustrations, the start of any area of memory is at the area's bottom. With that in mind, the master pointer in Figure 9.5 is shown pointing to the first address of the block's data, not at the start of the block's header. This is correct. The block header information is used by the Memory Manager. Your application will be interested in the block data.

Keeping Track of Relocatable Blocks

When the Memory Manager moves a relocatable block, the Memory Manager will make note of the block's new starting address by updating the fixed master pointer. Thus the master pointer will always hold the correct address of the relocatable block. The master pointer has the address of the moved block, but how does the handle variable (which is your program's means of keeping track of a relocatable block) also become aware of the block's new address? The handle, as it turns out, doesn't have to do anything to keep track of this change. The handle holds the address of the master pointer, and because the master pointer is fixed in the heap, the contents of the handle need never change (see Figure 9.6). For simplicity, this figure uses a little symbolism rather than using real addresses—assume that A, B, and C each represent a RAM address.

In the memory pictured to the left of the figure, the handle holds an address we'll call A. Looking at address A we see that this memory location holds a master pointer, as expected. Examining the contents of the master pointer reveals that it holds an address, B. At address B is a block of data. This is the double-indirection that a handle uses to lead to a block of data.

Now observe the right side of Figure 9.6. Here you can see that the relocatable block has been moved down in memory. When the Memory Manager performed this move, it updated the contents of the block's master pointer. The master pointer now properly holds the new starting address of the block; address C. And the handle? No change to its contents are necessary. It still points to the fixed master pointer. The unchanging handle uses the changing contents of the master pointer to always track down the moving block of data.

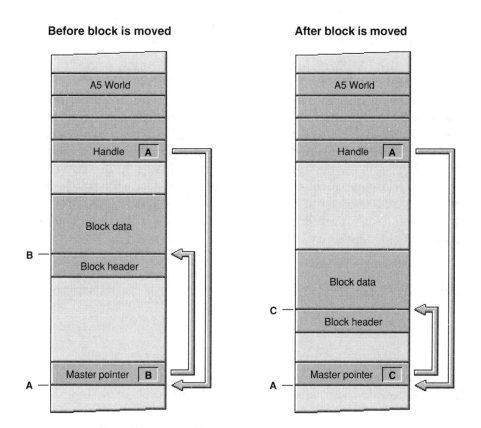

Figure 9.6 *When a relocatable block moves,
its master pointer is updated to hold the new block address.*

In Figure 9.6, note that the handle and the master pointer don't move—even after the block moves. The handle still sits comfortably on the stack, while the master pointer still remains at its original place in the heap.

Nonrelocatable Blocks

A block that is referenced by a handle is relocatable. A block that is referenced by a pointer is nonrelocatable. A nonrelocatable block never moves about in the heap. Instead, it remains at a fixed location until the program either explicitly disposes of it (as opposed to a relocatable block, which can be purged by the Memory Manager without intervention by your program) or until your program quits.

When the Memory Manager compacts memory, nonrelocatable blocks remain unmoved. Thus a nonrelocatable block has the undesirable side effect of creating an "island" in the middle of free memory. While the free memory on either side of a nonrelocatable block can eventually be used to hold other blocks, they can't be used to hold a single large block. For the efficient use of memory, it is best to use relocatable blocks, which enables the Memory Manager to use compaction to open up large areas of contiguous free space. Occasionally, however, you'll have no choice but to use nonrelocatable blocks. Any time your application uses a pointer variable, it will be working with a nonrelocatable block. Here's an example:

```
void  OpenNewWindow( short windID )
{
   WindowPtr  theWindow;

   theWindow = GetNewWindow( windID, nil, (WindowPtr)-1L );
   ...
}
```

Because a nonrelocatable block won't move in the heap, there's no need to use a double-indirection scheme to keep track of it. Instead, the pointer is enough, as shown in Figure 9.7. In this figure, a pointer variable (such as a variable of type `WindowPtr`) points to one of the two blocks of data in the heap.

A pointer, such as a `WindowPtr`, isn't called a master pointer. While both hold an address that leads to a block of memory, the master pointer is always fixed in the heap. As you can see in Figure 9.7, a "regular" pointer can be outside the heap.

Setting an Application's Heap Size

You'll find projects for two simple Macintosh programs in this chapter's code examples folder on the book's CD. The two programs, `PictMemBad68K` and `PictMemGood68K`, are very similar. In fact, the only difference is how they use memory. In this section, you'll see how to make a good first approximation of the heap size needs of `PictMemBad68K`. Later in this chapter, you'll use `ZoneRanger` for a better understanding of an application's heap requirements.

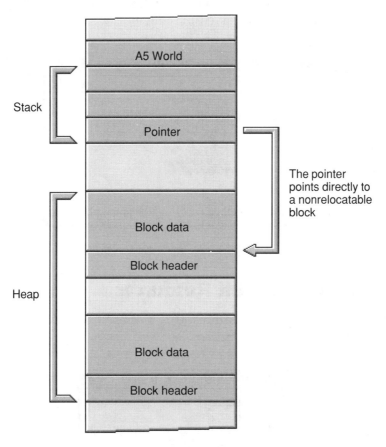

Figure 9.7 *A nonrelocatable block needs only a pointer to access it—not a handle.*

What the PictMemBad68K Program Does

Figure 9.8 shows what you'll see as `PictMemBad68K` runs. This trivial program displays a window, but no menu bar. Every time you click the mouse, a picture will be drawn to the window. The resource file for the project holds ten similar `PICT` resources. The only difference between the pictures is in the placement of the cylinder that crosses the

Metrowerks logo. As the user repeatedly clicks the mouse, the illusion of a cylinder moving across the logo is created. More important than the simple animation is the fact that you'll get visual feedback confirming that at each of the first ten mouse clicks a different PICT is being loaded into memory and displayed in the window.

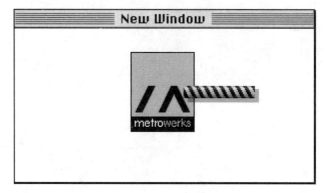

Figure 9.8 *The PictMemBad68K program displays a window with a picture in it.*

The PictMemBad68K Resources

The PictMemBad68K project requires just two resource types—WIND and PICT. Figure 9.9 shows the resource file.

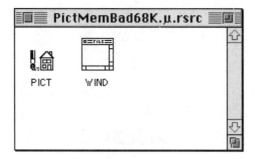

Figure 9.9 *The PictMemBad68K project resource file holds just two types of resources.*

PictMemBad68K includes ten PICT resources, numbered 128 through 137. Figure 9.10 shows a few of these pictures, as viewed from ResEdit.

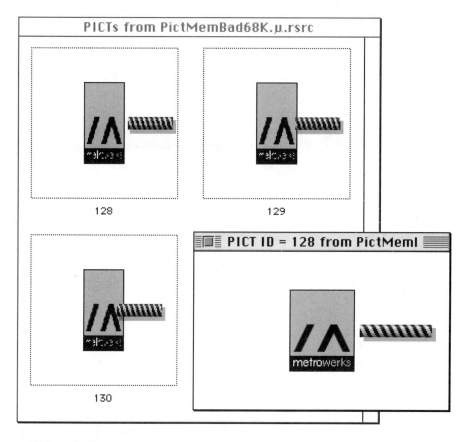

Figure 9.10 *The PictMemBad68K project resource file contains ten PICT resources.*

The PictMemBad68K.c Source Code

The PictMemBad68K.µ project holds a single source code file, the project resource file, and a single Metrowerks library. Figure 9.11 shows the PictMemBad68K project window.

NOTE

If you have access to a Mac, and you run the included PictMemBad68K program now, don't be surprised if the program doesn't work exactly as described (more on that later).

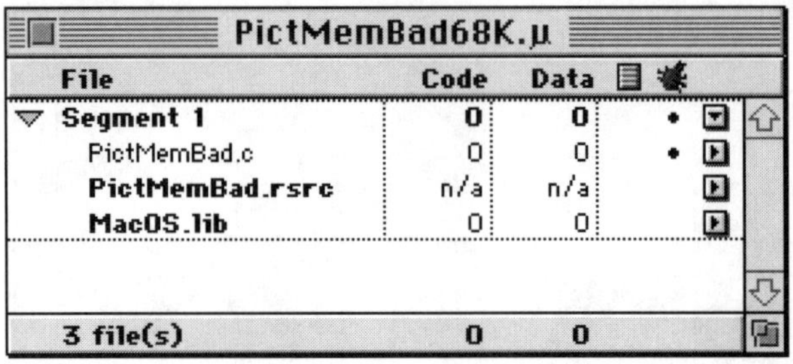

Figure 9.11 *The* `PictMemBad68K` *MW* `C/C++` 68K *project window.*

The `main()` routine found in the file `PictMemBad68K.c` begins by initializing the Toolbox and opening an empty window. Then it's off to the main event loop. Here's a look at the `PictMemBad68K main()` routine:

```
void  main( void )
{
   WindowPtr   theWindow;

   InitializeToolbox();

   theWindow = GetNewWindow( 128, nil, (WindowPtr)-1L );
   SetPort( theWindow );

   MainEventLoop();
}
```

The main event loop looks for just two event types: a key press or a click of the mouse button. When the user presses any key, the global variable gDone is set to true and the while loop—and program—terminate. If the event is instead a click of the mouse button, the program's DrawResourcePicture() routine is invoked.

```
void MainEventLoop( void )
{
   EventRecord   theEvent;

   while ( gDone == false )
   {
      WaitNextEvent( everyEvent, &theEvent, 15L, nil );

      switch (theEvent.what)
      {
         case keyDown:
```

```
                gDone = true;
                break;

            case mouseDown:
                DrawResourcePicture();
                break;
        }
    }
}
```

The purpose of DrawResourcePicture() is to load one of the ten PICT resources into memory and draw the picture to the program's window. A call to the Toolbox function GetPicture() takes care of the resource loading, while a call to the Toolbox routine DrawPicture() does the drawing. In between these calls, the size of the picture—its bounding rectangle—is determined by examining the picFrame field of the picture's Picture data structure. A rectangle (in window coordinates) in which to display the picture is then set up.

```
void  DrawResourcePicture( void )
{
    static  short  numPICTs;

    Rect        theRect;
    PicHandle   thePicture;
    short       theWidth;
    short       theHeight;
    short       theLeft = 35;
    short       theTop = 20;

    if ( numPICTs < 10 )
        ++numPICTs;
    else
        numPICTs = 1;

    thePicture = GetPicture( 127 + numPICTs );

    theRect = (**(thePicture)).picFrame;
    theWidth  = theRect.right - theRect.left;
    theHeight = theRect.bottom - theRect.top;
    SetRect( &theRect, theLeft, theTop,
             theLeft + theWidth, theTop + theHeight );

    DrawPicture( thePicture, &theRect );
}
```

`DrawResourcePicture()` uses a `static` variable named `numPICTs` to keep track of which `PICT` resource to load. Recall from your C programming experiences that a variable declared `static` is not destroyed after the function in which it is declared ends, as is the case with other local variables. Instead, it is initialized to a value of 0 at the first invocation of the function in which it resides and is kept in memory between function calls. Every time it is assigned a new value it retains that new value, even after the function ends. This means that the first time the main event loop invokes `DrawResourcePicture()`, the variable `numPICTs` will be initialized to 0 but will quickly be incremented to 1:

```
if ( numPICTs < 10 )
   numPICTs++;
else
   numPICTs = 1;
```

Next, the call to `GetPicture()` will load `PICT` 128 into memory and return a handle to the relocatable block that holds the `PICT` data:

```
thePicture = GetPicture( 127 + numPICTs );
```

After determining the size of the picture and setting a rectangle in which to draw it, a call to `DrawPicture()` does the drawing:

```
DrawPicture( thePicture, &theRect );
```

The first time `DrawResourcePicture()` gets called, `numPICTs` gets incremented from 0 to 1 and `PICT` 128 will be drawn. The second time, `numPICTs` will be incremented from 1 to 2 and `PICT` 129 is drawn. The first ten key presses will thus result in the display of each of the ten resource pictures. On the eleventh key press, `numPICTs` will have a value of 10 and will get set back to a value of 1 to restart the animation cycle.

Setting the Application's Heap Size

A programming integrated development environment like CodeWarrior lets a programmer easily set the size of an application's heap before building the application. With a project open, select **Preferences** from the Edit menu, then click on the **Project** icon in the icon list of the preferences dialog box. The Project panel has two edit boxes that let you set the preferred heap size and the minimum heap size for the application that is to be built. Figure 9.12 shows that the default values supplied by CodeWarrior are 384K for both the preferred heap size and the minimum heap size.

N O T E   Determining the heap requirements of an application is an inexact science. For determining application heap size, a study like the one done here, along with the use of a memory-watching tool like ZoneRanger, will almost always suffice. If you need still more tips on the determination of heap size, refer to *Inside Macintosh: Memory* and the M&T book *Macintosh Programming Techniques*.

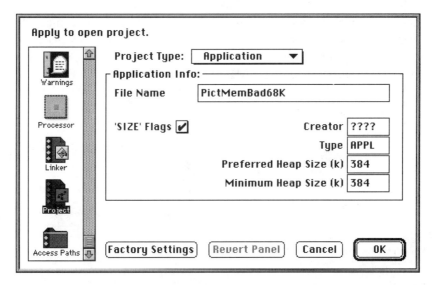

Figure 9.12   *The CodeWarrior Project panel in the Preferences dialog box allows you to set your application's heap size.*

The preferred heap size is the number of bytes that the operating system will attempt to allocate for your application when the program is launched. If that amount of free, contiguous RAM is unavailable on the user's Mac, an amount between the minimum heap size and the preferred heap size will be reserved. While the default values of 384 KB often suffice, your application may need more or less. If it needs more, the application may quit unexpectedly. If it needs less, then your application will be consuming more of the user's RAM than necessary, and it may prohibit the user from running a different program concurrently with yours.

Estimating an Application's Heap Requirements

If you click once on the icon of any application that is on your hard drive and then select **Get Info** from the File menu in the Finder, you'll set the Info dialog box for that application. There you can see the amount of memory that will be devoted to that one application. While an application may occasionally use the default values of 384 KB, it is more likely that it will request more or less memory. In Figure 9.13, you can see that Apple's TeachText text editor prefers to be given 600 KB of memory (but will run on as little as 192 KB), while the Metrowerks MW C/C++ 68K compiler attempts to reserve a heap 2 MB (2048 KB) in size (but will still launch if only 1.5 MB is available).

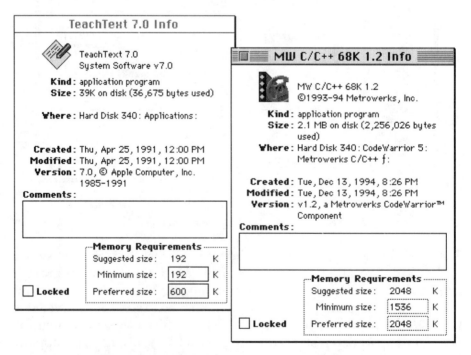

Figure 9.13 *The Get Info menu item from the Finder's File menu tells you how much memory an application requires.*

NOTE Don't try to make a correlation between the amount of disk space an application occupies and the size of its heap. An application's heap size depends on what the application loads into memory. A small application may be required to load more than just its own executable code into memory. It may need to also reserve space for the loading of, say, several large graphics files, or resources from an external resource file. Note in Figure 9.13 that TeachText occupies only 39 KB of disk space, yet it needs 192 KB of heap space, and it would prefer 600 KB!

One means of estimating the minimum amount of heap space an application needs is to look at the application's resources and determine how much memory they will occupy. Here's the quick method I'll use to get a rough idea of how much heap space PictMemBad68K will need:

- Add up the size of all CODE resources that have their preload attribute set.
- Allow for the loading of some of the other CODE resources
- Add up the size of the largest PICT that will be loaded
- Determine the amount of memory needed for other resources
- Add an appropriate "buffer" of memory to play it safe

NOTE Programmers who will be creating fat applications or PowerPC-only applications should read this section for general techniques, then read the last section in this chapter—"ZoneRanger and the Power Mac"—for PowerPC-specific tips.

When your CodeWarrior integrated development environment compiles and links a project, the resulting application consists of all of the resources from the project's resource file (or files), as well as two or more CODE resources. Each CODE resource is a segment of executable code—the end result of your compiled source code. Any of these CODE resources that are marked as preload will be loaded into the application heap when the application launches. An application's heap must be large enough to accommodate all of the CODE resources that are marked as preloaded. CodeWarrior will allow you to mark any segment to be preloaded, and it will always mark CODE resource 1, which holds the start of your application, as preloaded.

Figure 9.14 shows some of the CODE resources for the graphics program MacDraw Pro, as viewed when the application is opened with Resorcerer. In this figure, you can see that MacDraw Pro has 20 CODE resources, totaling about 330 KB, that will preload when the program is launched. From this you can safely conclude that the heap size for MacDraw Pro will need to be at least 330 KB in size—and more likely much higher. Additional heap space must also be reserved to hold at least some of the other CODE resources as well.

NOTE For 680x0 applications, all of the program's executable code need not be loaded into memory at once; only code marked as preloaded will be loaded at application startup. Other code will be loaded as needed, and purged (if marked purgeable) when it is not in use and unavailable memory is being requested by the program. Again, *Inside Macintosh: Memory* and *Macintosh Programming Techniques* provide details on memory management for 680x0 applications.

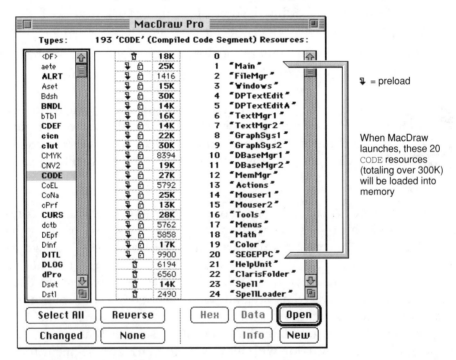

Figure 9.14 *Most commercial applications, such as* Claris MacDraw Pro, *have several* CODE *resources that are marked to preload.*

If you build the `PictMemBad68K` application and then open it with a resource editor, you'll see that it has just one `CODE` resource that gets preloaded. Figure 9.15 shows that this `CODE` resource, with an ID of 1, is less than 2 KB in size. Because `PictMemBad68K` is such a trivial program, it needs less than 2 KB to hold its preloaded code. The Info dialog box shown in this figure was opened by selecting **Get Info** from the File menu of `ResEdit`. Figure 9.16 provides a similar view of `CODE 1`, this time from `Resorcerer`. To view the Info window from `Resorcerer`, select **Get Info** from the Edit menu.

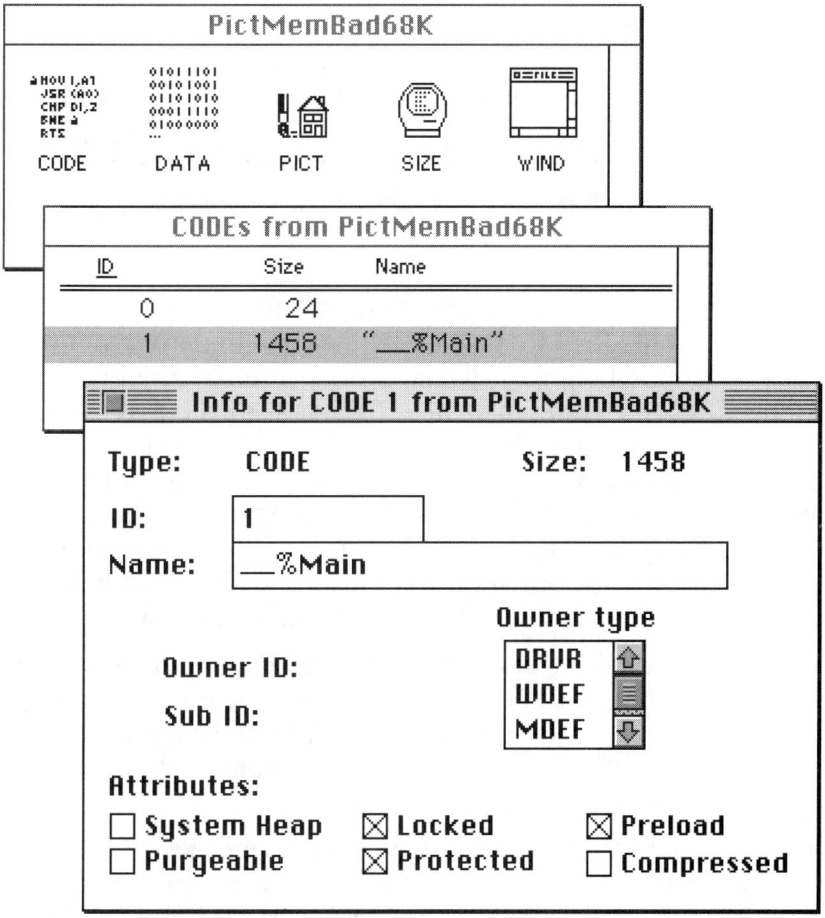

Figure 9.15 *The* `PictMemBad68K` *application's one preload* `CODE` *resource, viewed from* `ResEdit`.

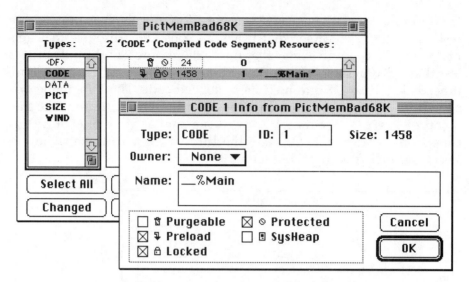

Figure 9.16 *The* PictMemBad68K *application's one preload* CODE *resource, viewed from* Resorcerer.

Besides loading its own executable code at startup, the PictMemBad68K application will load PICT data into the heap as the program executes. Because the application only displays one picture at any given time, I won't need to determine the total size of all of the PICT resources. Instead, I'll rely on a quick look at the PICT resources to tell me that the program will only need about 5 KB of heap space to hold even the largest picture. Figure 9.17 shows the PICT resources from ResEdit (with **by ID** rather than **by PICT** selected from the View menu). Figure 9.18 shows the PICT information from Resorcerer (with **Show 'PICT' data** unchecked and **Show sizes** checked in the View menu).

Another object that will appear in the heap is the data for the one window that PictMemBad68K uses. Opening a new window means a WindowRecord gets loaded into memory, and the WIND resource information gets copied to that record. A window occupies well under 1 KB of memory, so the window is not a concern.

The PictMemBad68K application has less than 2 KB of code, won't display more than 5 KB of picture information at any one time, and will display only one window. Additionally, because PictMemBad68K doesn't work with files, it won't require heap space to hold data from other files. From this information, what can be concluded about the memory requirement of PictMemBad68K? Obviously, it's quite low. If I leave the heap size at the default value of 384 KB, I'll be creating an application that probably wastes about one third of a megabyte of the user's RAM; so instead, I'll use CodeWarrior to change the heap size.

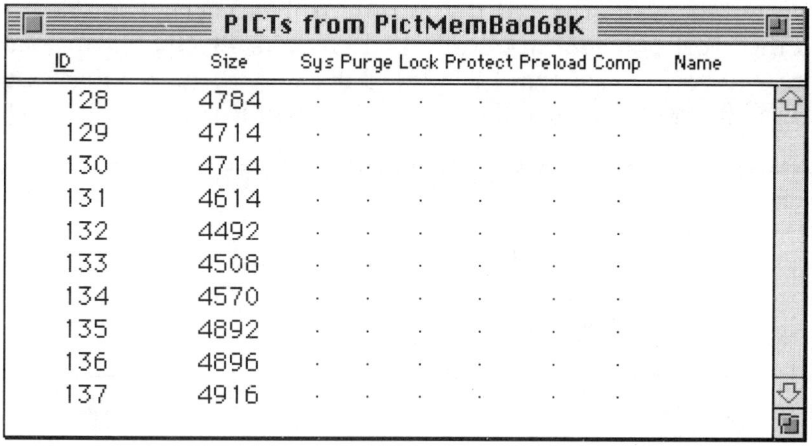

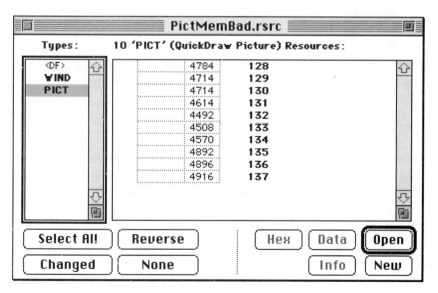

Figure 9.17 *The size of each* PictMemBad68K PICT *resource, viewed from* ResEdit.

Figure 9.18 *The size of each* PictMemBad68K
PICT *resource, viewed from* Resorcerer.

Changing an Application's Heap Size

To tell CodeWarrior to generate a version of PictMemBad68K that uses a smaller heap, I'll select **Preferences** from the MW C/C++ 68K compiler's Edit menu, click the **Project** icon, and enter a much smaller number for the preferred heap size and the minimum heap size. Though I don't think the PictMemBad68K application will require 48 KB of heap space, in Figure 9.19 you can see that I've played it safe and entered that value. If I'm right, the net savings to the user is 336 KB of RAM (384 KB – 48 KB).

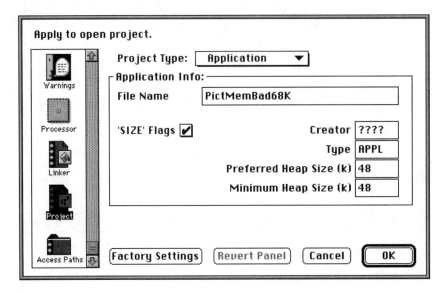

Figure 9.19 *An application's heap size can be changed by using the CodeWarrior Preferences dialog box.*

After selecting **Make** from the Project menu, I returned to the Finder. There I clicked once on the new version of PictMemBad68K and selected **Get Info** from the Finder's File menu. The numbers in the Info dialog box confirm that the system will indeed allocate only 48 KB to PictMemBad68K, as shown in Figure 9.20.

There's a second way to change the heap size of an application. After the application is built, you can open the application with a resource editor and change the values in the last **N O T E** two fields of the application's SIZE resource.

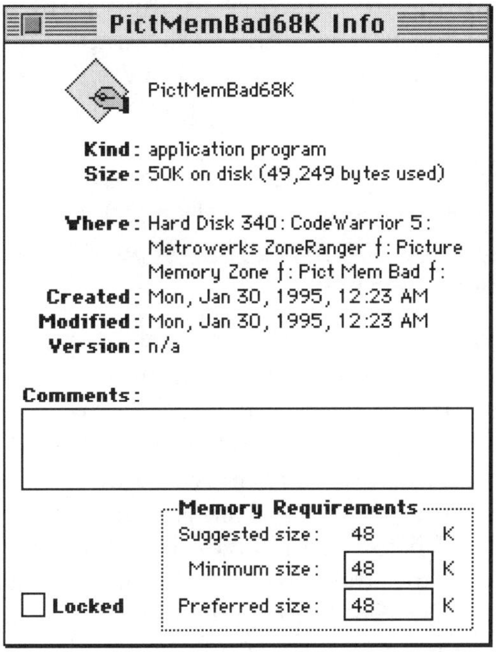

```
┌──────────────────────────────────────────────┐
│ ▦ ≡≡≡≡≡    PictMemBad68K Info    ≡≡≡≡≡ ▩ │
├──────────────────────────────────────────────┤
│                                                │
│   ◇◇◇                                          │
│   ◇ ◈ ◇   PictMemBad68K                        │
│   ◇◇◇                                          │
│                                                │
│        Kind : application program              │
│        Size : 50K on disk (49,249 bytes used)  │
│                                                │
│       Where : Hard Disk 340 : CodeWarrior 5 :  │
│               Metrowerks ZoneRanger ƒ : Picture│
│               Memory Zone ƒ : Pict Mem Bad ƒ : │
│     Created : Mon, Jan 30, 1995, 12:23 AM      │
│    Modified : Mon, Jan 30, 1995, 12:23 AM      │
│     Version : n/a                              │
│                                                │
│    Comments :                                  │
│   ┌──────────────────────────────────────┐    │
│   │                                      │    │
│   │                                      │    │
│   └──────────────────────────────────────┘    │
│              ┌── Memory Requirements ──────┐   │
│              │ Suggested size :   48    K  │   │
│              │ Minimum size : [ 48   ]  K  │   │
│   ☐ Locked   │ Preferred size : [ 48  ]  K │   │
│              └─────────────────────────────┘   │
└──────────────────────────────────────────────┘
```

Figure 9.20 *The Finder's Get Info dialog box reflects changes made to an application's heap size in CodeWarrior, after the application is rebuilt in CodeWarrior.*

Now it's time for a test run. Double-click on the `PictMemBad68K` icon to launch the application. When the empty window opens, click the mouse button to display the first of the ten pictures. Repeatedly click the mouse to display each picture. What happens after a few clicks? Most likely, either some mouse clicks don't display pictures or the application quits altogether. Why? You may have discovered the problem several pages back. But whether you have or haven't, read on to see how `ZoneRanger` can be used to track down a bug and determine an appropriate heap zone size.

ZoneRanger Basics

This chapter's Macintosh memory overview provides a background for the use of Metrowerks' impressive memory-watching software tool `ZoneRanger`.

N O T E Like all of the software in the CodeWarrior package, ZoneRanger is constantly being improved and upgraded. Included on the book's CD is version 1.2 of ZoneRanger copyright late 1994. If you're going to run ZoneRanger to follow along with the discussions in this chapter, and you also own the Metrowerks CodeWarrior CD (which may include a more recent version of ZoneRanger), use this book's version instead. That way what you see on screen will match what you read in this book.

When you launch ZoneRanger, the ZoneRanger Overview window will open. Listed in this window is the name of each application, or process, that is currently running. These are the processes that ZoneRanger tracks. You'll notice that the System, MultiFinder and Finder are always listed in this window, because as long as your Mac is running, so are these programs. Because ZoneRanger is of course executing, it too will be listed in the Overview window. If you have any other programs running, their names will also appear in this window. In Figure 9.21, you can see that besides the four applications that will always be named in the Overview window, I also have the program PictMemGood68K running.

	Name	Free Blocks	Pointers	Handles...	🔒	✏️	🗄️
🏠	System	153	411	1567	124	133	170
🏠	MultiFinder	4	2	81	11	5	0
🏠	Finder	12	12	91	11	25	42
🏠	MW ZoneRanger ...	13	8	155	9	6	19
🏠	PictMemGood68K	7	4	55	2	1	2

⬆ Each application that is currently running is a process that ZoneRanger tracks

Figure 9.21 *The ZoneRanger Overview window keeps track of all applications that are executing.*

You've seen that every application that is running (each process) on a Macintosh has its own application partition. Within this partition is the application heap. As each block in the heap begins with a block header, the application heap itself also begins with a header, called the *zone header*. This header provides the Memory Manager with information about the heap, such as its size in bytes. Because the application heap is able to expand and shrink as the application executes, the heap ends with a small block of memory, known as the *zone trailer*, which helps the Memory Manager keep track of the end of the heap. Collectively, the heap and its header and trailer are referred to as the *heap zone*. It is an application's heap zone that ZoneRanger monitors.

Figure 9.22 shows the ZoneRanger Overview window and three of the six pieces of memory-related information that ZoneRanger tracks for each process. From earlier in this chapter, you know that a heap, or zone, holds free memory, nonrelocatable blocks, and relocatable blocks. ZoneRanger labels these blocks as Free Blocks, Pointers, and Handles, respectively. Within each column appears the number of each type of block for each process. For example, in Figure 9.22 you can see that at this point in time the PictMemGood68K application's heap zone contains 7 free blocks, 4 nonrelocatable blocks (referenced by pointers), and 55 relocatable blocks (referenced by handles).

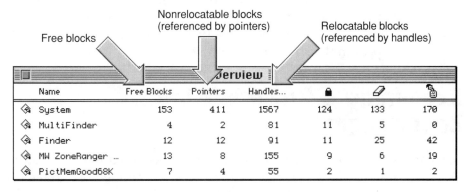

Name	Free Blocks	Pointers	Handles...	🔒	✏️	📑
System	153	411	1567	124	133	170
MultiFinder	4	2	81	11	5	0
Finder	12	12	91	11	25	42
MW ZoneRanger ...	13	8	155	9	6	19
PictMemGood68K	7	4	55	2	1	2

Figure 9.22 *The* ZoneRanger *Overview window tracks all the free blocks, nonrelocatable blocks, and relocatable blocks in the memory heap of each application that is running.*

Relocatable blocks have locked, purgeable, and resource attributes. ZoneRanger reports the number of blocks with each of these attributes for each process. Figure 9.23 points out the three attributes columns in the Overview window.

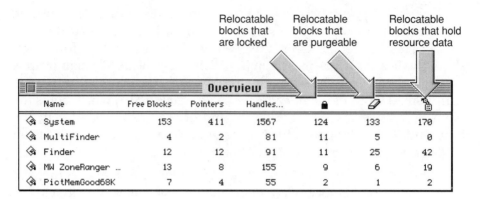

Figure 9.23 *The* ZoneRanger *Overview window tracks all the attributes of all of the relocatable blocks in each application that is running.*

N O T E The blocks in the three rightmost columns are all relocatable blocks referenced by handles. Yet for any one process (any one application), the total number of blocks in these three columns will not add up to the number of blocks in the Handles column for that same process. That's because many of the application's relocatable blocks may not have any of these three attributes set. That is, a block that is unlocked, unpurgeable, and holds data that isn't from a resource won't appear in the Attributes columns.

Examining a Process Using ZoneRanger

ZoneRanger is an application; you just double-click its icon to start it up. Once it's running, ZoneRanger will keep tabs on the memory usage of all applications that are currently running. ZoneRanger will also monitor any applications you start up after ZoneRanger is launched. Just a few sentences back you read (or, if you're following along on your Mac, you actually *saw*) that the PictMemBad68K application had problems displaying the pictures that it has stored in its resource fork. Here you'll see how ZoneRanger can help out.

Using the ZoneRanger Overview Window

To examine how `PictMemBad68K` uses memory, double-click on the `ZoneRanger` icon to launch the `ZoneRanger` application. Then, if you haven't already done so, launch the application to be examined—`PictMemBad68K`. When I did that, my screen displayed a `ZoneRanger` Overview window like the one pictured in Figure 9.24. Your Overview window will display the five processes shown in the figure. If you have other applications running, those also will be listed in your Overview window.

	Name	Free Blocks	Pointers	Handles...	🔒	✐	🗑
🔷	System	146	411	1567	124	132	171
🔷	MultiFinder	4	2	81	11	5	0
🔷	Finder	11	12	91	11	25	42
🔷	MW ZoneRanger ...	10	6	123	9	6	19
🔷	PictMemBad68K	8	4	55	2	1	2

Figure 9.24 *The* `ZoneRanger` *Overview window with the* `PictMemBad68K` *application running.*

Values in your Overview will differ from the ones shown in mine. Different system configurations will result in different numbers of blocks. Also, Macintosh memory is dynamic—blocks are relocated and purged periodically. As you view the Overview window, don't be surprised to see some of the values changing almost constantly.

Knowing the *number* of blocks of memory a program is using may or may not answer questions you have about that application. So `ZoneRanger` lets you view heap information in the Overview window in three different ways. Figure 9.25 shows the Configure menu. The first three items in the menu will alter the way in which heap memory usage is displayed in the Overview window. Figure 9.24 showed the Overview window with the **Display Block Counts** item checked. In Figure 9.25, you can see that I've changed the view to **Display Block Usage**.

```
┌─────────────────────────────────────┐
│ Configure                           │
│  Display Block Sizes                │
│  Display Block Counts               │
│ ✓Display Block Usage                │
│ ─────────────────────────────────  │
│ ✓Display Decimal                    │
│  Display Hexadecimal                │
│ ─────────────────────────────────  │
│ ✓Block View                    ⌘B   │
│  Grid View                     ⌘G   │
│ ─────────────────────────────────  │
│  Show Locked Handles           ⌘L   │
│  Show Purgeable Handles        ⌘P   │
│  Show Resource Handles         ⌘R   │
│ ─────────────────────────────────  │
│  Increase Resolution           ⌘]   │
│  Decrease Resolution           ⌘[   │
│ ─────────────────────────────────  │
│  Zoom In                       ⌘.   │
│  Zoom Out                      ⌘,   │
│ ─────────────────────────────────  │
│  Refresh Foreground            ▶    │
│  Refresh Background            ▶    │
└─────────────────────────────────────┘
```

Figure 9.25 *The ZoneRanger Configure menu.*

With **Display Block Usage** selected, the Overview window will use a scale to display blocks as a percentage of the total application heap. The application heap is the sum of an application's free blocks, nonrelocatable blocks, and relocatable blocks, as shown in Figure 9.26

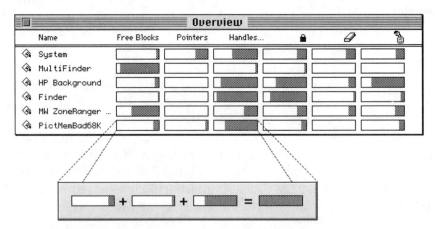

Figure 9.26 *The sum of the sizes of the free blocks, nonrelocatable blocks, and relocatable blocks equals the size of the heap at that moment.*

The Overview Window and PictMemBad68K

Now it's time to take a look at the heap of `PictMemBad68K`. With ZoneRanger running, check the Configure menu to verify that **Display Block Usage** is selected. Then click on the **Refresh Foreground** menu item in the same menu. A hierarchical menu will be displayed. You can slide the cursor to the right to see the choices of how often the ZoneRanger windows will be updated. Slide the mouse over this menu until **Always** is displayed (see Figure 9.27) and then release the mouse button. The **Refresh Foreground** item tells `ZoneRanger` how often to update the Overview window when another application (such as `PictMemBad68K`) is in the foreground. You can do the same for the **Refresh Background** menu item.

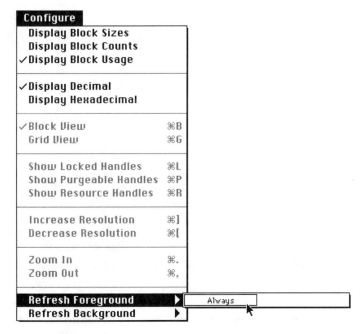

Figure 9.27 *The frequency at which the* ZoneRanger *windows are updated can be set in the Configure menu.*

If `PictMemBad68K` has been running and you've clicked the mouse button on its window to view the animation, press any key to quit the program; then launch it again. You'll want to view memory usage from the very start of the program—before pictures have been loaded and displayed. After restarting PictMemBad68K, click the mouse on the ZoneRanger Overview window to bring it to the front.

Next, click on the PictMemBad68K window so that a picture is displayed. Then, about every 2 seconds, click on the PictMemBad68K window so that a new picture is displayed. In between clicks, look at the ZoneRanger Overview window, taking note of the memory usage for each column in the PictMemBad68K row. As you click the mouse in PictMemBad68K, you should notice a trend developing in the Overview window. With each click of the mouse, the amount of memory shown in the Free Blocks display will be decreasing, while the amount of memory shown in the Handles display will be increasing. Figure 9.28 illustrates this.

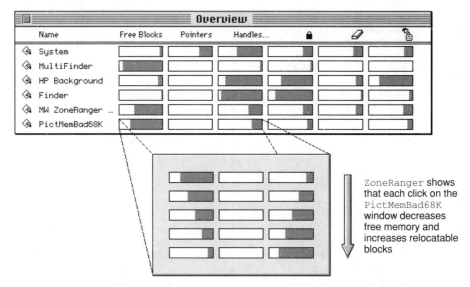

Figure 9.28 *As* PictMemBad68K *runs, its free memory is filled by relocatable blocks.*

Apparently, each picture that gets drawn is using, and retaining, a part of the application heap zone. To confirm this guess, I'll use ZoneRanger to examine the PictMemBad68K heap zone in greater detail.

Using the ZoneRanger Zone Window

If you click the mouse button while the cursor is over a process name in the ZoneRanger Overview window, a pop-up menu will appear. Among the menu items in this menu is an **Open Zone** item. Each process that is running has a zone—its own private heap zone. Selecting **Open Zone** opens a Zone window that provides a graphical look at the memory layout in that one zone. In Figure 9.29, I'm opening a zone for the `PictMemBad68K` program.

	Name	Free Blocks	Pointers	Handles...	🔒	🖊	🗑
	System	146	411	1567	124	132	171
	MultiFinder	4	2	81	11	5	0
	HP Background	1	1	15	3	9	10
	Finder	11	12	91	11	25	42
	MW ZoneRanger ...	10	6	123	9	6	19
	PictMemBad68K	8	4	55	2	1	2

Overview

Open Zone...

Compact
Purge
Compact and Purge

Bring To Front

Figure 9.29 *A Zone window can be opened for any application listed in the Overview window.*

If you haven't already done so, quit `PictMemBad68K` and restart it. Then click on its name in the Name column of the `ZoneRanger` Overview window. Select **Open Zone** from the pop-up menu. When you do, you'll see a Zone window that looks similar to the one shown in Figure 9.30. In that figure, I've added a key so that you can tell which shades of gray represent which type of block. I've also pointed out an example of each in the Zone window.

NOTE Don't expect your Zone window to look just like mine, even if you're running the same `PictMemBad68K` program. Remember, Macintosh memory is dynamic. The Memory Manager will attempt to make the best use of the memory available on your machine at the time you run the application, and throughout the running of it. What is the same, however, is the size of various blocks of memory. For example, while the same `PICT` resource may get loaded to a different address each time you run the same program, it will occupy the same amount of memory each time.

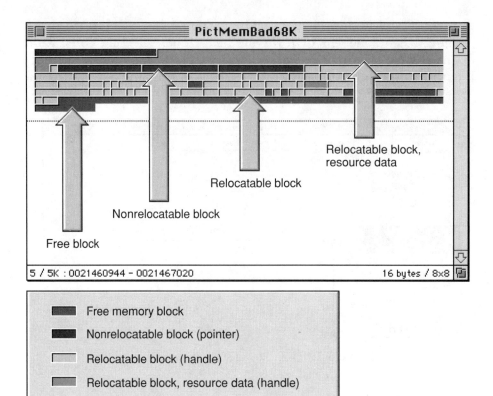

Figure 9.30 *A Zone window graphically exhibits
the types of blocks in an application's heap zone.*

 N O T E   If you're following along on screen, select **Legend** from the Apple menu of ZoneRanger. That will present you with a dialog box that describes which color represents which type of block.

If the display of the heap in the Zone window seems too small to be clearly legible, you can increase the area each block occupies by making selections from the Configure menu. You can repeatedly select **Increase Resolution** and **Zoom In** to enlarge the display size of each block. While I'm on the topic of the Configure menu, you can also select any one of the three **Show** commands to change the highlighting of a particular type of relocatable block. For example, if you want the Zone window to clarify which relocatable blocks hold resource data, select **Show Resource Handles**. Figure 9.31 shows these Configure menu items.

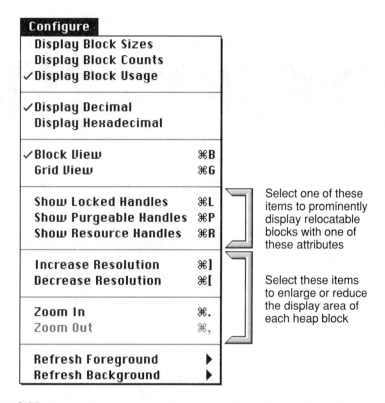

Figure 9.31 *The Configure menu has items used to change the shading of blocks and menu items to change the scale of the blocks in the Zone window.*

Getting Heap Block Information

Now let's see how the Zone window works. You can determine the type of block by its color. I checked **Show Resource Handles**, so my window displays all relocatable resource blocks in a color different than relocatable blocks that don't hold resource data. You can get still more information about a *particular* block by clicking on it and holding down the mouse button. That will bring up a pop-up list of information about that block. In Figure 9.32, I've clicked on the large block near the start of the `PictMemBad68K` program's heap zone.

Clicking on a block inverts the
block, and results in a popup that
holds information about that block

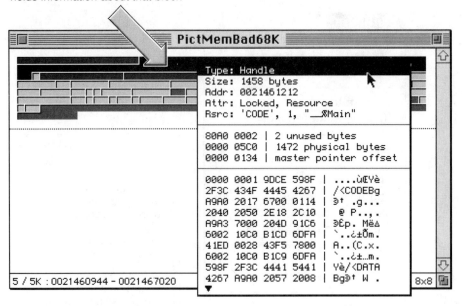

Figure 9.32 *Clicking on any block in the Zone window
displays a pop-up that holds information about that block.*

Let's take a look at the information in the pop-up in Figure 9.32. From
the information near the top of the pop-up I can see that this block is
accessed by a handle, is 1458 bytes in size, is locked, and holds a
resource of type CODE—with a resource ID of 1. Earlier in this chapter,
I opened PictMemBad68K with ResEdit to see how many CODE
resources were marked to be preloaded, and to get their size. Figure
9.33 shows that I found one CODE resource with its preload attribute
set—the CODE 1 resource. ZoneRanger confirms that this resource does
indeed get loaded. How can I be sure that it was preloaded? Preloaded
resources are placed in the heap right when the application launches, so they're found near the start of the heap just as the clicked-on
block was.

N O T E The more you know about Macintosh memory in general, the more things in particular ZoneRanger will help identify. If you hadn't read about the CODE 1 resource earlier in this chapter (and you didn't know of it before you read this book), the fact that there is a block of memory designated as Locked, Resource, CODE, 1, might mean little or nothing to you.

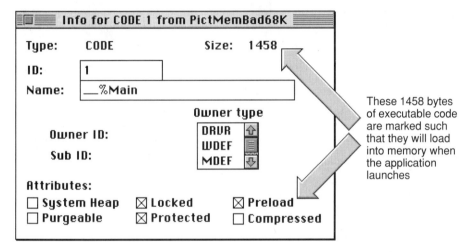

Figure 9.33 *The* PictMemBad68K *application has one CODE resource marked as preload.*

Before moving on to finding the PictMemBad68K memory problem, I'll click on one more memory block, just to feel comfortable with how the Zone window works. With **Show Resource Handles** checked in the Configure menu, ZoneRanger has given a distinctive shading to all relocatable blocks that hold resource data. For PictMemBad68K, there's only two such blocks, which are shown in Figure 9.34.

Aside from the CODE 1 resource (which I've found in memory), I know that PictMemBad68K holds a WIND resource. So it's a pretty safe bet that the WIND resource data will be in the other relocatable resource data block. Sure enough, when I click on that block, the pop-up that appears tells me that WIND 128 is at this location. Figure 9.35 illustrates this. In the figure, the small black section just above the cursor is the block that was clicked on.

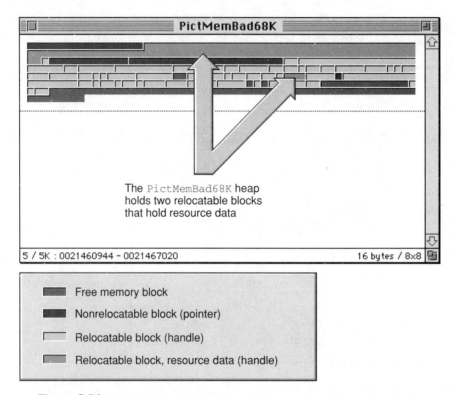

Figure 9.34 *The* PictMemBad68K *heap holds two relocatable resource blocks.*

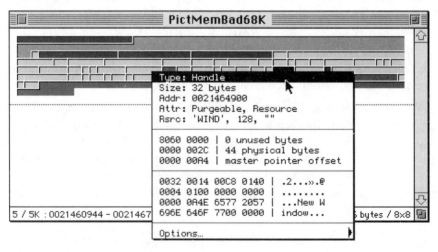

Figure 9.35 *Clicking on the second relocatable resource block in the*
PictMemBad68K *heap reveals that it holds* WIND *resource data.*

Finding the PictMemBad68K Memory Problem

If you've been experimenting with PictMemBad68K and ZoneRanger, and
you got a little ahead of me, quit PictMemBad68K and restart it. Then
click on its name in the Name column of the ZoneRanger Overview window and select **Open Zone** from the pop-up menu that appears. While
the contents of your Zone window may look different than the one
shown in Figure 9.36, it will have similarities. Most importantly, if you
have **Show Resource Handles** checked in the Configure menu, your
Zone window will show two relocatable blocks that hold resource data,
like the Zone window in the figure.

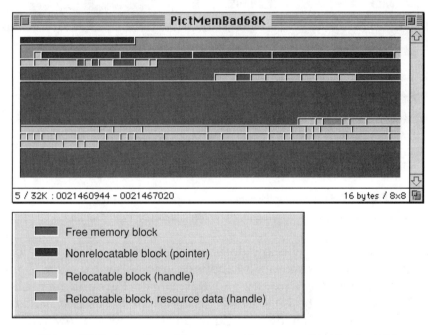

Figure 9.36 *Regardless of the amount of free memory* PictMemBad68K
currently has, it should have two relocatable resource blocks.

Now click on the PictMemBad68K window. In response to your mouse
click, a picture will be drawn in the PictMemBad68K window. The Zone
window should also update to show that memory has changed. You'll
notice that a new relocatable handle holding resource data has been
added to the zone heap. Clicking on the new block shows that it is a little less than 5 KB in size (4784 bytes) and is the resource data for the
displayed picture (see Figure 9.37).

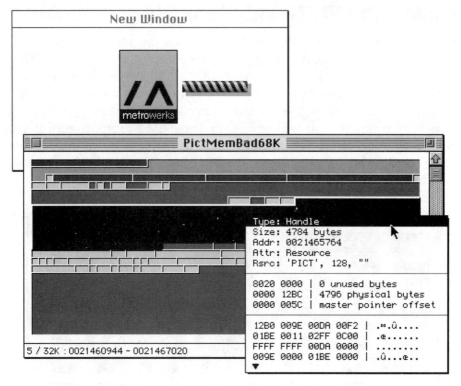

Figure 9.37 *Clicking the mouse over the* PictMemBad68K *window*
adds a new relocatable resource block to the Zone window.

NOTE If the Zone window doesn't update after clicking the mouse on the PictMemBad68K application window, try changing the **Refresh Foreground** and **Refresh Background** menu item values in the ZoneRanger Configure menu, as discussed earlier in this chapter. Clicking on the Zone window will also update it.

Now click on the PictMemBad68K window again. When you do, a different picture will be displayed in the PictMemBad68K window and another relocatable block of resource data will be added to the heap. The heap now holds four such blocks, as shown in Figure 9.38.

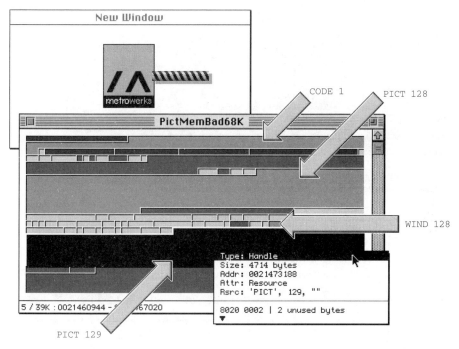

Figure 9.38 *A second click on the* `PictMemBad68K` *window adds a second relocatable resource block to the Zone window.*

At this point, you should have caught on that something is not right. Though the `PictMemBad68K` program is displaying only a single picture at a time, it is retaining the `PICT` data for more than one picture in memory. In fact, if you click the mouse a few more times, you'll see that the zone heap begins to fill with blocks of `PICT` data. Figure 9.39 shows the `PictMemBad68K` zone after five clicks of the mouse.

You can get a different view of memory by clicking on the `ZoneRanger` Overview window. There, I selected **Display Block Counts** from the Configure menu. Then I clicked on the block count in the relocatable resource blocks column of the `PictMemBad68K` process. As shown in Figure 9.40, `ZoneRanger` then displayed a pop-up that provided a summary of each resource data relocatable block currently in the zone heap.

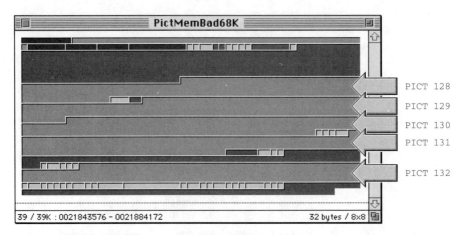

Figure 9.39 *Five clicks on the* PictMemBad68K *window result in five relocatable resource blocks appearing in the Zone window.*

	Name	Free Blocks	Pointers	Handles...	🔒	✏️	🗑️
	System	62	392	1142	116	138	149
	MultiFinder	5	2	140	25	32	0
	HP Background	1	1	15	3	9	10
	Finder	12	8	78	11	11	28
	MW ZoneRanger ...	11	6	121	9	5	17
	PictMemBad68K	11	5	60	2	0	7

Zone: PictMemBad68K
Count: 7
Size: 25776

Type	Size	Attr	Type	ID Name
Handle	1468	● L.R	'CODE'	000001 _%Main
Handle	4952	. ..R	'PICT'	000128
Handle	44	. .PR	'WIND'	000128
Handle	4900	. ..R	'PICT'	000129
Handle	4896	. ..R	'PICT'	000130
Handle	4796	. ..R	'PICT'	000131
Handle	4720	. ..R	'PICT'	000132

Options...

Figure 9.40 *Clicking on a block count in the resource column of the Overview window displays a pop-up that describes the resource type of each block.*

It should be clear to you that if the heap size of PictMemBad68K is set low, the application will soon run into trouble. Recall that I used

CodeWarrior to set the heap size to 48 KB. At close to 5 KB per displayed picture, the heap will soon become full, and either the program will terminate abruptly or it will simply fail to display each picture.

Correcting the PictMemBad68K Memory Problem

ZoneRanger's ability not only to show memory blocks, but also to show the size, type, and, in some cases, the exact contents, of blocks, helps you find memory-related programming bugs. In the case of PictMemBad68K, being able to see that memory blocks holding PICT data remained in memory after the pictures were drawn is what pinpointed the cause of PictMemBad68K's problems. Now, it's up to your Macintosh programming skills to relate this memory problem to the code that needs to be altered.

When a program is finished with a picture, the application should release the memory that was used to hold that picture's PICT data. Let's take a look at the DrawResourcePicture() routine from PictMemBad68K to see if that's being done:

```
void  DrawResourcePicture( void )
{
   static  short  numPICTs;

   Rect        theRect;
   PicHandle   thePicture;
   short       theWidth;
   short       theHeight;
   short       theLeft = 35;
   short       theTop = 20;

   if ( numPICTs < 10 )
      ++numPICTs;
   else
      numPICTs = 1;

   thePicture = GetPicture( 127 + numPICTs );

   theRect = (**(thePicture)).picFrame;
   theWidth  = theRect.right - theRect.left;
   theHeight  = theRect.bottom - theRect.top;
```

```
    SetRect( &theRect, theLeft, theTop,
            theLeft + theWidth, theTop + theHeight );

    DrawPicture( thePicture, &theRect );
}
```

You can see that the last line in `DrawResourcePicture()` is the call to the Toolbox routine `DrawPicture()`. I never did release the heap memory that was used in the call to `GetPicture()`. The remedy? I'll simply add a call to `ReleaseResource()` at the end of the function. `ReleaseResource()` requires a generic handle as its only parameter, so I'll typecast the `PicHandle` when I pass it:

```
void  DrawResourcePicture( void )
{
    ...
    ...
    thePicture = GetPicture( 127 + numPICTs );
    ...
    ...
    DrawPicture( thePicture, &theRect );

    ReleaseResource( (Handle)thePicture );
}
```

Is this really the solution? You can verify that it is by adding the call to `ReleaseResource()` and recompiling the program. Then again use `ZoneRanger` to observe the application's memory. This work is already done for you in the form of `PictMemGood68K`. You'll find this project and application on the book's CD. The only difference between the `PictMemBad68K` and `PictMemGood68K` programs is one line of code—the call to `ReleaseResource()`. Figure 9.41 is a look at the `PictMemGood68K` program, along with a `ZoneRanger` Zone window. In the figure, you can see that even with the last of the ten `PictMemGood68K` pictures displayed, there's still plenty of heap space left. The figure also shows that there are only two relocatable resource blocks in the heap—the `PICT` block is released immediately after a picture is drawn.

 As you run `PictMemGood68K`, keep an eye on the amount of free space in the `PictMemGood68K` Zone window. If, after putting the program through its paces, there is always an ample amount of free memory, you know that you can reduce the size of the application's heap. Quit `PictMemGood68K`, click

N O T E

on it once, then select **Get Info** from the Finder's File menu. Lower the minimum size and preferred size values, then test the program again. Quit `PictMemGood68K`, adjust the heap size, and rerun the program several times until you find the optimum heap size. Keep in mind that `PictMemGood68K` should always have a free block at least the size of the largest `PICT` resource it needs to load.

When you've found the ideal heap size, change the values in the MW C/C++ 68K compiler Preferences dialog box so that they match the heap size. Then, each time you make a new version of the program CodeWarrior will give the application the heap size you want. To guarantee that any program you write doesn't use too much of a user's RAM (or so little that it behaves erratically), examine it with `ZoneRanger`.

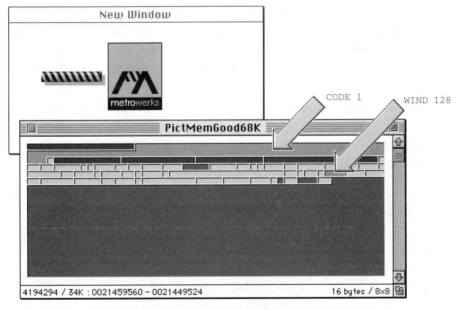

Figure 9.41 *When* `PictMemGood68K` *runs,*
it releases resource blocks immediately after using them.

Why Not Just Use the Debugger?

After using `ZoneRanger`, you may be wondering if it is really necessary to use a memory-watching tool like `ZoneRanger` when you're already familiar with source-level debugging. After all, a debugger is easy to use and it too displays the contents of memory. Let's again refer to the PictMemBad68K application for the answer.

If I wasn't using ZoneRanger and I compiled and ran the PictMemBad68K program, I would turn to MW Debug when I noticed that the program wasn't displaying the pictures properly. Making the assumption that the problem lies in the DrawResourcePicture() routine, I'd set a breakpoint at the call to GetPicture() and then start watching what happens as the program executes.

The first few times through DrawResourcePicture() I wouldn't notice any problems. Eventually, however, I'd step past GetPicture() and notice that the PicHandle variable thePicture was nil, as shown in Figure 9.42. I'd look at numPICTs and see that it had a value of 8, meaning GetPicture() had attempted to load PICT 135 (127 + 8) but failed to do so. Could it be that I forgot to add PICT 135 to the resource file? Or, if I did add it, is the PICT resource somehow corrupt? Neither of these possibilities would of course be true. A check of the resource file would eliminate the first potential problem, but determining if one or more of the PICT resources was corrupt might be more difficult.

The investigation continues. What happens after the eighth, ninth, and tenth mouse clicks, when each of these pictures fails to be drawn? The program cycles back to the first picture. If it does occur to me that perhaps there is a memory problem, those thoughts might be dashed when I see that the eleventh mouse click does in fact show that thePicture is no longer nil—the first picture is again loaded and displayed in the window.

What did ZoneRanger show that the debugger didn't? ZoneRanger provided a quick, graphical look at the entire heap of PictMemBad68K—not just the values of a few variables. And, because variables reside on the stack—not in the heap—the debugger didn't give the same kind of view of memory as the heap watcher. When watching the PictMemBad68K heap with ZoneRanger, you could easily see that the heap was rapidly filling up, something that the debugger didn't report. And when that eleventh mouse click took place, you already knew from the ZoneRanger Zone window that PICT 128 had never been released from memory. So even though PictMemBad68K didn't have enough free memory to load another PICT, the call to DrawPicture() still worked.

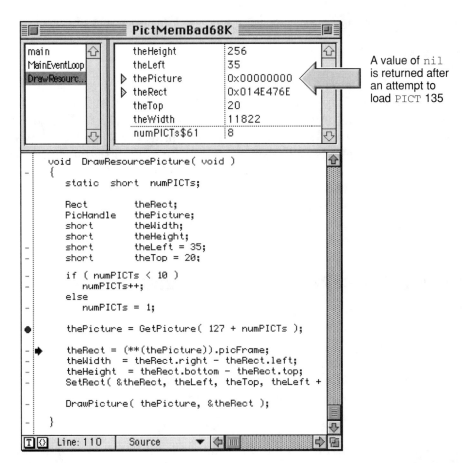

Figure 9.42 *The Metrowerks debugger reports that a call to* GetPicture() *has failed.*

Like any tool, ZoneRanger isn't to be used for all jobs. But it is helpful for a variety of tasks:

- To improve your understanding of how Macintosh memory is organized
- To get a complete, graphical view of what's going on in the heap
- To help, in conjunction with a debugger, track down memory-related bugs
- To help determine how large of a partition should be devoted to your program

ZoneRanger and Native PowerPC Programs

Whether you're using a 680x0-based Macintosh or a Power Macintosh, if you run a 680x0 application and ZoneRanger, you'll see results like those shown in the previous sections. If you own a Power Mac, and if you examine a native PowerPC application, however, ZoneRanger will reveal that the contents of the application heap are a little bit different. When a native PowerPC application is launched, it is given its own application partition in RAM, just as a 680x0 application is. If you examine this native PowerPC process with ZoneRanger, though, you will notice some differences between the contents of its heap zone and that of a 680x0 program.

Native PowerPC Applications and Memory

Like a 680x0 program, a native program is loaded into an application partition that has a stack and a heap. Unlike a 680x0 program, a native application doesn't use an A5 World; that's shown in Figure 9.43. Information that is held in the A5 World of a 680x0 application has been either moved or eliminated for native programs. Native application global variables, for example, are all held in a single nonrelocatable block in the application heap.

 The following discussion pertains to applications running on a Power Mac with virtual memory turned *off*. If you'd like to use ZoneRanger to examine any of your native PowerPC applications, first open the Memory control panel from the Apple menu. **N O T E** Click the **Off** radio button in the Virtual Memory section of the Control Panel, as shown in Figure 9.44. Then close the Control Panel and restart your Macintosh.

As you saw in Chapter 4, a 680x0 application has its executable code stored in CODE resources in its resource fork. When a 680x0 application launches, the CODE resources marked as preloaded will immediately be loaded into the application heap. As the program executes, other CODE resources will be loaded as needed (and possibly unloaded when unneeded). As the application needs other types of resources (WIND, MBAR, etc.), they will be loaded into the heap.

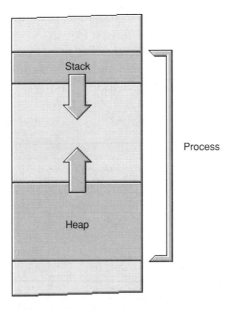

Figure 9.43 *Native applications don't have an A5 World.*

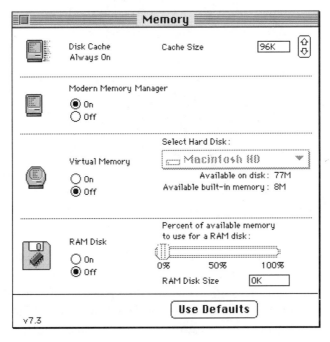

Figure 9.44 *The* Memory *Control Panel allows you to turn virtual memory on or off.*

A native PowerPC application has its executable code stored in the application's data fork. When a native PowerPC application launches, its executable code is loaded into one block of nonrelocatable memory in the application's heap, not into several relocatable blocks as it is for a 680x0 program. Like a 680x0 application, a native PowerPC application loads and uses resources as needed. Figure 9.45 provides a look at the heap of a PowerPC application that has its executable code and a few resources loaded.

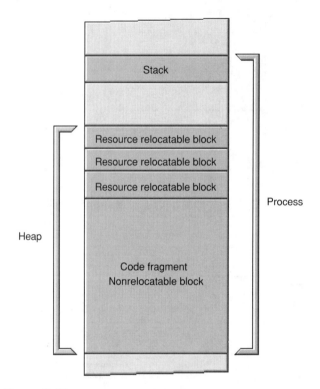

Figure 9.45 *A native application running on a Power Mac keeps its executable code in a nonrelocatable block in the heap.*

If you run a native PowerPC application on a Power Mac and then open a Zone window using ZoneRanger, you'll see a window much like the one shown in Figure 9.46. To verify this, run any of your own native applications (any program you've compiled with the Metrowerks MW C/C++ PPC compiler) or any commercial native program. One of the first blocks in the zone will be a nonrelocatable block. Because this block holds *all* of the executable code of the application, it may be quite large. Clicking on the block will tell you its size, as well as confirm that it is a block accessed by a pointer, rather than a handle.

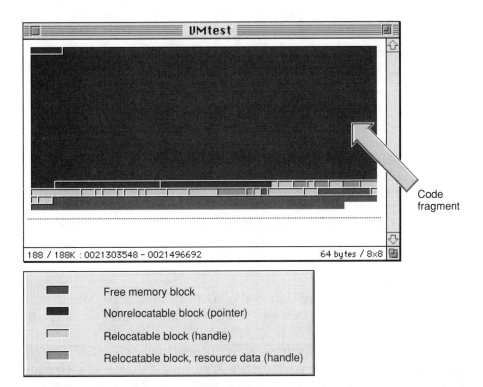

Figure 9.46 *When a native application runs on a Power Mac,* ZoneRanger *graphically illustrates that the program's code is stored in a single, nonrelocatable block.*

If you'd like further proof that the large, nonrelocatable block is indeed code, make note of the block's size and then quit the application. Launch your resource editor and open the application that you just tested with ZoneRanger. If you're using ResEdit, select **Get Info** from the File menu. If you're using Resorcerer, choose **File Info** from the File menu. Look at the size of the application's data fork (as shown using ResEdit in Figure 9.47) and compare it to the size of the large pointer block that you saw in the ZoneRanger Zone window. Because a native application stores its executable code in its data fork, these two values should be similar.

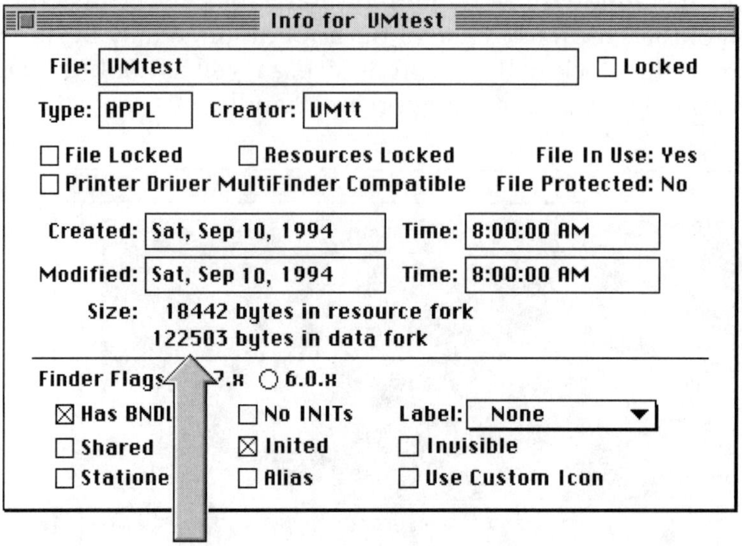

For a PowerPC application, this value usually tells the
approoximate size of the application's executable code

Figure 9.47 *The size of an application's data fork can be found by*
opening the application with either ResEdit *or* Resorcerer.

If you specify a heap size that is too small to hold the code for your
native application, the operating system will automatically enlarge the
heap to accommodate the code. Don't rely on this operating system service when establishing a heap size for your native application, though.
You should take note of your native application's data fork size and
include that value in the heap size. Remember, the application code
won't be the only block in the heap; you should allow room for
resources and any other data that your application will need.

Native PowerPC Applications and Virtual Memory

Macintosh computers equipped with a 68030, 68040, or a PowerPC
processor, and running a version of system software 7.0 or later, can use
virtual memory. Virtual memory allows the operating system to use
memory other than the Mac's physical RAM. To do this, the operating
system views a part of the hard drive memory as an extension of RAM.
This allows a user to run more applications concurrently than would be
possible without virtual memory.

If a Power Macintosh has virtual memory enabled (by turning it on in the Memory control panel and rebooting), the code fragment of a native application will *not* be loaded into the application heap when the program is launched. Instead, a part of RAM outside the application partition will be set aside to hold *some* of the application's executable code. A nonrelocatable block will then be established in the application heap to provide a link between the process and this externally located code section.

The code section for a process is not large enough to hold the entire code fragment of the application. If it were, there would be no net RAM savings. Instead, the code section is used as a holding area for parts, or *pages*, of the native application's code. As a program runs, the application's executable code remains on the hard drive—in the data fork of the application. When a part of an application's code needs to be executed, it is loaded into the code section of the process. When a different part of the application's code needs to run, the code currently in the code section is swapped with it. Figure 9.48 illustrates how a native application runs on a Power Mac with virtual memory enabled.

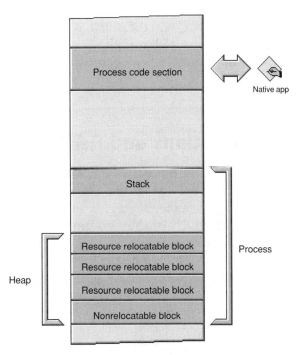

Figure 9.48 *A native application running on a Power Mac with virtual memory turned on will have its executable code stored in RAM outside of the heap, and in the application itself.*

The fact that your native application may not need any heap space for your application's code may tempt you to consider decreasing the size of your application's heap; don't do it. While many users of your PowerPC program may have virtual memory enabled, you can't make the assumption that all users will. You'll want to estimate your application's heap size with virtual memory turned off.

While the use of virtual memory is transparent to the end user (except for a slow down in program execution in some cases), it will be noticeable to you, the programmer, if you run `ZoneRanger`. Figure 9.49 shows the Zone window for the same native `VMtest` application that was used in the discussion of Power Mac memory with virtual memory turned off. If you compare Figure 9.49 with Figure 9.46, you'll see that the large nonrelocatable block found in Figure 9.46 is not present in Figure 9.49. That's because the `VMtest` application code is found outside the heap when virtual memory is turned on.

Because virtual memory is implemented in a way that makes its details transparent to the user, you won't have to consider any special virtual memory programming concerns when writing a native application. Your application will run whether virtual memory is enabled or not. Still, it's a good idea to be familiar with how virtual memory works, if for no other reason than to avoid the confusion of assuming code is missing from the heap when you examine your application with `ZoneRanger`!

Fat Binary Applications and RAM

While a fat binary application holds twice the code of either a 680x0 version or a PowerPC-only version of the same application, a fat app doesn't need a partition size twice as big as either of those versions. That's because no matter which of the two environments the fat app runs in (680x0 or PowerPC), only one of the two code versions (resource fork or data fork) will execute at any one time.

When your fat binary runs on a Power Mac, its entire code fragment will be loaded into memory. For that reason, you'll want to determine the application's heap size based on the PowerPC version of the code.

For a fat application, there's one additional consideration. Any CODE resources that are marked as preload and locked will be loaded into the heap and remain there, even though the application will use the native code from the application's data fork instead.

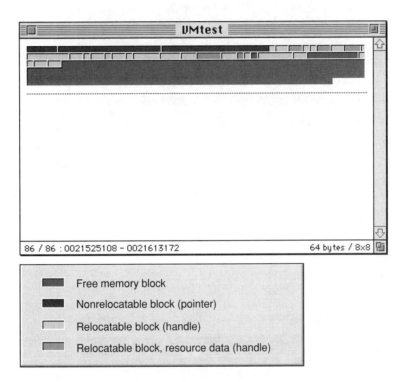

	Free memory block
	Nonrelocatable block (pointer)
	Relocatable block (handle)
	Relocatable block, resource data (handle)

Figure 9.49 ZoneRanger *demonstrates that a native application running on a Power Mac with virtual memory on will not have its code stored in its heap zone.*

In Figure 9.50, you can see that a fat binary named VMtestFat was launched on a Power Macintosh. ZoneRanger shows that the 680x0 CODE 1 resource has been loaded just before the PowerPC data fork code. This figure shows the heap with virtual memory turned off. Figure 9.51 shows the same application in a Power Mac's memory, this time with virtual memory enabled. For VMtestFat, it would be wise to add the byte size of the CODE 1 resource to the heap size of the VMtestFat application.

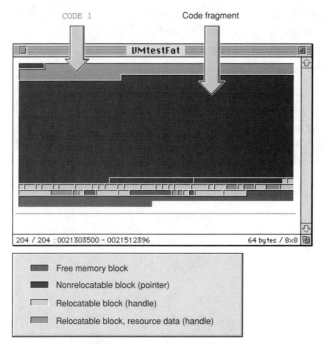

Figure 9.50 *A fat application running on a Power Mac with virtual memory turned off will have* CODE 1 *in its application heap.*

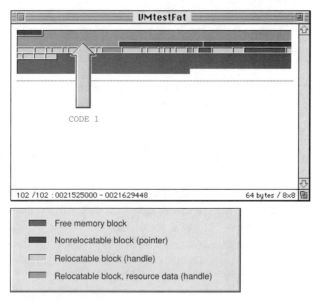

Figure 9.51 *A fat application running on a Power Mac with virtual memory enabled will also have* CODE 1 *in its application heap.*

Chapter Summary

Each Macintosh application that is executing is given its own memory partition. For a 680x0 application, this partition consists of an A5 World, a stack, and a heap. For a PowerPC application, there is no A5 World. The size of the heap—the largest part of the application partition—can be set by the programmer using the Project panel in the CodeWarrior Preferences dialog box. After rebuilding the application, the new heap size can be confirmed by selecting **Get Info** from the Finder's File menu.

An application's heap, or heap zone, holds blocks of memory. Each block is either nonrelocatable (it can't be moved by the Memory Manager), relocatable (it can be moved), or free (it is available to hold a nonrelocatable or relocatable block). Nonrelocatable blocks are accessed via pointers. Relocatable blocks are accessed using handles. A relocatable block may have (but doesn't have to have) any of the following three attributes: purgeable (it can be removed from memory by the Memory Manager), locked (it can not be moved or purged), or resource (it holds data obtained from a resource).

ZoneRanger is a software utility that is used as a memory checker. ZoneRanger is used to examine the heap zone of any application that is running on a Mac. ZoneRanger is useful because it provides a numerical and graphical look at how applications use memory.

Chapter 10

Profiler and
Program Timing

As you write a Mac program, you may have concerns about its execution speed—especially if it makes extensive use of graphics. If this is the case, you'll want to devote programming time and effort to optimizing your code, thereby eliminating unneeded code and replacing sluggish routines with faster ones. To handle this fine-tuning you'll want to rely on more than guesswork. Enter the CodeWarrior `Profiler`.

By adding a few `Profiler` function calls to your source code, you tell the Mac to keep track of processor timing information as your program executes. The `Profiler` monitors the amount of time spent in each function and saves this data to a file. This information is vital to determining which of your application-defined routines are the slowest. After quickly isolating the time-consuming functions, you'll know just where to devote your optimization energies. And when you rewrite a function in the hopes of speeding it up, you'll be able to again use the Profiler to verify that your efforts did in fact improve your program's performance.

Using the CodeWarrior Profiler

The CodeWarrior Profiler makes monitoring a program's execution speed simple. In short, you'll add a single library to your existing CodeWarrior project, include a few extra function calls in your source code, and then run your program. The timing results will all be saved to a single file that can be viewed using the CodeWarrior Profiler viewing application.

The CodeWarrior Profiler

The CodeWarrior Profiler consists of a library you add to your CodeWarrior project and a viewer application named CodeWarrior Profiler. The library holds the compiled code for a handful of Profiler functions that you invoke from the source code of whatever project you're working on.

The Profiler functions will monitor your program as it runs and will track and save information about the time your program spends in various parts of your program. They'll also create a file and save this information in it. When you quit your program, you'll run the CodeWarrior Profiler viewer application to open this file and view the results.

Figure 10.1 shows the Profiler file that is the result of profiling a simple Macintosh program—a program named ProfilerIntro68K, covered later in this chapter. The figure shows the file as viewed from the CodeWarrior Profiler application. The figure points out a few bits of information that can be garnished from the profile.

Adding Profiling to a Project

As mentioned, the Profiler isn't just an application; it's also code found in a library. When you link this library of code with the rest of a project's code, your program will be able to use the `profiler` functions that monitor processing time. That means you'll be able to determine how much time a program spends in each of your own application-defined functions. In Figure 10.2 you can see that the 68K version of the `Profiler` library has been added to a project named `ProfilerIntro68k.μ`. For PowerPC projects, you'll add the `profilerPPC.lib` library instead.

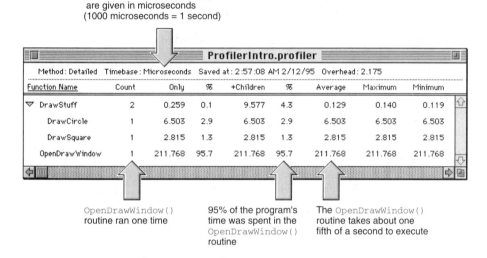

All values in the table
are given in microseconds
(1000 microseconds = 1 second)

ProfilerIntro.profiler

Method: Detailed   Timebase: Microseconds   Saved at: 2:57:08 AM 2/12/95   Overhead: 2.175

Function Name	Count	Only	%	+Children	%	Average	Maximum	Minimum
▽ DrawStuff	2	0.259	0.1	9.577	4.3	0.129	0.140	0.119
DrawCircle	1	6.503	2.9	6.503	2.9	6.503	6.503	6.503
DrawSquare	1	2.815	1.3	2.815	1.3	2.815	2.815	2.815
OpenDrawWindow	1	211.768	95.7	211.768	95.7	211.768	211.768	211.768

OpenDrawWindow()
routine ran one time

95% of the program's
time was spent in the
OpenDrawWindow()
routine

The OpenDrawWindow()
routine takes about one
fifth of a second to execute

Figure 10.1 *Some of the information that can be found in a Profiler output file.*

ProfilerIntro68K.μ

File	Code	Data	📄	🐛
▽ **Segment 1**	0	0	•	▼
ProfilerIntro.c	0	0	•	▶
ProfilerIntro.rsrc	n/a	n/a		▶
MacOS.lib	0	0		▶
profiler68k.lib	0	0		▶
4 file(s)	0	0		

Figure 10.2 *To add profiling capabilities to a 68-K project, add the profiler68k.lib library to it.*

After adding the appropriate `Profiler` library to your project, make sure that the **Generate Profiler Calls** check box is checked in the Processor panel of the Preferences dialog box. You can see this check box near the bottom of the MW C/C++ 68K compiler's Preferences dialog box in Figure 10.3. For the MW C/C++ PPC compiler, the check box is in a different location in this same panel.

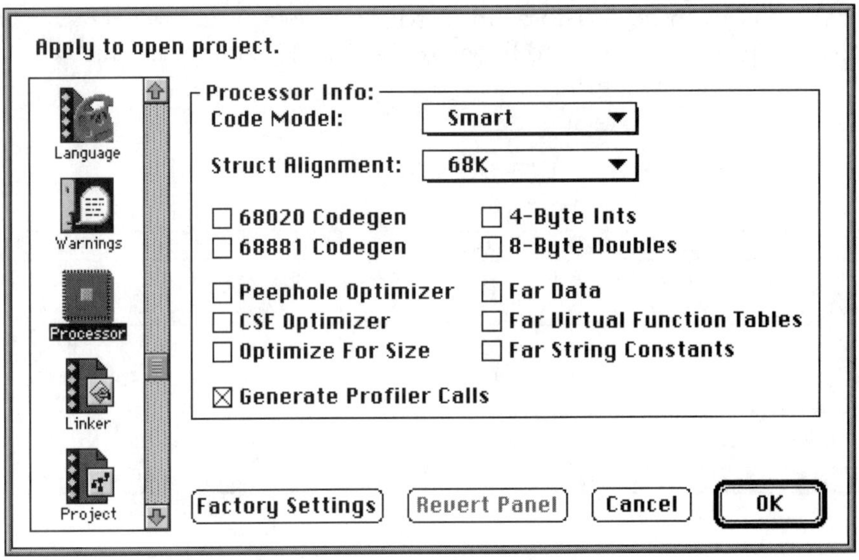

Figure 10.3 *Make sure the **Generate Profiler Calls** check box is checked for the project that is to be profiled.*

Finally, add the Profiler.h header file to your source code listing so that the function definitions are known to the compiler:

```
#include "Profiler.h"
```

The Profiler Functions

To communicate with the Profiler, you'll typically use just three functions:

ProfilerInit()	Prepares the Profiler for use and turns it on
ProfilerDump()	Creates a file and dumps the stored Profiler information to it
ProfilerTerm()	Turns the Profiler off

A few pages ahead you'll look at an example of how to add these calls to a Mac program. For now, here's a quick, abbreviated look at how they'd be used:

```
ProfilerInit( collectDetailed, bestTimeBase, 10, 10 );

// Code to monitor: can be any number of calls to the
// functions that make up your program

ProfilerDump("\pProfilerIntro.profiler");
ProfilerTerm();
```

The `ProfilerInit()` function requires four parameters. The first parameter is a constant that tells the `Profiler` whether to collect detailed (`collectDetailed`) or summary (`collectSummary`) timing information.

The second parameter to `ProfilerInit()` is a constant that tells the `Profiler` which *timebase* to use. A timebase is the means the `Profiler` uses for keeping track of time. The four available timebases range from somewhat crude (using the sixtieth second tick count available on all Macintoshes) to extremely accurate (using the built-in timing facilities found only on the PowerPC chip of a Power Mac). Typically you'll use the constant `bestTimeBase` to let the `Profiler` select the most accurate timebase available on the host machine.

The `Profiler` allocates memory for its own use—memory it uses to store timing information as your program runs. The third parameter to `ProfilerInit()` is used by the `Profiler` in its calculations of an appropriate buffer size. This parameter is the number of functions that will be profiled. If the `Profiler` will be watching your entire program, and your program defines 20 functions, this parameter should have a value of "at least" 20. Why "at least" 20? Because the `Profiler` may count a single function more than one time. If a function is called from within two functions, `Profiler` views it as two separate functions. In this snippet `Profiler` would assume it is to profile four functions: `DrawLargeShape()`, `DrawSmallShape()`, and `RequestShapeSize()`—twice:

```
void DrawLargeShape( void )
{
    RequestShapeSize( LARGE_SHAPE );

    // draw the large shape
}

void DrawSmallShape( void )
{
    RequestShapeSize( SMALL_SHAPE );

    // draw the small shape
}
```

NOTE Multiple calls to a routine, when made within the same function, aren't counted as separate functions by the `Profiler`. Thus `RequestShapeSize()` would only be considered one function in this snippet:

```
void DrawShapes( void )
{
   int  i;

   for ( i = 0; i < 10; i++ )
   {
      RequestShapeSize( UNKNOWN_SHAPE );

      // draw the shape
   }
}
```

The value of this third parameter does not have to be an exact match to the number of functions in your program. If you're profiling a large program, you can easily count the number of functions your program uses by counting the number of function prototypes, then adding a little to that value. You're best bet is to play it safe and use a value you feel is somewhat higher than the actual number of functions. It's better to have the `Profiler` allocate its buffer too big than too small.

The fourth parameter to `ProfilerInit()` is also used by the `Profiler` for allocating its own buffer. This parameter is the greatest number of functions that may be on the stack at any one time. This is the greatest length *call chain*, or *call tree*, in your program. For example, if function A calls function B, which in turn calls function C, the call chain is 3. If this is the longest chain in your program, then this final `ProfilerInit()` parameter should have a value of 3. Like the third parameter to `ProfilerInit()`, it's better to have this value too large rather than too small.

The second `Profiler` function you'll rely on is `ProfilerDump()`. When done profiling, call `ProfilerDump()` to send the collected timing information to a file. The only parameter to `ProfilerDump()` is a Pascal string that establishes the name of the file. While this can be any valid file name, you may want to consider including an extension of "prof" or "profiler" to make this file's identity obvious.

The last of the three commonly used `Profiler` routines is `ProfilerTerm()`. Before your program quits, call `ProfilerTerm()` to terminate profiling. Don't assume that quitting the program is enough to end profiling. A program that calls `ProfilerInit()` *must* also call `ProfilerTerm()`. If it doesn't, timers created by the `Profiler` may continue to run in the background and may eventually crash the user's Mac.

Adding Profiling to a Project

Checking **Generate Profiler Calls** in a project's Preferences dialog box sets a preprocessor variable named __profile__ to 1, or on. Unless your code explicitly changes the value of this variable, the `Profiler` will be considered on for every file in the current project.

N O T E

The Preferences check box should suit your needs. If you have to change the value of __profile__ in your code, though, use one of the following lines:

```
#pragma profile on    // enables  calls to the profiler

#pragma profile off   // disables calls to the profiler
```

To begin profiling, call `ProfilerInit()`. Before doing so, verify that the project is set up to be profiled by using the __profile__ variable with the #if preprocessor directive. If profiling is enabled, call `ProfilerInit()`. Then check to see if the call was successful by comparing the function's return value to the Apple constant noErr. If there was an error, you'll want to exit the program or post an alert. If there was no error, it's on to the code to profile:

```
OSErr  theErr;

#if __profile__
    theErr = ProfilerInit( collectDetailed, bestTimeBase, 10, 10 );
    if ( theErr != noErr )
      ExitToShell();
#endif

// your function calls here
```

N O T E

Note that the __profile__ preprocessor directive begins with two underscores and ends with two underscores.

When profiling is complete, again use the __profile__ variable in a check to ensure that profiling was turned on for this code. If it was, call `ProfilerDump()` and `ProfilerTerm()`. Here's how calls to the three `Profiler` routines you'll be using should look:

```
OSErr   theErr;

#if __profile__
    theErr = ProfilerInit( collectDetailed, bestTimeBase, 10, 10 );
    if ( theErr != noErr )
        ExitToShell();
#endif

// code to monitor

#if __profile__
    ProfilerDump("\pProfilerIntro.profiler");
    ProfilerTerm();
#endif
```

A Profiler Example

With the preliminaries out of the way, it's on to an example. The `ProfilerIntro68K` program found on the included CD is a simple application that opens a window and then draws a rectangle and circle in that window. Clicking the mouse button ends the program. The result of running `ProfilerIntro68K` is shown in Figure 10.4. The `ProfilerIntro68K.µ` project—with the `profiler68k.lib`—is shown in Figure 10.5.

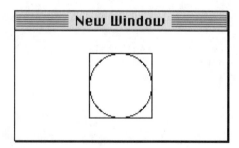

Figure 10.4 *Result of running the ProfilerIntro68K program.*

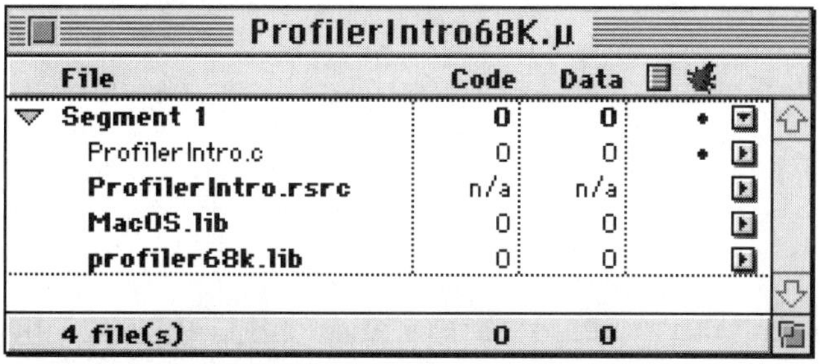

Figure 10.5 *The ProfilerIntro68K project.*

The ProfilerIntro68K Source Code

ProfilerIntro68K consists of main( ) and five application-defined functions—four of which will be profiled. Here's how the program's main( ) function would look if *no* profiling code was to be included:

```
void  main( void )
{
   InitializeToolbox();

   OpenDrawWindow();
   DrawStuff( 1 );
   DrawStuff( 2 );

   while ( !Button() )
      ;
}
```

With profiling, main( ) ends up looking like this instead:

```
void  main( void )
{
   OSErr  theErr;

   InitializeToolbox();

   #if __profile__
      theErr = ProfilerInit( collectDetailed, bestTimeBase, 10, 10 );
      if ( theErr != noErr )
         ExitToShell();
   #endif

   OpenDrawWindow();
   DrawStuff( 1 );
   DrawStuff( 2 );
```

```
#if __profile__
    ProfilerDump("\pProfilerIntro.profiler");
    ProfilerTerm();
#endif

    while ( !Button() )
        ;
}
```

Between the calls to ProfilerInit() and ProfilerTerm() lie two application-defined routines: OpenDrawWindow() and DrawStuff(). DrawStuff() itself invokes two other application-defined routines— DrawCircle() and DrawSquare()—bringing the total number of profiled functions to four. Figure 10.6 shows the functions that make up ProfilerIntro68K and highlights the four functions that will be profiled.

NOTE

The InitializeToolbox() function includes the standard Toolbox initialization code found in all Mac programs. There's little room for variance in this routine, so there's not much point in profiling it. It's here to stay, without change, so there's little need to see how much time is spent in the function. Remember, you don't *have* to profile your entire application—only the parts of interest to you.

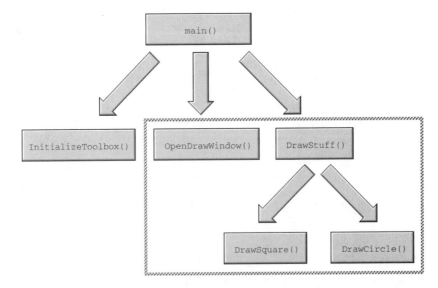

Figure 10.6 *The function hierarchy of ProfilerIntro68K, with emphasis on the functions to profile.*

Looking at Figure 10.6 you can see that four functions will be profiled, and the largest call tree is two: DrawStuff() invoking DrawSquare(), or DrawStuff() invoking DrawCircle(). That means I could pass ProfilerInit() the following parameters:

```
theErr = ProfilerInit( collectDetailed, bestTimeBase, 4, 2 );
```

Instead, I chose to call it as follows:

```
theErr = ProfilerInit( collectDetailed, bestTimeBase, 10, 10 );
```

As stated earlier, it's all right to have the Profiler allocate a little extra memory for its own buffer. In doing so, I also avoid having to keep careful track of how many functions my program calls as I add and modify routines in the ProfilerIntro68K program. If my program grows considerably, I'll reevaluate the values that get passed to ProfilerInit().

Before examining the Profiler output file, take a look at the code for the four functions that will be profiled. OpenDrawWindow() makes a call to the Toolbox routine GetNewWindow() to load the program's only resource—a WIND—into memory. DrawStuff() accepts a short parameter that determines which of two application-defined functions should be invoked. DrawSquare() does just that—draws a square in the center of the program's window. DrawCircle() draws a circle in the window's center.

```
void  OpenDrawWindow( void )
{
   WindowPtr  theWindow;

   theWindow = GetNewWindow( 128, nil, (WindowPtr)-1L );

   SetPort( theWindow );
}


void  DrawStuff( short shape )
{
   if ( shape == 1 )
      DrawCircle();
   else if ( shape == 2 )
      DrawSquare();
}


void  DrawSquare( void )
{
   Rect  theRect;
```

```
    SetRect( &theRect, 70, 20, 130, 80 );
    FrameRect( &theRect );
}


void  DrawCircle( void )
{
    Rect  theRect;

    SetRect( &theRect, 70, 20, 130, 80 );
    FrameOval( &theRect );
}
```

The Profiler Output File

After running `ProfilerIntro68K`, a new file will appear in the folder that holds the `ProfilerIntro68K` application—a file named `Profiler Intro.profiler`. This file was created by the call to `ProfilerDump()` in the `ProfilerIntro68K` program:

```
ProfilerDump("\pProfilerIntro.profiler");
```

To open the file, double-click on its icon. That will launch the CodeWarrior Profiler application—the program used to display and analyze `Profiler` files. Double-clicking the `ProfilerIntro.profiler` file will result in a window that looks like the one in Figure 10.7.

N O T E

If you run the include `ProfilerIntro68K` program and then open the resulting `Profiler` file, you'll notice that the values in your file don't match the values shown here. Values vary depending on factors such as the speed of your machine and whether virtual memory is turned on.

N O T E

Depending on the size of your monitor, you may have to use the horizontal scroll bar to see each column in the `Profiler` file.

`ProfilerIntro68K` consists of four application-defined routines that get profiled (`InitializeToolbox()` being the fifth routine, and the one function not profiled). Yet the `Profiler` window lists only two of the functions—`DrawStuff()` and `OpenDrawWindow()`. From the Profiler's point of view, these are *first-level*, or *level 1* functions, the functions that appear directly between the calls to `ProfilerInit()` and `ProfilerDump()`:

```
// ProfilerInit() called here

    OpenDrawWindow();
    DrawStuff( 1 );
    DrawStuff( 2 );

// ProfilerDump() called here
```

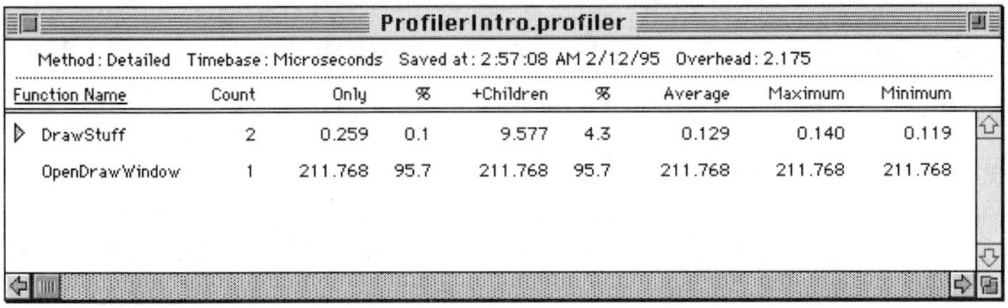

Function Name	Count	Only	%	+Children	%	Average	Maximum	Minimum
▷ DrawStuff	2	0.259	0.1	9.577	4.3	0.129	0.140	0.119
OpenDrawWindow	1	211.768	95.7	211.768	95.7	211.768	211.768	211.768

ProfilerIntro.profiler — Method: Detailed   Timebase: Microseconds   Saved at: 2:57:08 AM 2/12/95   Overhead: 2.175

Figure 10.7 *The Profiler file generated by the ProfilerIntro 68K program, as opened with the CodeWarrior Profiler application.*

When you open a Profiler file that holds detailed information (created using collectDetailed as the first parameter in the program's call to ProfilerInit()), the function hierarchy will be preserved. While only the names of the first-level functions will be displayed upon opening the file, you'll be able to see information about the functions that these first-level routines invoke. Back in Figure 10.7 you can see that DrawStuff(), which calls two other application-defined functions, has a small triangle to the left of its name. Clicking on this triangle displays the names of each application-defined function that DrawStuff() invokes, as shown in Figure 10.8.

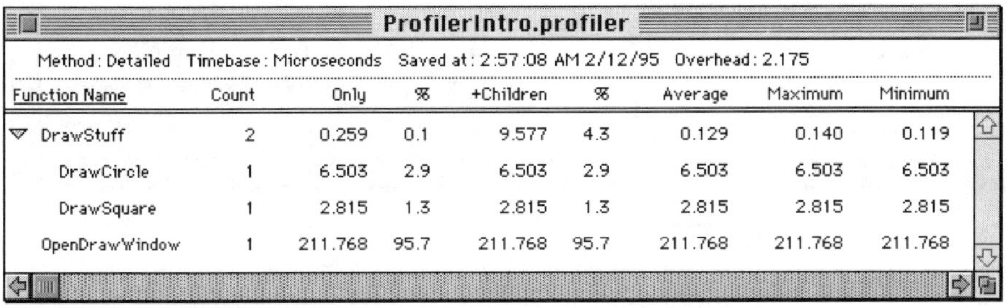

Function Name	Count	Only	%	+Children	%	Average	Maximum	Minimum
▽ DrawStuff	2	0.259	0.1	9.577	4.3	0.129	0.140	0.119
DrawCircle	1	6.503	2.9	6.503	2.9	6.503	6.503	6.503
DrawSquare	1	2.815	1.3	2.815	1.3	2.815	2.815	2.815
OpenDrawWindow	1	211.768	95.7	211.768	95.7	211.768	211.768	211.768

ProfilerIntro.profiler — Method: Detailed   Timebase: Microseconds   Saved at: 2:57:08 AM 2/12/95   Overhead: 2.175

Figure 10.8 *Clicking on a triangle by a function's name results in a display of that function's subordinate routines.*

Examining the Profiler Output File

After the function name column, a Profiler file has eight other columns. The first, Count, gives the number of times each function was invoked during the execution of the program.

The next column, Only, tells the amount of time spent in each function. The word "only" is used to denote that this value includes *only* the time spent in the one function listed in each row; it doesn't include any time spent in application-defined routines invoked by the function. To find out how much time was spent in a first-level function *and* all of its *children*, or *subordinate*, functions, look to the +Children column. In Figure 10.9 you can see that when the times spent in each of the two children functions of DrawStuff() (6.503 and 2.815 microseconds) are added to the time spent in DrawStuff() itself (0.259 microseconds), the total (9.577) is the same as the value listed in the +Children column for the DrawStuff() row.

NOTE Because the same routine can be called from more than one other function, a function can be a child of more than one first-level function. For example, if DrawCircle() was also called from OpenDrawWindow(), it would be considered a child of both DrawStuff() and OpenDrawWindow(). It would also appear indented, in its own row, under each of those first-level functions.

Time spent *only* in the function
named in each row—does *not* include
time spent in subordinate functions

	ProfilerIntro.profiler						
Method: Detailed Timebase: ┊econds Saved at: 2:57:08 AM 2/12/95 Overhead: 2.175							
Function Name	Count	Only	%	+Children	%	Average	Maximum	Minimum
▽ DrawStuff	2	0.259		9.577	4.3	0.129	0.140	0.119
DrawCircle	1	6.503	2.9	6.503	2.9	6.503	6.503	6.503
DrawSquare	1	2.815	1.3	2.815	1.3	2.815	2.815	2.815
OpenDrawWindow	1	21░ ░	95.7	211.768	95.7	211.768	211.768	211.768

The time spent in DrawStuff() and
its subordinate, or children functions, is
the time given in the +Children column

Figure 10.9 *The sum of the times for a function and the routines*
it invokes can be found in the function's +Children column.

The two percentage columns in the `Profiler` window report information in the same manner as the Only and +Children columns. The first percent column gives the percent of the time a program spends in the one function listed in a row. The second percent column—the one after the +Children column—gives the percent of the time a program spends in a function and all of the function's children. In Figure 10.10 you can see that the `DrawStuff()` function, less the calls to `DrawCircle()` and `DrawSquare()`, account for just 0.1% of the program's time. When the times spent in `DrawCircle()` and `DrawSquare()` (2.9% and 1.3%) are added to this value, the result is the time spent in `DrawStuff()` and its children (4.3%).

Like the Only column, the % column
refers to only the function named in
each row—not children functions

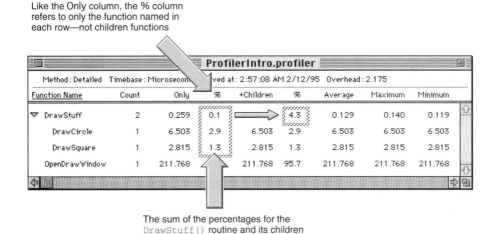

The sum of the percentages for the
`DrawStuff()` routine and its children
functions appears in the rightmost % column

Figure 10.10 *The sum of the percentages for a function and the routines it invokes can be found in the function's second % column.*

Clearly, the vast majority of the `ProfilerIntro68K` program's time is spent in the one execution of the `OpenDrawWindow()` function. More on this later....

N O T E

The last three columns in the `Profiler` window display the average, maximum, and minimum times spent in each function. If a function is executed only a single time, all three of these values will of course be the same for that one function.

A Further Look at the Profiler Output File

You can change the way in which information is displayed in a `Profiler` window by selecting menu items from the `CodeWarrior` `Profiler` View menu. If your program used the `collectDetailed` parameter in its call to `ProfilerInit()`, the resulting `Profiler` file will open with the **Detailed** menu item checked in the View menu. This item displays the application-defined functions with their hierarchy preserved. If you'd rather see all of your program's functions listed without regard for their function relationships, select **Summary** from the View menu. For the `ProfilerIntro68K` Profile file, the result would be as shown in Figure 10.11.

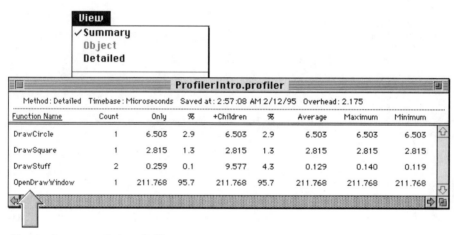

Choosing **Summary** displays all of the
profiled functions, in alphabetical order
and without regard for function hierarchy

Figure 10.11 *A Summary view shows all of a program's application defined routines, without regard for hierarchy.*

`Profiler` lists functions in alphabetical order. If you'd rather use a different criterion, choose one of the other **Sort** options in the View menu. When you do, the functions will be rearranged in the window, and the column that is used as the basis for the sort will be underlined. In Figure 10.12, the **by Maximum** menu item has been selected. This is a good way to sort the functions if you're working with a larger program and are interested in finding its slowest functions.

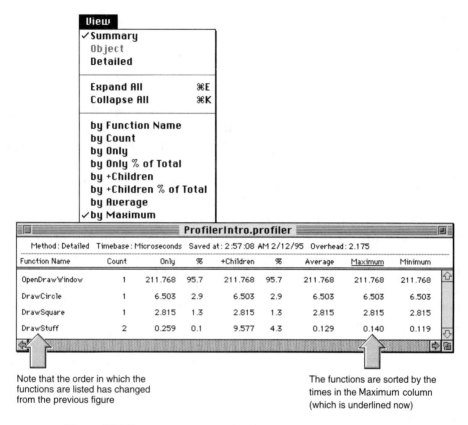

Figure 10.12 *Functions in a Profiler file can be sorted by any column.*

Speeding Up a Function

The four profiled functions in the `ProfilerIntro68K` program execute in a total time of less than a quarter of a second—not an ideal candidate for a program to devote time to fine tuning. But then, `ProfilerIntro68K` is simply a vehicle to demonstrate how `Profiler` works; it's not a real world application. Since it is a simple program, and one you're familiar with, I'll ignore its impractical nature and continue to use it in the following discussions. The techniques described on the following pages apply equally as well to your own much larger applications.

Getting a Sampling of a Function's Execution Time

One execution of a function may not provide an accurate representation of how long that function takes to execute. Why? There are several factors that can change the speed at which a function executes, including virtual memory. If you're going to make changes to a function in the hopes of speeding it up, you'll want to get an accurate idea of how long the original version of the function takes to run. Only then will you know if your changes have improved or diminished the function's speed.

Because a function's execution time can vary from one running to the next, you might want to place a call to the function in a loop. Then, compile and run the program. When complete, view the resulting `Profiler` file and look at the average time the function took to execute. I've done that for the `OpenDrawWindow()` function in the `ProfilerIntro68K` program. To preserve my original program, I've copied the entire folder that houses the `ProfilerIntro68K` project and renamed the files. The new program, called `WindowResource68K`, can be found on the book's CD.

N O T E

If you can stand the suspense, the reasoning behind this new version's name will be evident in just a bit....

The source code for `WindowResource68K` is the same as that of `ProfilerIntro68K` except for the addition of two lines of code and the changing of one in the `main()` function. The additions include a declaration of an `int` variable and a `for` loop that invokes `OpenDrawWindow()` 20 times. The one change consists of a new `Profiler` file name in the `ProfilerDump()` function. Here's the new version of `main()`—the additions are shown in larger type:

```
void  main( void )
{
   int    i;
   OSErr  theErr;

   InitializeToolbox();

   #if __profile__
       theErr = ProfilerInit( collectDetailed, bestTimeBase, 10, 10 );
```

```
        if ( theErr != noErr )
            ExitToShell();
    #endif

    for ( i = 0; i < 20; i++ )
        OpenDrawWindow();

    DrawStuff( 1 );
    DrawStuff( 2 );

    #if __profile__
        ProfilerDump("\pWindowRes.profiler");
        ProfilerTerm();
    #endif

    while ( !Button() )
        ;
}
```

The third parameter to `ProfilerInit()`—the number of functions called—hasn't changed. My overestimate of 10 is still valid. Though `OpenDrawWindow()` is called 10 times, the `Profiler` views it as only one function. That's because all 10 calls are made from the same routine—`main()`.

Recall that earlier I found that `OpenDrawWindow()` took about 211 microseconds, or just over a fifth of a second, to execute on my Macintosh. After running the `WindowResource68K` program, I now see that on an average, this function takes closer to a quarter of a second to run. This value of 240 microseconds (shown in Figure 10.13) is the number I'll use in comparisons to subsequent versions of the `OpenDrawWindow()` function.

The looping method is a good way to compare an average time of one version of a function to the average time of another version of that same function. If you aren't interested in which version of a function is quicker, but instead want to know the execution time of a function "as is," then you might want to reconsider putting it in a loop. If the function won't appear in a loop in the actual program, then don't place it in a loop during testing. Why? The same code is repeatedly being executed, so it might end up in cache memory. Thus the average time would be lower than the time for a single execution of the same function.

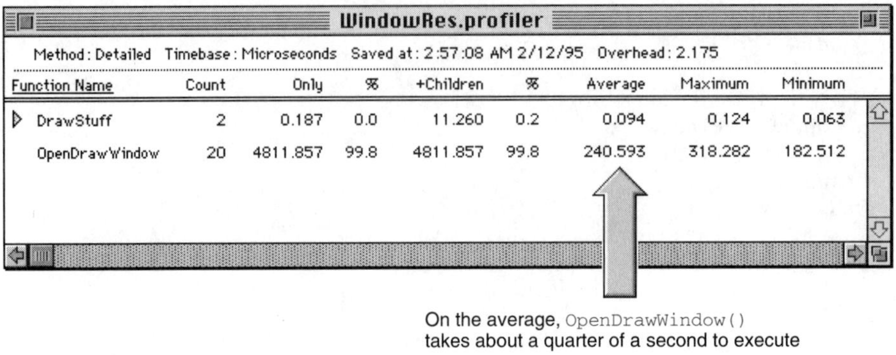

On the average, `OpenDrawWindow()`
takes about a quarter of a second to execute

Figure 10.13 *The Profiler file shows that the OpenDrawWindow()
function takes a quarter of a second to run.*

Improving the OpenDrawWindow() Function?

Why the question mark in this sections heading? When you attempt to fine-tune a function, there's no guarantee that your improved version will be just that—improved. But it never hurts to try.

`OpenDrawWindow()` consists of just three lines of code. Your own functions will of course be larger and will afford you more opportunities (and challenges) for fine-tuning. Still, even this short piece of code, shown below, may open to improvement.

```
void  OpenDrawWindow( void )
{
    WindowPtr  theWindow;

    theWindow = GetNewWindow( 128, nil, (WindowPtr)-1L );

    SetPort( theWindow );
}
```

In a Macintosh program there are two ways to open a window. You can use a call to the Toolbox function `GetNewWindow()` to load window information from a `WIND` resource into memory, or you can use a call to the Toolbox function `NewWindow()`, passing in the window information as parameters to the function. `ProfilerIntro68K` uses `GetNewWindow()`. `WindowResource68K`, created to test the timing of the `ProfilerIntro68K` version of `OpenDrawWindow()`, does the same.

As written, `ProfilerIntro68K` gets its window information from a `WIND` resource. That means the program has to locate a particular resource (`WIND 128`) and call `GetResource()` to load the information contained in that resource into memory. A call to `NewWindow()`, on the other hand, doesn't have to access any resources. In theory, this sounds quicker. Here's how `OpenDrawWindow()` looks if a call to `NewWindow()` is substituted for the call to `GetNewWindow()`:

```
void  OpenDrawWindow( void )
{
   WindowPtr   theWindow;
   Rect        theRect;

   SetRect( &theRect, 10, 40, 210, 140 );
   theWindow = NewWindow( nil, &theRect, "\pNew Window", true,
                     documentProc, (WindowPtr)-1L, false, nil );

   SetPort( theWindow );
}
```

Does the theory hold up in practice? To see, I've copied the folder that holds the `WindowResource68K` files to create a new CodeWarrior project. The source code for this project has the same `for` loop that is found in the `WindowResource68K` source code—the loop that executes `OpenDraw Window()` 20 times. The difference is in the `OpenDrawWindow()` routines. The `WindowCode68K` version uses `NewWindow()`, as shown above.

After compiling and running the `WindowCode68K` program, it's time to examine the `Profiler` file. Figure 10.14 shows that this new version of `OpenDrawWindow()` takes an average of about 150 microseconds to run—just under one seventh of a second. That's down from the `GetNewWindow()` version of `OpenDrawWindow()`, which took about 240 microseconds, or a quarter of a second.

Is a potential savings of about a tenth of a second (150 microseconds from 240 microseconds) worth the abandonment of my practice of using a resource editor to create easily modifiable windows? Probably not. But then, the true purpose of this exercise wasn't really to dramatically speed up the `ProfilerIntro68K` program; it was to see the *steps* to take to speed up a function. Those same steps, outlined as follows, can be applied to routines that will really benefit from small time savings. In particular, graphics routines and functions that perform calculations that keep the user waiting for results are prime candidates for optimization.

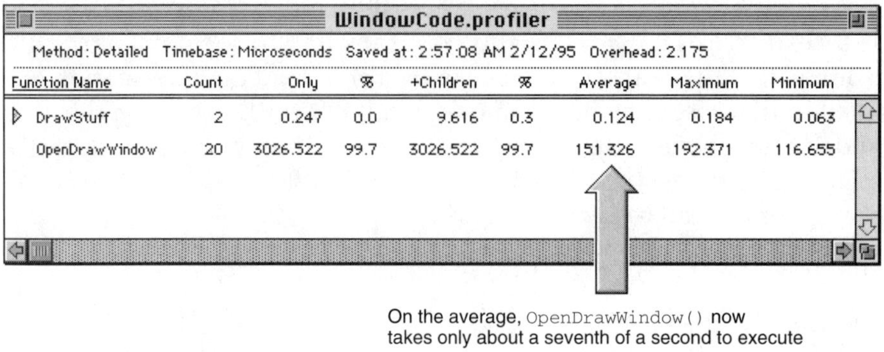

On the average, `OpenDrawWindow()` now
takes only about a seventh of a second to execute

Figure 10.14 *After making changes to the* `OpenDrawWindow()`
function, its execution time is decreased.

Here are the steps you'll want to follow when using `Profiler` to help
speed up your program.

- Profile the functions in your application.
- Determine the average execution time of a function you feel is slowing down your program.
- Analyze the function to see where improvements might be made.
- Make the change or changes and determine the average execution time of the new version of the function.
- Compare the execution times of the two versions of the function and decide if the time savings justify the changes.

Determining Which Part of a Function Is Slow

If the `Profiler` shows that one of your application-defined functions
seems slow, but you aren't sure which lines of code are causing the sluggish performance, move the contents of the one function into two or
more new functions. Then call these new routines from the original function. Consider a program that has a function named `DrawObjects()`.
This routine draws two objects in a window. For this example the specific code used to perform the drawing isn't important, so I'll show the
`DrawObjects()` routine as follows:

```
void DrawObjects( void )
{
   // code to draw 1st object
   // code to draw 2nd object
}
```

Profiling the DrawObjects() function shows that the routine takes more than 1500 microseconds to execute. That's longer than a second and a half—a time period that's too long for the quick updating of a window. Figure 10.15 shows that by profiling DrawObjects() I can find the time this routine takes to run, but no details of *where* the time-consuming code lies is revealed.

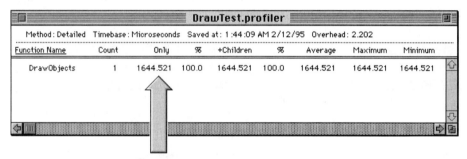

Doesn't indicate which code in this function
is responsible for the majority of this time

Figure 10.15 *The Profiler gives the total execution time for a function.*

To confine my fine-tuning efforts to the slow code, I'll break up the DrawObjects() code into two new functions: DrawObjectOne() and DrawObjectTwo(). Then I'll have DrawObjects() call both these new routines, as shown here:

```
void DrawObjects( void )
{
   DrawObjectOne();
   DrawObjectTwo();
}

void DrawObjectOne( void )
{
   // code to draw 1st object
}
```

```
void DrawObjectTwo( void )
{
    // code to draw 2nd object
}
```

As far as program execution, the end result will of course be the same as the original version of DrawObjects(). With the new version, however, the Profiler will be able to report the execution time in a more helpful manner. As shown in Figure 10.16, it's the code that draws the first object that takes the most time. This is the code I'll want to expend the greatest effort on improving. After I've sped up DrawObjectOne(), I can move the code from DrawObjectOne() and DrawObjectTwo() back into DrawObjects().

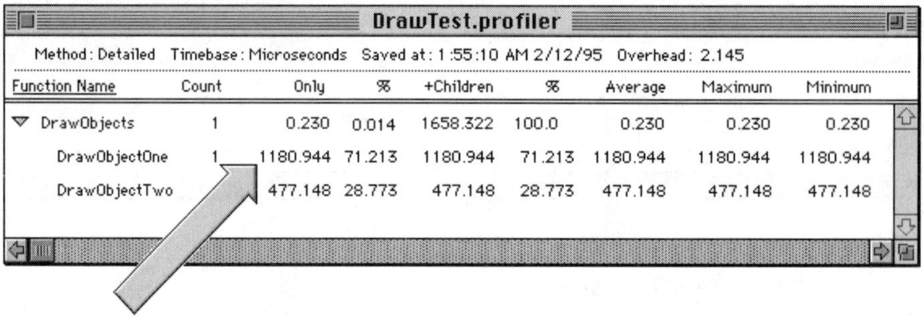

Now it's clear that the code that draws the first of two objects is the time-consuming code

Figure 10.16 *Dividing the contents of a single function into two separate functions helps determine where the slow code is located.*

Analyzing the Drawing Time of PICTs

The Profiler is a great utility for examining an existing Mac project and determining where speed enhancements can be made. But it's also a good code exploration tool. For example, you can write a short test program that performs one task, then profile it to see if your way of doing things is efficient. In this section I'll profile a test program that opens PICT resources and displays them in a window. I'll profile the program to see how fast this task is carried out by the Toolbox routines GetPicture() and DrawPicture(), and to see just what effect picture byte size has on drawing time.

Creating a Simple Test Program

To test the speed of a few routines or of a programming technique of yours, you don't need to write a full-blown Macintosh application. Instead, quickly set up a simple project that forgoes the event loop and terminates with the click of the mouse button. You can use the Toolbox routine Button() to check to see if the mouse button is down. If it's not (!), then carry on with the loop (;):

```
while ( !Button() )
   ;
```

If the code you'll be testing uses the mouse button, the preceding strategy won't work—the mouse button click will instead end your test program. In that case you can replace the preceding while loop with a loop that looks for the press of a particular key, such as "q" for "quit":

```
unsigned char   theKeyMap[16];
Boolean  quitKeyPressed = false;
short    keyNum = 12;

while ( quitKeyPressed == false )
{
   GetKeys( (long *)theKeyMap );
   quitKeyPressed = (theKeyMap[keyNum >> 3] >> (keyNum & 7)) & 1;
}
```

> Yes, it does look ugly. Briefly, here's what's going on. The Toolbox function GetKeys() fills 16 bytes (128 bits) with information about the current state of the keyboard. Each bit tells whether one particular key is pressed (bit equals 1) or not pressed (bit equals 0). The C language can be used to readily access bytes, but not bits. So a little bit shifting and bit masking needs to be done to examine any single bit. The above code is looking to see if the "q" key is pressed. On a Macintosh keyboard, the key number of the "q" key is $0C, or 12. Each pass through the above loop checks the state of the keyboard to see if the "q" key has been pressed. For more information on keyboard key numbering, refer to *Inside Macintosh: Macintosh Toolbox Essentials*.

Next, write the function that is to be tested, and then invoke it. Place the call to it between the calls to ProfilerInit() and ProfilerDump(). Run the program, then examine the Profiler file to see how fast your code executes.

The PictureResource68K Test Program

You might guess that DrawPicture() will take longer to draw a larger picture to a window than a smaller picture. But how much longer? Will a picture that is twice as large in pixel size take twice as long to draw? What about a picture that is twice as large in byte size? To answer these questions, I've written a short program named PictureResource68K that loads two PICT resources and draws them to a window.

PictureResource68K loads two pictures, PICT resources with IDs of 128 and 129, into memory and draws them to the same window, one on top of the other. Figure 10.17 shows the two PICT resources in Resorcerer. In Figure 10.18 you can see that the PictureResource68K program draws picture 129 (the small Metrowerks picture) over picture 128 (the larger airplane picture).

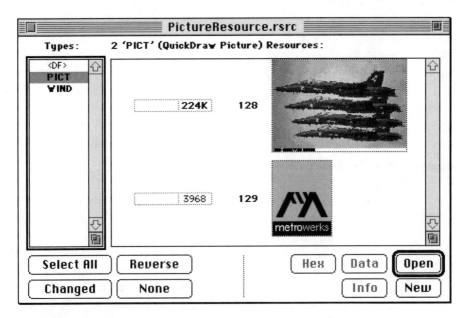

Figure 10.17 *The two PICT resources used by the PictureResource68K project.*

 If your program works with large PICT resources, don't forget to set your application's heap accordingly, as discussed in Chapter 9. The largest PICT resource in the Picture Resource68K program is about 225K, so the 384K heap that **N O T E** CodeWarrior defaults to is large enough.

Figure 10.18 *The result of running the PictureResource68K program.*

To profile my code, I've written a single function named `DrawStuff()` and placed it between the three standard `Profiler` functions. Below is a look at the `PictureResource68K` program's `main()` routine. Notice that I've kept the program simple by using the `Button()` routine to end the program at the first click of the mouse button.

```
void  main( void )
{
   WindowPtr  theWindow;
   OSErr      theErr;

   InitializeToolbox();

   theWindow = GetNewWindow( 128, nil, (WindowPtr)-1L );

   SetPort( theWindow );

   #if __profile__
      theErr = ProfilerInit( collectDetailed, bestTimeBase, 10, 10 );
      if ( theErr != noErr )
         ExitToShell();
```

```
#endif

DrawStuff();

#if __profile__
    ProfilerDump("\pPictRes.profiler");
    ProfilerTerm();
#endif

while ( !Button() )
    ;
}
```

DrawStuff() calls an application-defined routine named GetPicture
Resource() to load a single picture into memory and to obtain the rectangle that holds the pictures boundary. GetPictureResource() accepts
a PICT ID and a pointer to a rectangle as its two parameters, and it
returns a handle to the loaded picture. A second application-defined
routine, DrawPicture128(), uses the returned picture handle and rectangle to draw the picture to a window. These steps are repeated for a
second picture—one with an ID of 129.

```
void  DrawStuff( void )
{
    PicHandle   thePicture;
    Rect        pictRect;

    thePicture = GetPictureResource( 128, &pictRect );
    DrawPicture128( thePicture, pictRect );

    thePicture = GetPictureResource( 129, &pictRect);
    DrawPicture129( thePicture, pictRect );

    ReleaseResource( (Handle)thePicture );
}
```

Here's a look at GetPictureResource(). I'm not concerned with the
four boundaries of the rectangle entering the routine. Instead, I'm
counting on GetPictureResource() to fill the pictRect variable with
the loaded pictures boundaries. Notice that a pointer to a rectangle is
passed to the routine rather than a rectangle. That way, the changes
made to the rectangle's boundaries will show up back in the calling
routine, DrawStuff().

```
PicHandle  GetPictureResource( short pictID, Rect *pictRect )
{
    Rect        theRect;
    PicHandle   thePicture;
    short       theWidth;
    short       theHeight;

    thePicture = GetPicture( pictID );

    theRect = (**(thePicture)).picFrame;
    theWidth  = theRect.right - theRect.left;
    theHeight = theRect.bottom - theRect.top;
    SetRect( pictRect, 0, 0, theWidth, theHeight );

    return ( thePicture );
}
```

After `GetPictureResource()` returns the picture handle and picture boundary rectangle, a call is made to `DrawPicture128()` to draw the picture to the window. After `DrawStuff()` calls `GetPictureResource()` and `DrawPicture128()` to draw the first picture, it then calls `GetPictureResource()` and `DrawPicture129()` to draw the second picture.

```
void  DrawPicture128( PicHandle thePicture, Rect pictRect )
{
    DrawPicture( thePicture, &pictRect );
}


void  DrawPicture129( PicHandle thePicture, Rect pictRect )
{
    DrawPicture( thePicture, &pictRect );
}
```

Figure 10.19 shows how `DrawStuff()`, `DrawPictureResource()`, and `DrawPicture128()` work together to draw a picture with resource ID 128.

The two drawing routines, `DrawPicture128()` and `DrawPicture129()` are identical, so I could easily have used a single function. But that would have defeated the point of the program. I'm using the `Profiler` to compare the time it takes to draw two different-sized pictures. When the program completes, I'll be looking at the timing information for the two functions.

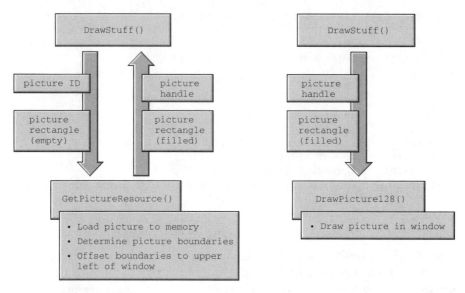

Figure 10.19 *The functionality of the PictureResource68K program.*

N O T E Since DrawPicture128() consists of nothing more than a call to the Toolbox routine DrawPicture(), I could also have omitted the DrawPicture128() function altogether and just included the call to DrawPicture() in DrawStuff(), like this, right?

```
thePicture = GetPictureResource( 128, &pictRect );
DrawPicture( thePicture, &pictRect );
```

Wrong! Sure, the program would work. But since the picture-drawing code would now be buried in the DrawStuff() routine, along with other code, the Profiler wouldn't be able to profile how long the drawing of PICT 128 took. I've intentionally isolated the picture-drawing code in its own routine so that the Profiler could keep track of the execution time of this code—apart from all other code.

Examining the PictureResource68K Profiler Output

After running PictureResource68K, double-click on the PictRes.profiler file that appears in the PictureResource68K directory. When you do, you'll see a window similar to the one shown in Figure 10.20. Of most interest to you will be the columns that show the speed at which

`DrawPicture128()` and `DrawPicture129()` ran. From the figure, you can see that on my Macintosh the larger airplane picture took more than 800 microseconds—more than three quarters of a second—to draw, while the small Metrowerks picture took just 30 microseconds to draw. As guessed, it takes the Toolbox longer to draw a large picture than a small picture, though you might not have suspected the difference in time would be so great.

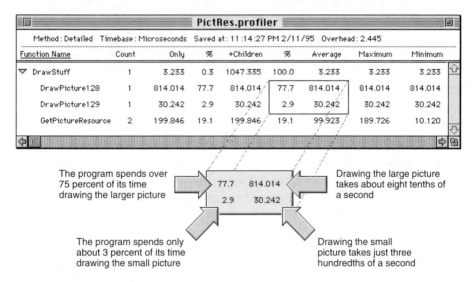

Figure 10.20 *The Profiler clearly shows the speed at which each function runs.*

Also of interest in Figure 10.20 is the timing of the `GetPicture Resource()` function. This function executes twice—one time to load each of the two `PICT` resources. By looking at the Maximum and Minimum columns you can see that it took much longer for `GetPicture Resource()` to load one of the two pictures. While you might have a pretty good idea which picture took longer to load, you'd need to do a copy and paste on `GetPictureResource()` to create `GetPicture Resource128()` and `GetPictureResource129()` routines to verify your suspicions.

What would happen if you put a call to `GetPictureResource()` inside a loop to get an average execution time? The result might surprise you. While the Maximum column might show a value such as 180 microseconds, the Minimum column would show a value *much* smaller, perhaps 1 microsecond or less. That's because of how the GetPicture() Toolbox function works. If the PICT resource GetPicture() is to load is already in memory (as it would be after the first iteration of the loop), GetPicture() doesn't reload it—it just returns the handle to the picture.

To get timing information for two different pictures, just open the PictureResource68K program (not the project resource file) with a resource editor and either cut out the original two pictures or renumber them. Then paste in the new PICT resources. Give the new pictures IDs of 128 and 129, then save the program and quit the resource editor. Rerun PictureResource68K. When you look at the new Profiler file that gets generated, the DrawPicture128() and DrawPicture129() routines will now show the times for the drawing of these two pictures.

You can use PictureResource68K to study the drawing times for all different types of pictures. For example, you can make two copies of the same picture: one in color, one in grayscale. Add these two pictures to the PictureResource68K program and compare the drawing times of color versus grayscale.

N O T E

To make a grayscale copy of a picture, open the picture using a graphics program. Then change the color level of your monitor from color to gray using the Monitors Control Panel. Next, do a screen dump (**Command-Shift-3**). Open the resulting PICT file with your graphics program and select and copy the area that holds your picture.

Profiler and the Event Loop

All of the Profiler examples to this point have been short, simple programs that end when the user clicks the mouse button. This is adequate for the purpose of demonstrating how the Profiler works, and for short test programs like the PICT resource timer program Picture Resourse68K. But your Mac applications will of course be larger and, more importantly, won't end when the user clicks the mouse button. That doesn't present a problem for the Profiler. In fact, profiling an event-driven Mac application is quite simple.

The EventLoop68K Program

On this book's CD you'll find a program named EventLoop68K. The program displays two menus—the Apple and File menus. The Apple menu holds the **About** menu item, as well as all of the user's Apple Menu Item folder items. The File menu has a single item—**Quit**. When you run EventLoop68K, an empty, draggable window will open. Figure 10.21 shows the program's menus and window. The program watches for update events (updateEvt) and mouse down events (mouseDown), and responds to each. EventLoop68K is a standard event-driven Mac program that takes up a couple of pages of source code.

NOTE The intent of this section isn't to discuss in detail the code that makes up a basic Mac program, but rather to find out how the Profiler can be used to gain an understanding of an event-driven program. For that reason the entire listing of EventLoop68K isn't given here. If you're interested, open the EventLoop.c source code file on the included CD.

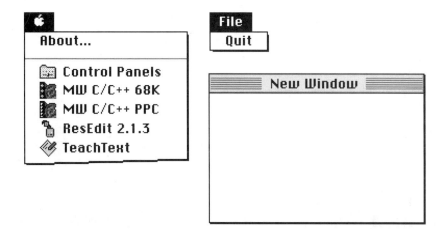

Figure 10.21 *The menus and window of the EventLoop68K program.*

EventLoop68K consists of a main() function and eight other application-defined routines. Their function prototypes are listed as follows.

```
void   InitializeToolbox( void );
void   SetUpMenuBar( void );
void   EventLoop( void );
```

```
void  HandleUpdate( void );
void  HandleMouseDown( void );
void  HandleMenuChoice ( long );
void  HandleAppleChoice( short );
void  HandleFileChoice( short );
```

The `main()` function initializes the Toolbox, sets up the menu bar, opens a window, and then jumps into the main event loop. To profile an event-driven program, you can use the same three `Profiler` functions that have been used throughout this chapter. Now, just place the call to the event loop routine between them. Here's how `EventLoop68K` does that:

```
void  main( void )
{
   WindowPtr   theWindow;
   OSErr       theErr;

   InitializeToolbox();
   SetUpMenuBar();

   theWindow = GetNewWindow( WIND_ID, nil, (WindowPtr)-1L );
   SetPort( theWindow );

#if __profile__
    theErr = ProfilerInit( collectDetailed, bestTimeBase, 10, 10 );
    if ( theErr != noErr )
        ExitToShell();
#endif

   EventLoop();

#if __profile__
    ProfilerDump("\pEventLoop.profiler");
    ProfilerTerm();
#endif
```

Function Dependencies and the Profiler

To test the profiling, I ran `EventLoop68K` and put the program through its paces. I clicked on the window, dragged it, and released the mouse button. I did that a second time. Then I selected the **About** menu item from the Apple menu. Next, I selected the **Scrapbook** from the Apple menu. Finally, I chose **Quit** from the File menu. All of this action was followed by the `Profiler` and saved to a file named `EventLoop.profiler`. Figure

10.22 shows what that file looks like for my sample running of EventLoop68K.

Function Name	Count	Only	%	+Children	%	Average	Maximum	Minimum
▽ EventLoop	1	17027.783	74.1	22973.144	100.0	17027.783	17027.783	17027.783
▽ HandleMouseDown	5	4427.267	19.3	5937.919	25.8	885.453	1288.354	451.685
▽ HandleMenuChoice	3	13.884	0.1	1510.652	6.6	4.628	4.682	4.586
HandleAppleChoice	2	1496.768	6.5	1496.768	6.5	748.384	766.009	730.759
HandleFileChoice	1	0.000	0.0	0.000	0.0	0.000	0.000	0.000
HandleUpdate	1	7.442	0.0	7.442	0.0	7.442	7.442	7.442

EventLoop.profiler
Method: Detailed   Timebase: Microseconds   Saved at: 8:59:12 PM 2/18/95   Overhead: 9.492

Figure 10.22 *The Profiler output file for the EventLoop68K program.*

Before looking at the values in the columns of the Profiler window, take notice of the levels at which the EventLoop68K application-defined functions are listed under Function Name. At the first level is the EventLoop() function. At the second level are HandleMouseDown() and Handle Update(). The third level lists HandleMenuChoice(), while the fourth level shows HandleAppleChoice() and HandleFileChoice(). Figure 10.23 emphasizes how the Profiler displays a program's functional hierarchy. Figure 10.24 gives you another way of viewing the hierarchy.

The functional hierarchy displayed in the Profiler window is itself a good tool for analyzing a large program. It clearly shows a program's flow of control as well as its function dependencies. If one of your programs isn't behaving as expected, simply profiling it and looking at the Function Name column of the generated Profiler file may be enough to help you find any flaws in your logic.

Examining the Profiler Output

From the time profiling began (just after the program's window opened) until profiling ended, my test running of the EventLoop68K program took about 23 seconds. In this section I'll look at those 23 seconds, not to find a way to reduce the execution time of any routines, but rather to gain a better understanding of how an event-driven program operates.

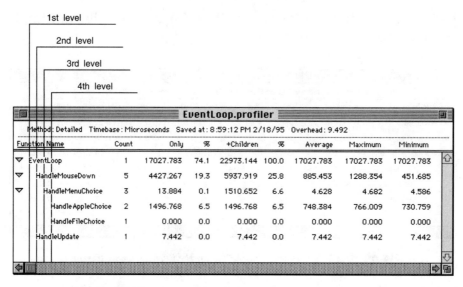

Figure 10.23 *Profiler displays functions by hierarchy, or level.*

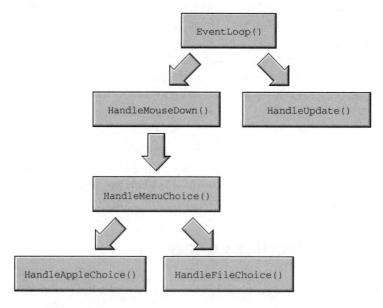

Figure 10.24 *Another way of displaying a program's function hierarchy.*

Once the EventLoop68K program invokes EventLoop()—the main event loop routine—the program stays in this routine (and the rou-

tine's children) until the program ends. The event loop consists of a
`while` loop that cycles continuously until a global variable named
`gAllDone` is set to `true` (by the user selecting **Quit** from the File menu).
Even when no action is taking place, the program is still running the
event loop, waiting for a new event to take place. This means that as
long as the program is running, the `Profiler` will be logging time to
the `EventLoop()` routine and its children. For example, if the user runs
`EventLoop68K` for 60 seconds before quitting, the `EventLoop()` routine's +Children column will have a value of 60,000 microseconds.

Just as the time in the `EventLoop()` +Children column will be high,
so will the time spent in the `EventLoop()` routine itself (as logged in the
`EventLoop()` Only column). This long period of time in the `EventLoop()`
routine doesn't mean the routine is flawed—it's just the nature of an
event-driven program. If you want to reduce the execution time of a program, you'll look at routines other than the event loop. Figure 10.25
shows that for the 23 seconds I ran the `EventLoop68K` program (see the
+Children column), the program spent about 17 seconds cycling through
the `while` loop in the `EventLoop()` routine.

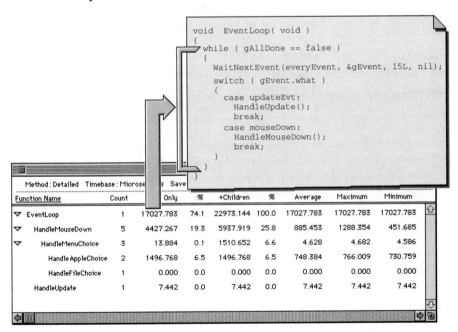

Figure 10.25 *Much of the EventLoop68K program's execution
time is spent cycling through the event loop.*

The `Profiler` output file shows that `HandleMouseDown()` takes about 4.5 seconds to execute (4427 microseconds) five times. This relatively long period of time isn't due to a poorly written function, though. Instead, the time is dependent on how long the user holds down the mouse button when making a menu selection and when dragging a window. When the user clicks on a menu, `HandleMouseDown()` calls the Toolbox function `MenuSelect()`. This routine gains and maintains control of the program until the user releases the mouse button, whether that's a half second or a hundred seconds. The same is true of the Toolbox function `DragWindow()`. When the user clicks on a window's title bar and drags a window, `DragWindow()` executes until the user releases the mouse button.

Figure 10.26 shows what `HandleMouseDown()` looks like and serves as a reminder that it is the routine's calls to the two Toolbox functions that are responsible for the routine's execution time.

When running `EventLoop68K`, I clicked the mouse five times. Three of the five executions of `HandleMouseDown()` are devoted to menu item selections (`inMenuBar`), while the other two executions handle window dragging (`inDrag`).

Looking at the Only column for the `HandleMenuChoice()` function shows that this routine uses only about 14 microseconds of CPU time to execute three times. That's because there's not much to `HandleMenuChoice()`. The bulk of the work is done using the Toolbox routines `HiWord()` and `LoWord()` to extract the menu and menu item from the one long variable `menuChoice`. The `Profiler` file shows that excluding the time spent in subordinate functions, `HandleMenuChoice()` took about 14 microseconds to run, while the function and its children routines together took over 1500 microseconds. This should cause you to guess that it must be the children functions of `HandleMenuChoice()` that do the real work. Figure 10.27 adds emphasis to this point.

`HandleMenuChoice()` takes very little time to run; it's the routine's children that take time. Actually, as you can see in Figure 10.28, only one of its two children functions uses much time. The `HandleAppleChoice()` executes two times, at a cost of about 750 microseconds (three fourths of a second) each time. The `HandleFileChoice()` function appears to take zero time! In fact, it executes so quickly that its execution time is less than the accuracy at which `Profiler` can measure, so `Profiler` simply enters 0.0 for the timing.

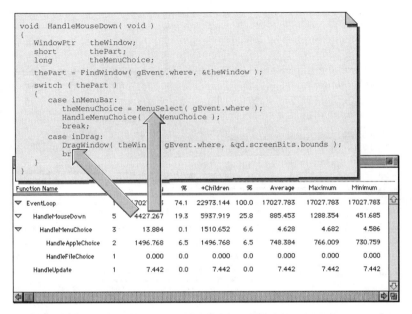

Figure 10.26 *The MenuSelect() and DragWindow() Toolbox functions are responsible for the length of execution of the HandleMouseDown() routine.*

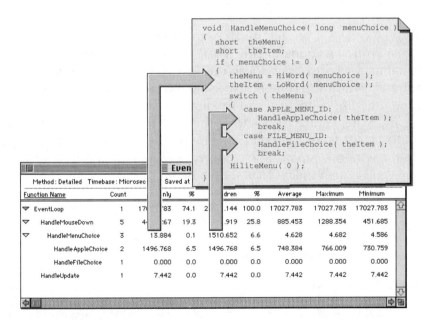

Figure 10.27 *The HandleMenuChoice() function does little work; instead, its subordinate routines take care of menu selections.*

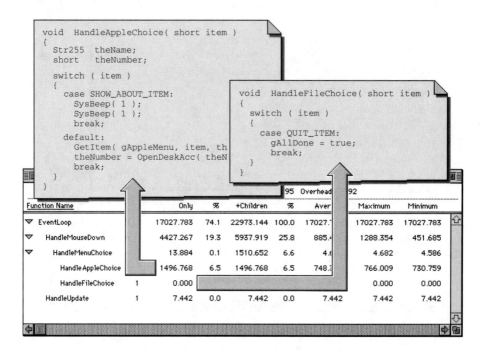

Figure 10.28 *HandleAppleChoice() uses CPU time, while HandleFileChoice() uses almost none.*

Finally, you can see from Figure 10.29 that the `HandleUpdate()` function takes just 7 microseconds to run. That's because this function is set up for updating a window, but doesn't do any drawing. If `HandleUpdate()` *did* redraw a window's contents, the single comment would be replaced with the drawing code, or a call to an application-defined routine that did the drawing. Figure 10.29 shows the code for the `EventLoop68K` version of `HandleUpdate()`. If you'd like to modify it so that it draws a picture to the window, replace the commented line with a call to a routine like `UpdatePictureWindow()`, as shown here:

```
void  HandleUpdate( void )
{
    WindowPtr   theWindow;

    theWindow = ( WindowPtr )gEvent.message;

    BeginUpdate( theWindow );
        EraseRgn( theWindow->visRgn );
        UpdatePictureWindow();              // call routine to draw picture
    EndUpdate( theWindow );
}
```

```
void  UpdatePictureWindow( void )
{
   PicHandle   thePicture;
   Rect        theRect;
   short       theWidth;
   short       theHeight;

   thePicture = GetPicture( 128 );
   theRect = (**(thePicture)).picFrame;
   theWidth = theRect.right - theRect.left;
   theHeight = theRect.bottom - theRect.top;
   SetRect( &theRect, 0, 0, theWidth, theHeight );
   DrawPicture( thePicture, &theRect );
   ReleaseResource( (Handle)thePicture );
}
```

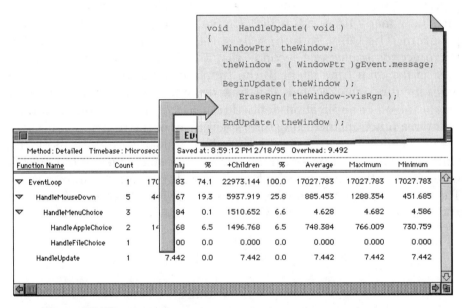

Figure 10.29 *If HandleUpdate() included code to redraw a window's contents,
its execution time could be much higher.*

Chapter Summary

The time that each application-defined routine takes to execute can easily be determined for any program. To do so, follow these steps:

1. Add the appropriate `Profiler` library (profiler68k.lib or
profilerPPC.lib) to the project to profile.

2. Make sure the **Generate Profiler Calls** check box is checked in the Processor panel of the Preferences dialog box.

3. Include the `profiler` header file `Profiler.h` in the project's source code.

4. Call `ProfilerInit()` *before* any calls are made to the functions to profile.

5. Call `ProfilerDump()` and `ProfilerTerm()` *after* all function's are profiled.

6. Open the resulting `Profiler` file with the CodeWarrior `Profiler` application.

The output file generated by the `Profiler` reveals much about how processor time is being spent in an application. The Count column indicates how many times a function was called during the running of the program. The Only column tells the time, in microseconds (1000 microseconds equals one second), that a function took to execute. This time is the total time spent in the function, regardless of how many times the function executed. This time doesn't include the time spent in any of the other application-defined routines. To find out the total time spent in a function, including time spent in all of the function's subordinate, or children, functions, look to the +Children column. Both the Only and +Children times can be viewed as percentages of the overall time spent in the program—look at the % columns for this information. The remaining three columns of the `Profiler` file—Average, Maximum, and Minimum—are self-explanatory.

Index

4-Byte Ints checkbox, 47-48
68881 Codegen checkbox, 47
68K projects
    adding file to, 18-19
    building application, 21
    compiling, 21
    creating, 16, 32
    linking, 21
    naming, 16, 32
    running application, 21
680x0, defined, 2
8-Byte Doubles checkbox, 47-48

A

A5 register, 272
A5 World, 271, 272, 318
Access Paths panel, 120-121
AddResMenu() Toolbox function, 129, 164
address, order of, 273, 278
allocation, 272-273
animation, 282
Apple Development Products ƒ folder, 9
Apple Universal Header files
    changes to, 77
    defined, 24, 57
    Dialogs.h, 29
    Events.h, 29
    knowledge of, 57
    modification of, 58, 59, 66
    number of, 25
    opening, 63-64
    precompiled, 27

QuickDraw.h, 29
searching, 64, 68-70, 73-75
Sound.h, 29
Toolbox relationship, 29
type mismatch error and, 58
Windows.h, 26, 29
application
    compiling, 21
    generating, 2
    linking, 21
    naming, 20, 24
    PowerPC-only, 4
    running, 21
application-defined functions, 36
application frameworks
    defined, 129-130
    see also PowerPlant application
        framework
application heap, 269, 272-275, 280-281,
    286-295
assignment versus comparison, 93
author's incompetence, 58
Automobile application-defined class,
    197-201

B

block
    attributes, 275
    header, 273
    size, 274
breakpoints, 89
building applications, 21, 24, 119-124
Button() Toolbox function, 355

C

Call Chain pane, 88
casting
    defined, 66
    Handle to SndListHandle, 66
cfrg resource, 113-115, 124-125
ChangingValues example program
    debugging, 91-94
    introduced, 86
    Source pane and, 88-89
children functions, 342-343
CODE resource, 112-116, 123-125, 289-292,
        306-308
Code Fragment Manager, 35
code, optimizing, 6
code fragment, 113, 323
CodeWarrior development environment
    Bronze, 2-3
    CD contents, 4-9
    editions, 2
    Gold, 2-3
    subscription, 4
command numbers, 175, 177, 189
commanders, 191-196
compaction, 275, 280
compiling, 21
conditional directives, 117-118
console window, 50-53
Constructor
    defined, 7, 142, 237
    files, 237, 242
    panes, adding, 250
    panes, learning about, 237-241
    PPob, creating with, 241-246
    views, adding, 243
    window attributes, editing, 245
Control menu, 89-91, 97
cout() ANSI function, 257
CreateTestPaneStream() application-
        defined function
ctype.h ANSI header file, 44
current statement arrow, 89

D

data fork, 112-116
data structures

start of in memory, 100
    studying with debugger, 82
debugger, *see* MW Debug
Debugger INIT extension and, 83
Delay() Toolbox function, 67, 70-71
DelaySound example program
    error in, 71-75
    introduced, 70
dereferencing handles, 277
derived classes, 148, 160
desktop pattern, 32
development environment, 1
DragWindow() Toolbox function, 366
DrawMenuBar() Toolbox function, 129, 164
DrawPicture() Toolbox function, 285-286,
        314
DrawString() Toolbox function, 105-106, 247

E

EmptyWindow example program
    68K project file, 15-21
    building, 21, 24
    introduced, 12
    libraries and, 18-19, 21
    PPC project file, 21-24
    resources, 12-15
    source code, 17-18
emulation mode, 3, 116
Enable Debugging menu item, 85, 87, 91
errors
    DelaySound example program, in,
        71-75
    function call does not match prototype
        error, 71
    PlaySound example program, in, 59, 62
    Project File not found error, 120
    semantic, 85
    syntax, 85
    type mismatch error and, 58, 63-67
event-driven programming, 284-285
EventLoop example program
    introduced, 361
    profiling, 362-369
    resources, 361
executable code
    68K applications, storage of, 112-113

fat binaries, storage of, 114-116
PowerPC applications, storage of, 113-114
storage of, 112-116
Extensions folder, 83

F

fat binary applications
cfrg resource, 113-115
creating, 119-124
data fork, 114, 125-126
defined, 12, 111
emulation mode, 116
executable code, 114-116
native mode, 116
resource editor, examining, 124-125
resource fork, 114, 124-126
fgColor field, 108
folders
ANSI (2i) ƒ folder, 47, 49
Apple Development Products ƒ folder, 9
Extensions folder, 83
MacOS 68K ƒ folder, 18
MacOS PPC ƒ folder, 21
Metrowerks C/C++ ƒ folder, 5-7
Metrowerks PowerPlant ƒ folder, 7
Metrowerks Utilities ƒ folder, 7
More Cool Tools/Demos ƒ folder, 8
PowerPlant Library ƒ folder, 134, 143
Private Templates folder, 178
Profiler Library ƒ folder, 6
Runtime PPC ƒ folder, 21
System Folder, 83-84
forks, 112-116
FrameRect() Toolbox function, 247, 261
function call does not match prototype
error, 71
function overloading, 157
function prototypes
parameters types in, 64
requiring, 38

G

garbage, memory contents, 99
Generate Profiler Calls checkbox, 332, 335
GetDateTime() Toolbox function, 67
GetDefaultOutputVolume() Toolbox

function, 77-78
GetKeys() Toolbox function, 353
GetNewMBar() Toolbox function, 129
GetNewWindow() Toolbox function, 26,
30, 100
GetPicture() Toolbox function, 276, 285-
286, 316
GetSoundVol() Toolbox function, 76
global variables, 272
GrafPort data type
defined, 100
fgColor field, 108
fields of, 100-102, 104
manipulating field values, 106-110
pnLoc field, 104-106
struct definition, 104
WindowPtr relationship, 100
WindowRecord relationship, 100

H

handles, 275-278
header files
opening in CodeWarrior, 63-64
heap size
problems, 310-313
setting, 286-287, 294
heap zone, 297
HideWindow() Toolbox function, 92, 94
HiWord() Toolbox function, 366

I

#ifdef conditional directive, 117-118
#include compiler directive, 26, 37
instruction set, 3
Int16 data type, 147
Int32 data type, 147
InterfaceLib library
adding to project, 21, 33, 35
defined, 30

K

keyDown event type constant, 152
kFullVolume constant, 77
killing program execution, 90, 94

L

LApplication PowerPlant class
    constructor, 160-163
    defined, 148
    deriving class from, 148-149
    instance of, 149
    ObeyCommand() member function,
        197-210
    Run() member function, 149-154
Language panel, 27, 38-39
libraries
    ANSI (2i) C++.68K.Lib, 49
    ANSI (2i) C.68K.Lib, 49
    ANSI (2i) ƒ folder, 47, 49
    ANSI C++.PPC.Lib, 44
    ANSI C.PPC.Lib, 44
    ANSI projects and, 43-50
    C++ projects and, 42
    CPlusPlus.lib, 42, 49
    defined, 30
    InterfaceLib library, 21, 30, 33, 35
    MacOS.lib library, 18-20, 30, 34, 41
    MWCRuntime.Lib library, 21, 23, 35
    PPLibrary68K PowerPlant library, 137
    profiler68K.lib library, 331
    profilerPPC.lib library, 331
    SIOUX.68K.Lib, 51
    SIOUX.PPC.Lib, 50
Locals pane, 88-89, 95-98
LoWord() Toolbox function, 366
LPane PowerPlant class
    ClickSelf() member function, 256-257,
        261-263
    defined, 255
    DrawSelf() member function, 256-257,
        260-261
    Hide() member function, 256
    LCommander class and, 255
    ResizeFrame() member function, 256
    Show() member function, 256
LWindows PowerPlant class
    Close() member function, 154-155
    CreateWindow() member function,
        154-155, 162
    defined, 154
    IsVisible() member function, 230-232
    objects of, 250
    Show() member function, 154-155, 162
    WindowPtr comparison, 154-155

M

MacDraw Pro application, 290
MacHeaders68K, 27-28,30, 40, 72
MacHeadersPPC, 27-28
Macintosh Drag and Drop, 83
Macintosh Toolbox
    adding new functions, 29
    calling conventions, 25
    defined, 25
    function prototypes, 25, 37
    number of functions, 29
    ROM and, 25-26, 29-30, 41
    System file and, 29-30
    Universal Header file relationship, 29
Macintosh Toolbox functions
    AddResMenu() Toolbox function, 129,
        164
    Button() Toolbox function, 355
    Delay() Toolbox function, 67, 70-71
    DragWindow() Toolbox function, 366
    DrawMenuBar() Toolbox function, 129,
        164
    DrawPicture() Toolbox function, 285-
        286, 314
    DrawString() Toolbox function, 105-
        106, 247
    FrameRect() Toolbox function, 247, 261
    GetDateTime() Toolbox function, 67
    GetDefaultOutputVolume() Toolbox
        function, 77-78
    GetKeys() Toolbox function, 353
    GetNewMBar() Toolbox function, 129
    GetNewWindow() Toolbox function,
        26, 30, 100
    GetPicture() Toolbox function, 276,
        285-286, 316
    GetSoundVol() Toolbox function, 76

HideWindow() Toolbox function, 92, 94
HiWord() Toolbox function, 366
LoWord() Toolbox function, 366
MenuSelect() Toolbox function, 174,
    366
MoveTo() Toolbox function, 105
NewWindow() Toolbox function, 86,
    97, 100
ReleaseResource() Toolbox function,
    314
SetDefaultOutputVolume() Toolbox
    function, 77-78
SetMenuBar() Toolbox function, 129,
    164
SetRect() Toolbox function, 99
SetSoundVol() Toolbox function, 30-31,
    37, 41, 76
ShowWindow() Toolbox function, 92
SndPlay() Toolbox function, 29
StillDown() Toolbox function, 262
SysBeep() Toolbox function, 37
TickCount() Toolbox function, 67
WaitNextEvent() Toolbox function, 151
MacOS 68K *f* folder, 18
MacOS PPC *f* folder, 21
MacOS.lib library
    adding to project, 18-20, 34
    defined, 30, 41
MacRecorder sound digitizer, 61
main event loop, 151
master pointer, 278-279
Mcmd resource
    adding, 174-188
    command numbers, 175, 177, 189
    ResEdit and, 184-188, 227-228
    Resorcerer and, 178-184, 227-228
memory
    A5 register, 272
    A5 World, 271, 272, 318
    address order in, 100
    address, order of, 273, 278
    allocation, 272-273
    application heap, 269, 272-275, 280-281,
        286-295
    block attributes, 275

block header, 273
block size, 274
blocks, 272-275
code fragment, 323
compaction, 275, 280
data structure, start of in, 100
dereferencing handles, 277
fat binaries, 324-326
free, 271, 275
global variables, 272
handles, 275-278
heap zone, 297
locked/unlocked, 275
low memory, 273
master pointer, 278-279
native applications and, 318-326
nonrelocatable blocks, 274, 279-280
overview, 270-272
partitions, 269, 271
pointers versus master pointers, 280
pointers, 279-280
PowerPC code, 320
processes, 271
purgeable/unpurgeable, 275
relocatable blocks, 274-279
resource data, 275
see also ZoneRanger
stack, 271, 272
studying with debugger, 95-110
virtual memory, 318, 322
zone header, 297
zone trailer, 297
MenuSelect() Toolbox function, 174, 366
Metrowerks C/C++ *f* folder, 5-7
Metrowerks PowerPlant *f* folder, 7
Metrowerks Profiler, *see* Profiler
Metrowerks Utilities *f* folder, 7
Metrowerks ZoneRanger, *see* ZoneRanger
minimum head size, 287
modes, 116
More Cool Tools/Demos *f* folder, 8
mouseDown event type constant, 152
MoveTo() Toolbox function, 105
MW Debug
    breakpoints, 89

Call Chain pane, 88
Control menu, 89-91, 97
current statement arrow, 89
data structures, study with, 82
Debugger INIT extension and, 83
defined, 81, 85
Enable Debugging menu item, 85,
    87, 91
installing, 82-84
killing program execution, 90, 94
Locals pane, 88-89, 95-98
Macintosh Drag and Drop and, 83
nub files, 82-84
Object SupportLib and, 84
panes, 88
pointer variables and, 98-99, 102, 105
Power Mac DebugServices and, 84
PPCTraceEnable and, 84
Program window, 87
Source pane, 88
starting, 85, 87, 91
stepping through program, 90-91, 105
stopping program execution, 90
support files, 82
SYM files, 88
SYM window, 87
toolbar, 87, 89
variables, changing values of, 106-108
versions of, 82
MWCRuntime.Lib library
adding to project, 21, 23, 35
defined, 35

N

native mode, 3, 116
NewPlaySound example program
    building a fat binary, 119-124
    conditional directives, 117-118
    introduced, 75
    resources, 122-123
NewWindow() Toolbox function, 86, 97,
    100
nub files, 82-84

O

Object SupportLib and, 84
online services
    sound files from, 61
    source code examples from, 58-59
optimizing code
OSUtils.h Universal Header file, 37
overriding class member functions, 197-
    201
Overview window, 296-300

P

panes
    alias, 252-253, 258-259
    CalcLocalFrameRect() member func-
        tion, 260
    construct-from-stream function, 259-
        260
    container, 237
    creating, 241-246, 250-253
    creation function, 259
    defined, 141-142, 236
    dragging, 247-249, 262-263
    IDs, 238-239, 249, 252
    LPane class, 236
    LView class, 236, 241
    PPob, 237-241
    registering, 258-260
    subpanes, 237, 242
    view relationship, 236-237, 241
partitions, 269, 271
picFrame Picture data field, 285
PICT resource, 276, 285-286, 292, 311, 313-
    314, 316
PictMemBad example program
    introduced, 281
    loading PICTs, 285-286, 292
    memory problem, 309-315
    resources, 282-283
    source code, 283-286
    ZoneRanger and, 301
PictMemGood example program

introduced, 314
Picture data structure, 285
PlaySound example program
  68K project, 59
  error in, 62
  introduced, 59
  resource file, 60
pnLoc field, 104-106
pointers versus master pointers, 280
Power Mac DebugServices and, 84
powerc conditional directive, 117-118
PowerPC
  defined, 2
PowerPC-only applications, 4
PowerPlant class member functions
  CalcLocalFrameRect(), 260
  Close(), 154-155
  CreateWindow(), 154-155, 162
  DrawSelf(), 256-257, 260-261
  FindCommandStatus(), 205, 210-214
  Hide(), 256
  IsVisible(), 230-232
  ObeyCommand(), 197-210
  RegisterClass(), 161, 258
  ResizeFrame(), 256
  Run(), 149-154, 163
  Show(), 154-155, 162, 256
  SwitchTarget(), 262
PowerPlant application framework
  #pragma once directive, 158-160
  aedt resource, 138-139
  ALRT resource, 139
  application-specific menus, 188-191
  chain of command, 194-196
  checking menu items, 211
  class naming convention, 144-145
  classes, 134-137, 143-158
  command numbers, 175, 177, 189
  commanders, 191-196
  commands, menu items as, 171, 192
  constructor, 259
  containers, 237
  .cp/.h file relationship, 144, 165-166, 254
  CreateWindow() member function, 162

data types, 146-148
defined, 129-130, 134, 171
derived classes, 148, 160
DITL resource, 139
drawing with, 235
FindCommandStatus() member function, 205, 210-214
header files, 164-165
Int16 data type, 147
Int32 data type, 147
IsVisible() member function, 230-232
LApplication class, 148-154, 160
LCommander class, 196-197
library/source code relationship, 136-137
LWindow class, 154-155
main event loop, 151
MBAR resource, 139, 173-178
Mcmd resource, 138-139, 173-188
member function access, 155-157
MENU resource, 139, 173-178
menu handling, 129-130, 171-234
menu items, adding, 226-233
menu updating, 210-211
naming program, 217
ObeyCommand() member function, 197-210
objects, 192-193
overriding member functions, 201-204, 210-214, 256
panes, 236-246, 255-263
PPob resource, 133, 141-142, 161-162
PP_Messages.h header file, 176, 191
projects, 133-137, 167-168
RegisterClass() member function, 161, 258
registering pane classes, 161, 258-260
ResIDT data type, 147
resource file, 138-141
resources, 133, 137-142
Run() member function, 149-154, 163
scroll bars, 236-237
see also LApplication PowerPlant class
see also LWindow PowerPlant class
source code/library relationship, 136-137

static member functions, 155-157
streams, 257-260
SwitchTarget() member function, 262
target objects, 172, 192, 194-197
this keyword, 163
TMPL templates, 177-178, 184
Toolbox functions and, 157-158
Toolbox initialization, 157
top level containers, 237
updating, 236
UQDGlobals class, 155-157
utility classes, 156
variable naming convention, 146
WIND resource, 133, 141, 162
PowerPlant Library ƒ folder, 134, 143
PP_Messages.h header file, 176, 191
PPC projects
  adding file to, 21
  building application, 24
  creating, 21
  naming, 21
PPCTraceEnable and, 84
PPDemoPane example program
  .cp/.h file relationship, 254
  header file, 263, 265-266
  introduced, 247
  pane, dragging, 247-249
  PPob file, 249-253
  project file, 253-254
  resources, 254-255
  source code, 263-267
PPIntro example program
  application class, 160-163
  header file, 164-165
  introduced, 130-132
  Mcmd resource, 173, 175
  PPob resource file, 142
  project file, 133-137
  resources, 138-141
  source code, 132-133, 165-167
  window, creating, 161-163
PPLibrary68K PowerPlant library, 137
PPMenu example program
  FindCommandStatus() member
    function, 212-214

header file, 221-222
menus, adding, 189-191, 218-220
ObeyCommand() member function,
    206-210
PowerPC project file, 225
project file, 215-217
resources, 217-220
source code, 222-225
PPMoreMenus example program
  introduced, 226
  menu items, adding, 226-233
  PowerPC project file, 233
PPob resource
  Constructor and, 142
  containment hierarchy, 237
  creating, 241-246
  defined, 141
  LPane objects and, 239
  LWindow objects and, 238, 240
  panes and, 141
  register classes and, 161
  resource editors and, 246-247
precompiled header files
  defined, 27
  MacHeaders68K, 27-28, 30, 40
  MacHeadersPPC, 27-28
preferences dialog box
  4-Byte Ints checkbox, 47-48
  8-Byte Doubles checkbox, 47-48
  68881 Codegen checkbox, 47
  Access Paths panel, 120-121
  Generate Profiler Calls checkbox,
    332, 335
  heap size, setting, 286-287, 294
  Language panel, 27, 38-39
  naming program from, 20, 24
  precompiled header files and, 27
  prefix file, adding, 27, 39-41
  Processor panel, 332
  Project panel, 20, 24, 38, 286, 294
  Require Function Prototypes
    checkbox, 38
preferred heap size, 287
prefix file, adding, 27, 39-41
preload resource attribute, 115

Private Templates folder, 178
Process Manager, 113-114
processes, 271
Processor panel, 332
Profiler
 __profile__ preprocessor directive, 335
 adding to project, 335-336
 application, 330
 children functions, 342-343
 defined, 6, 329-330
 detailed versus summary output, 344
 event loop and, 360-362
 function dependencies, 362-363
 functions, programmer interface,
  330, 332
 library, 330
 optimizing code, 348-350
 output file, 340-345, 358-360, 363-369
 PICT drawing time analysis, 352-360
 profiler.h header file, 332
 profiler68K.lib library, 331
 ProfilerDump() profiler function,
  332, 334
 ProfilerInit() profiler function, 332-334
 profilerPPC.lib library, 331
 ProfilerTerm() profiler function, 332, 335
 timing functions, 345-350
 timing part of a function, 350-352
Profiler Library ƒ folder, 6
ProfilerIntro example program
 introduced, 336
 profiler output file, 340-345
 source code, 337-340
Program window, 87
programs, *see* applications
Project File not found error, 120
Project panel, 20, 24, 38, 286, 294
project stationary, 54-55
projects
 68K, 12
 defined, 11
 file types in, 24
 opening source code files from, 39
 PPC, 12
 removing files from, 41

Q

QuickDraw.h Universal Header file, 104, 108

R

ReadCommanNumber PowerPlant function, 175
Rect data type
 defined, 99
 viewing contents of, 99
ReleaseResource() Toolbox function, 314
Require Function Prototypes check box, 38
ResEdit
 adding resource, 13
 creating file, 13
 defined, 8-9
ResIDT data type, 147
Resorcerer
 adding resource, 14
 creating file, 14
 defined, 8-9
 removing file, 217
resource files
 adding to project, 18, 21
 defined, 12
 opening from within a project, 60
resource fork, 112-116
resource types
 aedt, 138-139
 ALRT, 139
 cfrg, 113-115, 124-125
 CODE, 112-116, 123-125, 289-292, 306-308
 DITL, 139
 MBAR, 139, 173-178
 Mcmd, 138-139, 173-188, 227-228
 MENU, 139, 173-178
 PICT, 276, 285-286, 292, 311, 313-314, 316
 PPob, 133, 141-142, 161-162, 237-247
 SIZE, 294
 snd , 60
 WIND, 13-14, 133, 141, 162, 292
ROM chips, 25, 26, 29-30, 41
Runtime PPC ƒ folder, 21

S

scope resolution operator, 156, 158
scroll bars, 236-237
search dialog box
  collapsing, 68
  expanding, 68
  Multi-File Search list, 70
search sets
  creating, 68-69
  defined, 68
  saving, 70
  selecting, 73
  using, 73-77
searching
  multiple files, 68
  see also search sets
Segment Manager, 112
semantic errors, 85
SetDefaultOutputVolume() Toolbox
    function, 77-78
SetMenuBar() Toolbox function, 129, 164
SetRect() Toolbox function, 99
SetSoundVol() Toolbox function, 30-31,
    37, 41, 76
SetVolume example program
  68K project file, 32-35, 38
  introduced, 29-31
  PPC project file, 35
  SetSoundVol() Toolbox function, 37
  source code, 36-38
  SysBeep() Toolbox function, 37
ShowWindow() Toolbox function, 92
SIOUX, 50-53
SIZE resource, 294
snd resource
  defined, 60
  ID range, 60
SndChannelPtr data type, 64, 66
SndListHandle data type, 64, 66
SndPlay() Toolbox function, 29
Sound control panel, 31, 37
sound files
  copying sound resources from, 60
  defined, 60
  obtaining, 61

Sound.h Universal Header file, 30, 37,
    76-77
source code files
  creating, 17, 33
  naming, 17, 33
  reusing, 23, 33, 117
Source pane, 88
speaker
  beeping, 31, 37
  changing volume, 31, 37, 76, 78
  saving current volume, 76, 78
Standard Input Output User eXchange,
    50-53
static member functions, 155-157, 161
static variables, 286
stepping through program, 90-91, 105
StillDown() Toolbox function, 262
stopping program execution, 90
SYM files, 88
SYM window, 87
syntax errors, 85
SysBeep() Toolbox function, 37
System 7, 41
System Folder, 83-84
systemwide features, 32

T

target objects, 172, 192, 194-197
Telephone sound file, 60
this keyword, 163
TickCount() Toolbox function, 67
toolbar, 87, 89
Toolbox, *see* Macintosh Toolbox
top level containers, 237
touched files, 64
toupper() ANSI function, 44
type mismatch error
  correcting, 63-67
  function prototype and, 63

U

updateEvt event type constant, 152

V

variables, changing values of, 106-108
Vehicle application-defined class, 197-201
virtual memory, 318, 322

W

WaitNextEvent() Toolbox function, 151
WIND resource, 292
WindowPtr data type
  contents of, 97
  defined, 100
  GrafPort relationship, 100
  nil value, 96-97
  WindowRecord relationship, 100
WindowRecord data type
  defined, 100
  GrafPort relationship, 100
  WindowPtr relationship, 100
windows
  coloring of, 108
  data structures and, 100-110
  open, checking, 96-97
  see also GrafPort data structure
  see also WindowPtr data structure
  see also WindowRecord data structure
  visibility, checking, 230-232

Z

zone
  header, 297
  trailer, 297
Zone window, 302-305, 309
ZoneRanger
  block count, 299
  block information, 305-307
  block usage, 299-300
  debugger, versus, 315-317
  defined, 7, 269, 295, 298
  display relocatable blocks, 305
  heap problems, 310-313
  heap zone, 297

Overview window, 296-300
PowerPC applications and, 318-326
refreshing window, 301, 310
resolution, 304
uses for, 317
Zone window, 302-305, 309
zooming in, 304

Software License Agreement

PLEASE READ THIS LICENSE CAREFULLY BEFORE USING THE SOFTWARE. BY USING THE SOFTWARE, YOU ARE AGREEING TO BE BOUND BY THE TERMS OF THIS LICENSE. IF YOU DO NOT AGREE TO THE TERMS OF THIS LICENSE, PROMPTLY RETURN THE UNUSED SOFTWARE TO THE PLACE WHERE YOU OBTAINED IT AND YOUR MONEY WILL BE REFUNDED.

1. License. The application, demonstration, system and other software accompanying this License, whether on disk, in read only memory, or on any other media (the "Software") the related documentation and fonts are licensed to you by Metrowerks. You own the disk on which the Software and fonts are recorded but Metrowerks and/or Metrowerks' Licensor retain title to the Software, related documentation and fonts. This License allows you to use the Software and fonts on a single Apple computer and make one copy of the Software and fonts in machine-readable form for backup purposes only. You must reproduce on such copy the Metrowerks copyright notice and any other proprietary legends that were on the original copy of the Software and fonts. You may also transfer all your license rights in the Software and fonts, the backup copy of the Software and fonts, the related documentation and a copy of this License to another party, provided the other party reads and agrees to accept the terms and conditions of this License.

2. Restrictions. The Software contains copyrighted material, trade secrets and other proprietary material. In order to protect them, and except as permitted by applicable legislation, you may not decompile, reverse engineer, disassemble or otherwise reduce the Software to a human-perceivable form. You may not modify, network, rent, lease, loan, distribute or create derivative works based upon the Software in whole or in part. You may not electronically transmit the Software from one computer to another or over a network.

3. Termination. This License is effective until terminated. You may terminate this License at any time by destroying the Software, related documentation and fonts and all copies thereof. This License will terminate immediately without notice

from Metrowerks if you fail to comply with any provision of this License. Upon termination you must destroy the Software, related documentation and fonts and all copies thereof.

4. Export Law Assurances. You agree and certify that neither the Software nor any other technical data received from Metrowerks, nor the direct product thereof, will be exported outside the United States except as authorized and as permitted by the laws and regulations of the United States. If the Software has been rightfully obtained by you outside of the United States, you agree that you will not re-export the Software nor any other technical data received from Metrowerks, nor the direct product thereof, except as permitted by the laws and regulations of the United States and the laws and regulations of the jurisdiction in which you obtained the Software.

5. Government End Users. If you are acquiring the Software and fonts on behalf of any unit or agency of the United States Government, the following provisions apply. The Government agrees: (i) if the Software and fonts are supplied to the Department of Defense (DoD), the Software and fonts are classified as "Commercial Computer Software" and the Government is acquiring only "restricted rights" in the Software, its documentation and fonts as that term is defined in Clause 252.227-7013(c)(1) of the DFARS; and (ii) if the Software and fonts are supplied to any unit or agency of the United States Government other than DoD, the Government's rights in the Software, its documentation and fonts will be as defined in Clause 52.227-19(c)(2) of the FAR or, in the case of NASA, in Clause 18-52.227-86(d) of the NASA Supplement to the FAR.

6. Limited Warranty on Media. Metrowerks warrants the diskettes and/or compact disc on which the Software and fonts are recorded to be free from defects in materials and workmanship under normal use for a period of ninety (90) days from the date of purchase as evidenced by a copy of the receipt. Metrowerks' entire liability and your exclusive remedy will be replacement of the diskettes and/or compact disc not meeting Metrowerks' limited warranty and which is returned to Metrowerks or a Metrowerks authorized representative with a copy of the receipt. Metrowerks will have no responsibility to replace a disk/disc damaged by accident, abuse or misapplication. ANY

IMPLIED WARRANTIES ON THE DISKETTES AND/OR COM-
PACT DISC, INCLUDING THE IMPLIED WARRANTIES OF
MERCHANTABILITY AND FITNESS FOR A PARTICULAR
PURPOSE, ARE LIMITED IN DURATION TO NINETY (90)
DAYS FROM THE DATE OF DELIVERY. THIS WARRANTY
GIVES YOU SPECIFIC LEGAL RIGHTS, AND YOU MAY ALSO
HAVE OTHER RIGHTS WHICH VARY BY JURISDICTION.

7. Disclaimer of Warranty on Apple Software. You expressly
acknowledge and agree that use of the Software and fonts is at
your sole risk. Except as is stated above, the Software, related
documentation and fonts are provided "AS IS" and without
warranty of any kind and Metrowerks and Metrowerks'
Licensor(s) (for the purposes of provisions 7 and 8,
Metrowerks and Metrowerks' Licensor(s) shall be collectively
referred to as "Metrowerks") EXPRESSLY DISCLAIM ALL
OTHER WARRANTIES, EXPRESS OR IMPLIED, INCLUD-
ING, BUT NOT LIMITED TO, THE IMPLIED WARRANTIES
OF MERCHANTABILITY AND FITNESS FOR A PARTICU-
LAR PURPOSE. [LICENSEE NAME] DOES NOT WARRANT
THAT THE FUNCTIONS CONTAINED IN THE SOFTWARE
WILL MEET YOUR REQUIREMENTS, OR THAT THE OPER-
ATION OF THE SOFTWARE WILL BE UNINTERRUPTED OR
ERROR-FREE, OR THAT DEFECTS IN THE SOFTWARE AND
THE FONTS WILL BE CORRECTED. FURTHERMORE,
[LICENSEE NAME] DOES NOT WARRANT OR MAKE ANY
REPRESENTATIONS REGARDING THE USE OR THE
RESULTS OF THE USE OF THE SOFTWARE AND FONTS OR
RELATED DOCUMENTATION IN TERMS OF THEIR COR-
RECTNESS, ACCURACY, RELIABILITY, OR OTHERWISE.
NO ORAL OR WRITTEN INFORMATION OR ADVICE
GIVEN BY METROWERKS OR AN AUTHORIZED REPRE-
SENTATIVE THEREOF SHALL CREATE A WARRANTY OR
IN ANY WAY INCREASE THE SCOPE OF THIS WARRANTY.
SHOULD THE SOFTWARE PROVE DEFECTIVE, YOU (AND
NOT METROWERKS OR AN AUTHORIZED REPRESENTA-
TIVE THEREOF) ASSUME THE ENTIRE COST OF ALL NEC-
ESSARY SERVICING, REPAIR OR CORRECTION. SOME
JURISDICTIONS DO NOT ALLOW THE EXCLUSION OF
IMPLIED WARRANTIES, SO THE ABOVE EXCLUSION MAY
NOT APPLY TO YOU.

8. Limitation of Liability. UNDER NO CIRCUMSTANCES INCLUDING NEGLIGENCE, SHALL METROWERKS BE LIABLE FOR ANY INCIDENTAL, SPECIAL OR CONSE-QUENTIAL DAMAGES THAT RESULT FROM THE USE OR INABILITY TO USE THE SOFTWARE OR RELATED DOCU-MENTATION, EVEN IF METROWERKS OR AN AUTHO-RIZED REPRESENTATIVE THEREOF HAS BEEN ADVISED OF THE POSSIBILITY OF SUCH DAMAGES. SOME JURIS-DICTIONS DO NOT ALLOW THE LIMITATION OR EXCLU-SION OF LIABILITY FOR INCIDENTAL OR CONSEQUEN-TIAL DAMAGES SO THE ABOVE LIMITATION OR EXCLU-SION MAY NOT APPLY TO YOU.

In no event shall Metrowerks' total liability to you for all dam-ages, losses, and causes of action (whether in contract, tort (including negligence) or otherwise) exceed that portion of the amount paid by you which is fairly attributable to the Software and fonts.

9. Controlling Law and Severability. This License shall be gov-erned by and construed in accordance with the laws of the United States and the State of California, as applied to agree-ments entered into and to be performed entirely within California between California residents. If for any reason a court of competent jurisdiction finds any provision of this License, or portion thereof, to be unenforceable, that provision of the License shall be enforced to the maximum extent permis-sible so as to effect the intent of the parties, and the remainder of this License shall continue in full force and effect.

10. Complete Agreement. This License constitutes the entire agree-ment between the parties with respect to the use of the Software, the related documentation and fonts, and supersedes all prior or contemporaneous understandings or agreements, written or oral, regarding such subject matter. No amendment to or modification of this License will be binding unless in writing and signed by a duly authorized representative of Metrowerks.

About This CD

The CD that accompanies this book contains a limited version of both the 68K and PowerPC CodeWarrior C/C++ compilers. "Limited" means that while the compilers can be used to work with any of the twenty example projects that are also on the CD, you won't be able to create new projects of your own. To get the full-featured versions of these compilers—as well as numerous programming tools, extensive documentation, and technical support—you'll want to purchase the complete Metrowerks CodeWarrior CD. Until then, you can use these compilers to learn about Metrowerks, experiment with different compiler features, and learn more about Macintosh programming,

The two compilers that are on this CD run on either a 68K Mac (a Macintosh driven by either a Motorola 68020, 68030, or 68040 processor) or any Macintosh that has a PowerPC processor. So it doesn't matter what kind of Mac you have—as long as you have several megabytes of free RAM and System 7.1 or later installed.

Once you've popped the CD into your CD-ROM drive, read Chapter 1 to get an idea of what the many programs and files on the CD are for. Then move on to Chapter 2 to see how to write a Macintosh program using CodeWarrior!